Build Your Own Ruby On Rails Web Applications

by Patrick Lenz

Build Your Own Ruby On Rails Web Applications

by Patrick Lenz

Copyright © 2007 SitePoint Pty. Ltd.

Expert Reviewer: Luke Redpath
Managing Editor: Simon Mackie
Technical Editor: Matthew Magain
Technical Director: Kevin Yank
Printing History:
   First Edition: January 2007

Editor: Georgina Laidlaw
Index Editor: Max McMaster
Cover Design: Alex Walker

Published by SitePoint Pty. Ltd.

424 Smith Street Collingwood
VIC Australia 3066
Web: www.sitepoint.com
Email: business@sitepoint.com

ISBN 978-0-9758419-5-2
Printed and bound in the United States of America

About the Author

Patrick Lenz has been developing web applications for ten years. Founder and lead developer of the freshmeat.net software portal, he and his Rails consultancy and application development company, limited overload,[1] were responsible for a major relaunch of eins.de, Germany's biggest infotainment community, which is now one of the most popular Ruby on Rails sites in Europe.

Patrick lives in Wiesbaden, Germany, with his wife Alice and his daughter Gwendolyn.

When not working in front of a computer, he can often be seen with a camera in his hand, either taking artsy pictures or documenting the progress of his baby girl conquering the world.[2] He also enjoys cars, music, and extended weekend brunches with friends.

His weblog can be found at http://poocs.net/.

About the Expert Reviewer

Luke Redpath is a programmer with over seven years' experience in the web design and development field. A recovering PHP and ASP developer, Luke has been using Ruby and Rails professionally for nearly two years and has released and contributed to several Ruby libraries and Rails plugins, including UJS—the Rails unobtrusive JavaScript plugin.[3] He currently resides in North London, UK with his long-term partner Julie.

About the Technical Editor

Before joining the SitePoint team as a technical editor, Matthew Magain worked as a software developer for IBM and also spent several years teaching English in Japan. He is the organizer for Melbourne's Web Standards Group,[4] and enjoys swimming, listening to classical jazz, and drinking Coopers Pale Ale, though not all at the same time. Matthew lives with his wife Kimberley and their daughter Sophia.

About the Technical Director

As Technical Director for SitePoint, Kevin Yank oversees all of its technical publications—books, articles, newsletters, and blogs. He has written over 50 articles for SitePoint, but is best known for his book, *Build Your Own Database Driven Website Using PHP & MySQL*.[5] Kevin lives in Melbourne, Australia, and enjoys performing improvised comedy theater and flying light aircraft.

---

[1] http://limited-overload.de/
[2] His pictures are regularly published to Flickr and are available at http://flickr.com/photos/scoop/
[3] http://www.ujs4rails.com/
[4] http://webstandardsgroup.org/
[5] http://www.sitepoint.com/books/phpmysql1/

About SitePoint

SitePoint specializes in publishing fun, practical, and easy-to-understand content for web professionals. Visit http://www.sitepoint.com/ to access our books, newsletters, articles, and community forums.

To my daughter Gwendolyn
and my wife Alice.

Table of Contents

Preface

Ruby on Rails has shaken up the web development industry in a huge way—especially when you consider that version 1.0 of Rails was only released in December 2005. The huge waves of enthusiasm for the new framework, originally in weblogs and later in the more traditional media, are probably the reason why this book is in your hands.

This book will lead you through the components that make up the Rails framework by building a clone of the popular story-sharing web site digg.com. This will give you a chance to get your feet wet building a simple, yet comprehensive web application using Ruby on Rails.

Does this book cover Ajax? Absolutely! Rails has tight integration with the latest web technologies including Ajax, as well as pretty animations, and features such as auto-completion and in-line editing. If that's all Greek to you, don't worry. I'll get you started, and by the time you finish this book, you'll be able to discuss all things Web 2.0 with your friends and coworkers, and impress your grandparents with geeky vocabulary.

Who Should Read this Book?

This book is intended for anyone who's eager to learn more about Ruby on Rails in a practical sense. It's equally well suited to design-oriented people looking to build web applications as it is to people who are unhappy with the range of programming languages or frameworks that they're using, and are looking for alternatives that bring the fun back into programming.

I don't expect you to be an expert programmer—this isn't a pro-level book. It's written specifically for beginning to intermediate web developers who, though they're familiar with HTML and CSS, aren't necessarily fond of—or experienced with—any server-side technologies such as PHP or Perl.

As we go along, you'll get an understanding of the components that make up the Ruby on Rails framework, learn the basics of the Ruby programming language, and come to grips with the tools recommended for use in Ruby on Rails development. All these topics are covered within the context of building a robust application that addresses real-world problems.

In terms of software installation, I'll cover the installation basics of Ruby, Ruby on Rails, and the MySQL database server on Mac OS X, Windows, and Linux. All you need to have pre-installed on your system are your favorite text editor and a web browser.

What you'll Learn

Web development has never been easier, or as much fun as it is using Ruby on Rails. In this book, you'll learn to make use of the latest Web 2.0 techniques, and the concise Ruby programming language, to build interactive, database driven web sites that are a pleasure to build, use, and maintain.

Also, as web sites tend to evolve over time, I'll teach you how to make sure you don't wreak havoc with a careless change to your application code—we'll implement automated testing facilities and learn how to debug problems that arise within your application.

What's in this Book?

Chapter 1: Introducing Ruby on Rails
This chapter touches on the history of the Rails framework, which—believe it or not—is actually rather interesting! I'll explain some of the key concepts behind Rails and shed some light on the features that we're planning to build into our example application.

Chapter 2: Getting Started
Here's where the real action starts! In this chapter, I'll walk you through the installation of the various pieces of software required to turn your Mac or PC into a powerful Ruby on Rails development machine. I'll also show you how to set up the database for our example application, so that you can start your application for the first time, in all its naked glory.

Chapter 3: Introducing Ruby
Ruby on Rails is built on the object oriented programming language Ruby, so it helps to know a bit about both object oriented programming and the Ruby syntax. This chapter will give you a solid grounding in both—and if you'd like to get your hands dirty, you can play along at home using the interactive Ruby console.

Chapter 4: Rails Revealed

In this chapter, we start to peel back the layers of the Rails framework. I'll talk about the separation of environments in each of the application's life cycles, and introduce you to the model-view-controller architecture that forms the basis of a Rails application's organization. I'll also help you to establish a database connection so that your application can begin storing and retrieving data, and I'll show you some GUI tools that can be used to manage your database content outside Rails.

Chapter 5: Models, Views, and Controllers

In this chapter, we'll generate our first few lines of code. We'll create a class for storing data, a view for displaying the data, and a controller to handle the interaction between the two.

Chapter 6: Helpers, Forms, and Layouts

This chapter starts off by looking at how Rails's built-in helpers can reduce the amount of code required to create functionality for your application. I'll show you how to use one of the helpers to create a fully functioning form, and we'll style the end result with some CSS so that it looks good! I'll then show you how to write unit and functional tests to verify that the application is working as expected.

Chapter 7: Ajax and Web 2.0

Let's face it, this chapter is the reason you bought this book! Well, it won't fail to disappoint. I'll walk you through the steps involved in adding to our app some nifty effects that use Ajax to update parts of a page without reloading the entire page. Along the way, I'll explain the different relationships that you can establish between your objects, and we'll make sure that our application uses clean URLs.

Chapter 8: Protective Measures

In this chapter, I'll show you how to keep out the bad guys by adding simple user authentication to our application. We'll cover sessions and cookies, and we'll see first-hand how database migrations allow for the iterative evolution of a database schema.

Chapter 9: Advanced Topics

This chapter will give our example application a chance to shine. We'll add a stack of functionality, and in the process, we'll learn about model callbacks and join models.

Chapter 10: Plugins

In this chapter, I'll show you how to add a plugin—a component that provides features that expand the functionality of your application—to the example application. We'll also talk about some of the more advanced associations that are available to your models.

Chapter 11: Debugging, Testing and Benchmarking

This chapter will cover testing and benchmarking, as well as the reasons behind completing comprehensive testing of all your code. We'll also walk through a couple of examples that show how to debug your application when something goes wrong.

Chapter 12: Deployment

Now that you've developed a feature-packed, fully functional application, you'll want to deploy it so that other people can use it. In this chapter, I'll introduce you to the options available for deploying your application to a production server, and walk you through the steps involved in taking your application to the world.

The Book's Web Site

Head over to http://www.sitepoint.com/books/rails1/ for easy access to various resources supporting this book.

The Code Archive

The code archive for this book, which can be downloaded from http://www.sitepoint.com/books/rails1/archive/, contains each and every line of example source code that's printed in this book. If you want to cheat (or save yourself from carpal tunnel syndrome), go ahead and download the code to your hard drive.

Updates and Errata

While everyone involved in producing a technical book like this goes to an enormous amount of effort to ensure the accuracy of its content, books tend to have errors. Fortunately, the Corrections and Typos page located at http://www.sitepoint.com/books/rails1/errata.php is the most current, comprehensive reference for spelling and code-related errors that observant readers have reported to us.

The SitePoint Forums

If you have a problem understanding any of the discussion or examples in this book, try asking your question in the SitePoint Forums, at http://www.sitepoint.com/forums/. There, the enthusiastic and friendly community will be able to help you with all things Rails.

The SitePoint Newsletters

In addition to books like this one, SitePoint publishes free email newsletters including *The SitePoint Tribune* and *The SitePoint Tech Times*. In them, you'll read about the latest news, product releases, trends, tips, and techniques for all aspects of web development.

You can count on gaining some useful Rails articles and tips from these resources, but if you're interested in learning other technologies, or aspects of web development and business, you'll find them especially valuable. Sign up to one or more SitePoint newsletters at http://www.sitepoint.com/newsletter/.

Your Feedback

If you can't find your answer through the forums, or if you wish to contact us for any other reason, write to books@sitepoint.com. We have a well-manned email support system set up to track your inquiries, and if our support staff members are unable to answer your question, they'll send it straight to me. Suggestions for improvements, as well as notices of any mistakes you may find, are especially welcome.

Acknowledgements

Thanks to SitePoint for giving me the chance to write this book. I'm pretty confident that the old "build a house, get a child, plant a tree" phrase could also be interpreted as "rent a house, get a child, write a book on tree leaves," so I'm truly grateful for this opportunity.

In particular, thanks to Technical Editor Matthew Magain for his crisp, sharp commentary, and Managing Editor Simon Mackie for applying an appropriate measure of brute force to me and my drafts—dedication that ensured that this book is in the best shape possible.

To the Rails Core team, for making my developer life enjoyable again by putting together this amazing framework in almost no time, and laying the foundation on which this book could be written, thank you.

Finally, thanks must go to my family, especially Alice and Gwen, for giving me so much strength, motivation, and confidence in what I'm doing. Thank you for bearing the fact that I was barely seen away from a computer for so many months.

1

Introducing Ruby on Rails

Though it hasn't been long since Ruby on Rails was first released, it's already become a household name (well, in developers' households, anyway). Within that time, hundreds of thousands of developers the world over have adopted—and adored—this new framework, and I hope that, through the course of this book, you'll come to understand the reasons why. Before we jump into writing any code, let's take a stroll down memory lane, as we meet Ruby on Rails and explore a little of its history.

First, what exactly *is* Ruby on Rails?

The short—and fairly technical—answer is that Ruby on Rails (often abbreviated to *Rails*) is a *full-stack web application framework, written in Ruby*. However, depending on your previous programming experience (and your mastery of techno-jargon), that answer might not make a whole lot of sense to you. Besides, the Ruby on Rails movement really needs to be viewed in the context of web development in general if it is to be fully appreciated.

So, let me define a few of those terms, and give you a brief history lesson along the way. Then we'll tackle the question of why learning Rails is one of the smartest things you could do for your career as a web developer.

❏ A **web application** is a software application that's accessed using a web browser over a network. In most cases, that network is the Internet, but it could also be a corporate intranet. A big buzz has sprung up around web applications recently, due mostly to the increased availability of broadband Internet access and the proliferation of faster desktop machines in people's homes. We can only assume that you're interested in writing such a web application, because you've bought this book!

❑ A **framework** can be viewed as the foundation of a web application. It takes care of many of the low-level details that can become repetitive and boring to code, allowing the developer to focus on building the application's functionality.

A framework gives the developer classes that implement common functions used in *every* web application, including:

❑ database abstraction (ensuring that queries work regardless of whether the database is MySQL, Oracle, DB2, or something else)

❑ templating (reusing presentational code throughout the application)

❑ management of user sessions

❑ generation of "clean" URLs

A framework also defines the architecture of an application—something that can be useful for those of us who constantly fret over which file is best stored in which folder.

In a sense, a framework is an application that has been started for you—and a well-designed one at that. The structure, plus the code that takes care of the boring stuff, has already been written, and it's up to us to finish it off!

❑ **Full-stack** refers to the extent of the functionality the Rails framework provides. You see, there are frameworks, and then there are frameworks. Some provide great functionality on the server, but leave you high and dry on the client side; others are terrific at enhancing the user experience on the client machine, but don't extend to the business logic and database interactions on the server.

If you've ever used a framework before, chances are that you're familiar with the model-view-controller (MVC) architecture (if you're not, don't worry—we'll discuss it in Chapter 5). Rails covers *everything* in the MVC paradigm, from database abstraction to template rendering, and everything in between.

❑ **Ruby** is an open source, object oriented scripting language that Yukihiro Matsumoto invented in the early 1990s. We'll be learning both Ruby *and* Rails as we progress through the book (remember, Rails is written in Ruby).

Ruby makes programming flexible and intuitive, and with it, we can write code that's readable by both humans and machines. Matsumoto clearly envisioned Ruby to be a programming language that would entail very little mental overhead for humans, which is why Ruby programmers tend to be happy programmers.

What Does Ruby Look Like?

If you're experienced in programming with other languages, such as PHP or Java, you can probably make some sense of the following Ruby code, although some parts of it may look new:

File: **01-ruby-sample.rb** (excerpt)

```
>> "What does Ruby syntax look like?".reverse
=> "?ekil kool xatnys ybuR seod tahW"
>> 8 * 5
=> 40
>> 3.times { puts "cheer!" }
cheer!
cheer!
cheer!
>> %w(one two three).each { |word| puts word.upcase }
ONE
TWO
THREE
```

Don't worry too much about the details of programming in Ruby for now—we'll cover all of the Ruby basics in Chapter 3.

History

Ruby on Rails originated as an application named Basecamp,[1] a hosted project-management solution created by Danish web developer David Heinemeier Hansson for former design shop 37signals.[2] Due largely to Basecamp's success, 37signals has since moved into application development and production, and Heinemeier Hansson has become a partner in the company.

---

[1] http://www.basecamphq.com/
[2] http://www.37signals.com/

When I say "originated," I mean that Rails wasn't initially created as a stand-alone framework. It was *extracted* from a real application that was already in use, so that it could be used to build other applications that 37signals had in mind.[3] Heinemeier Hansson saw the potential to make his job (and life) easier by extracting common functionality such as database abstraction and templating into what later became the first public release of Ruby on Rails.

He decided to release Rails as open source software to "fundamentally remake the way web sites are built."[4] The first beta version of Rails was initially released in July 2004, with the 1.0 release following on December 13, 2005. At the time of writing, more than 300,000 copies of Rails have been downloaded, and that number is climbing.

The fact that the Rails framework was extracted from Basecamp is considered by the lively Rails community to represent one of the framework's inherent strengths: Rails was already solving *real* problems when it was released. Rails wasn't built in isolation, so its success wasn't a result of developers taking the framework, building applications with it, and then finding—and resolving—its shortcomings. Rails had already proven itself to be a useful, coherent, and comprehensive framework.

While Heinemeier Hansson pioneered Rails and still leads the Rails-related programming efforts, the framework has benefited greatly from being released as open source software. Over time, developers working with Rails have submitted thousands of extensions and bug fixes to the Rails development repository.[5] The repository is closely guarded by the Rails core team, which consists of about twelve highly skilled, professional developers chosen from the crowd of contributors, and led, by Heinemeier Hansson.

So, now you know what Rails is, and how it came about. But why would you invest your precious time in learning how to use it?

I'm glad you asked.

---

[3] Backpack [http://www.backpackit.com/], Ta-da List [http://www.tadalist.com/], Campfire [http://www.campfirenow.com/], and Writeboard [http://www.writeboard.com/] are other hosted applications written in Rails by 37signals.
[4] http://www.wired.com/wired/archive/14.04/start.html?pg=3
[5] The Rails repository, located at http://dev.rubyonrails.org/, is used to track bugs and enhancement requests.

Development Principles

Rails supports several software principles that make it stand out over other web development frameworks. Those principles are:

❑ convention over configuration

❑ don't repeat yourself

❑ agile development

Because of these principles, Ruby on Rails is a framework that really does save developers time and effort. Let's look at each of those principles in turn to understand how.

Convention Over Configuration

The concept of **convention over configuration** refers to the fact that Rails assumes a number of defaults for the way one should build a typical web application.

You see, many other frameworks (such as the Java-based Struts or the Python-based Zope) require you to step through a lengthy configuration process before you can get started with even the simplest of applications. The configuration information is usually stored in a handful of XML files, and these files can become quite large and cumbersome to maintain. In many cases, you're forced to repeat the entire configuration process whenever you start a new project.

While Rails was originally extracted from an existing application, excessive architectural work went into the framework later on. Heinemeier Hansson purposely created Rails in such a way that it doesn't need excessive configuration, as long as some standard conventions are followed. The result is that no lengthy configuration files are required. In fact, if you have no need to change these defaults, Rails really only needs a single (and short) configuration file in order to run your application. The file is used to establish a database connection: it supplies Rails with the necessary database server type, server name, user name, and password for each environment, and that's it. An example of a configuration file is shown on the following page. (We'll talk more about the contents of this configuration file in Chapter 4.)

Other conventions that are prescribed by Rails include the naming of database-related items, and the process by which **controllers** find their corresponding **models** and **views**.

File: **02-database.yml**

```
development:
  adapter: mysql
  database: rails_development
  username: root
  password:
  host: localhost
test:
  adapter: mysql
  database: rails_test
  username: root
  password:
  host: localhost
production:
  adapter: mysql
  database: rails_production
  username: root
  password:
  host: localhost
```

Controllers? Models? Views? *Huh?*

Model-view-controller (MVC) is a software architecture (also referred to as a design pattern) that separates an application's *data model* (model), *user interface* (view), and *control logic* (controller) into three distinct components.

Here's an example: when your browser requests a web page from an MVC-architected application, it's talking exclusively to the controller. The controller gathers the required data from one or more models and renders the response to your request through a view. This separation of components means that any change that's made to one component has a minimal effect on the other two.

We'll talk at length about the MVC architecture and the benefits it yields to Rails applications in Chapter 5.

Rails is also considered to be *opinionated software*, a term that has been coined to refer to software that isn't everything to everyone. Heinemeier Hansson and his core team ruthlessly reject contributions to the framework that don't comply with their vision of where Rails is headed, or aren't sufficiently applicable to be useful for the majority of Rails developers. This is a good way to fight a phenomenon that is known among software developers as **bloat**—the tendency for a software package to implement extraneous features just for the sake of including them.

Don't Repeat Yourself

Rails supports the principles of **DRY** (Don't Repeat Yourself) programming. When you decide to change the behavior of an application that's based on the DRY principle, you shouldn't need to modify application code in more than one authoritative location.

While this might sound complicated at first, it's actually pretty simple. For example, instead of copying and pasting code with a similar or even identical functionality, you develop your application in such a way that this functionality is stored once, in a central location, and is referenced from each portion of the application that needs to use it. This way, if the original behavior needs to change, you need only make modifications in one location, rather than in various places throughout your application (some of which you may easily overlook).

One example of how Rails supports the DRY principle is that, unlike Java, it doesn't force you to repeat your **database schema definition** within your application.[6] Rails considers your database to be the authoritative source of information about data storage, and is clever enough to ask the database for any information it might need to ensure that it treats your data correctly.

Rails also adheres to the DRY principle when it comes to implementing cutting-edge techniques such as **Ajax** (Asynchronous JavaScript and XML). Ajax is an approach that allows your web application to replace content in the user's browser dynamically, or to exchange form data with the server without reloading the page. Developers often find themselves duplicating code while creating Ajax applications: after all, the web site should function in browsers that *don't* support Ajax, as well as those that do, and the code required to display the results to both types of browser is, for the most part, identical. Rails makes it easy to treat each browser generation appropriately without duplicating any code.

Agile Development

More traditional approaches to software development (such as iterative development and the waterfall model) usually attempt to sketch out a long-running and

---

[6] A database schema definition describes how the storage of an application's data is structured. Think of it as a number of spreadsheets, each of which contains rows and columns that define the various pieces of data, and identify where each data item is stored.

rather static plan for an application's goals and needs using predictive methods. These development models usually approach applications from the bottom-up (that is, by working on the data first).

In contrast, **Agile** development methods use an *adaptive* approach. Small teams (typically consisting of fewer than ten developers) iteratively complete small units of the project. Before starting an iteration, the team re-evaluates the priorities for the application that's being built (these priorities may have shifted during the previous iteration, so they may need adjustment). Agile developers also architect their applications from the top-down, starting with the design (which may be as simple as a sketch of the interface on a sheet of paper).

When an application is built using Agile methods, it's less likely to veer out of control during the development cycle, due to the ongoing efforts of the team to adjust priorities. By spending less time creating functional specifications and long-running schedules, developers using Agile methodologies can really jump-start an application's development.

Here are a few examples that illustrate how Rails lends itself to Agile development practices:

❑ You can start to work on the layout of your Rails application before making any decisions about data storage (even though these decisions might change at a later stage). You don't have to repeat this layout work when you start adding functionality to your screen designs—everything evolves dynamically with your requirements.

❑ Unlike code written in C or Java, Rails applications don't need to go through a compilation step in order to be executable. Ruby code is interpreted on the fly, so it doesn't need any form of binary compilation to make it executable. Changing code during development provides developers with immediate feedback, which can significantly boost the speed of application development.

❑ Rails provides a comprehensive framework for the automated testing of application code. Developers who make use of this testing framework can be confident that they're not causing functionality to break when they change existing code—even if they weren't the ones who originally developed it.

❑ Refactoring (rewriting code with an emphasis on optimization) existing Rails application code to better cope with changed priorities, or to implement new features for a development project, can be done much more easily when developers adhere to the DRY principles we discussed above. This is because far fewer changes are required when a certain functionality is implemented just once, and is then reused elsewhere as required.

If your head is spinning from trying to digest these principles, don't worry—we're going to reinforce them continually throughout this book, as we step through building our very own web application in Ruby on Rails!

Building the Example Web Application

As you read this book, I expect you'll be itching to put the techniques we discuss into practice. For this reason, I've planned a fully functional web application that we'll build together through the ensuing chapters. The key concepts, approaches, and methodologies we'll discuss will have a role to play in the sample application, and we'll implement them progressively as your skills improve over the course of this book.

The application we'll build will be a functional clone of the popular story-sharing web site, digg.com, and I've included all necessary files for this application in this book's code archive.

What is digg?

digg.com (or just "digg") describes itself as follows:[7]

> Digg is a user-driven social content web site. OK, so what the heck does that mean? Well, everything on digg is submitted by the digg user community (that would be you). After you submit content, other digg users read your submission and digg what they like best.

> If your story rocks and receives enough diggs, it is promoted to the front page for the millions of digg visitors to see.

Basically, if you want to tell the world about something interesting you found on the Internet—be it your own weblog post or a news story from a major publication—you can submit its URL to digg, along with a short summary of the item. Your story sits in a queue, waiting for other users to "digg" it (give your item a positive vote). As well as voting for a story, users can comment on the story, creating lively discussions within digg.

---

[7] http://digg.com/about/

As soon as the number of "diggs" for a story crosses a certain threshold, it's automatically promoted to the digg homepage, where it attracts a far greater number of readers than the story-queuing area receives. Figure 1.1 shows a snapshot of the digg homepage.

Figure 1.1. The original digg.com

The digg Effect

Due to the huge number of visitors that digg receives, web sites that are listed on the front page may suffer from what is known as the "digg effect"—many sites' servers cannot cope with the sudden surge in traffic, and become inaccessible until the number of simultaneous visitors dies down (or the hosting company boosts the site's capacity to deal with the increase in traffic).

digg was launched in December 2004, and has since been listed in the Alexa traffic rankings as one of the top 200 web sites on the Internet.[8]

---

[8] http://www.alexa.com/data/details/traffic_details?url=digg.com

I didn't decide to show you how to develop your own digg clone just because the site is popular with Internet users, though; digg's feature set is not particularly complicated, but it's sufficient to let us gain first-hand experience with the most important and useful facets of the Ruby on Rails framework.

And while your application might not be able to compete with the original site, reusing this sample project to share links within your family, company, or college class is perfectly conceivable, and hopefully you'll learn enough along the way to branch out and build other types of applications, too.

Features of the Example Application

As I mentioned, we want our application to accept user-submitted links to stories on the Web. We also want to allow other users to vote on the submitted items. In order to meet these objectives, we'll implement the following features as we work through this book:

❑ We'll build a database back end that permanently stores every story, user, vote, etc. (This way, nothing is lost when you close your browser and shut the application down.)

❑ We'll build a story submission interface, which is a form that's available only to users who have registered and logged in.

❑ We'll develop a simplistic layout, as is typical for "Web 2.0" applications. We'll style it with Cascading Style Sheets (CSS) and enhance it with visual effects.

❑ We'll create clean URLs for all the pages on our site. **Clean URLs** (also known as search engine friendly URLs) are usually brief and easily read when they appear in the browser status bar. (An example of a clean URL is http://del.icio.us/popular/software, which I'm sure you'll agree is a lot nicer than http://www.amazon.com/gp/homepage.html/103-0615814-1415024/.)

❑ We'll create a user registration system that lets new users sign up, and allows existing users to log in with their usernames and passwords.

❑ We'll create two different views: the homepage of our application, and the story queue containing stories that haven't yet received enough votes to appear on the homepage.

❏ We'll give users the ability to check voting history on per-user and per-story bases.

❏ We'll facilitate the tagging of stories, and give users the ability to view only those stories that relate to "programming" or "food," for example (for a definition of tagging, see the note below).

It's quite a list, and the result will be one slick web application! Some of the features rely upon others being in place, and we'll implement each feature as a practical example when we look at a new aspect of Rails.

What is Tagging?

Tagging can be thought of as a free-form categorization method. Instead of the site's owners creating a fixed content categorization scheme (often represented as a tree), users are allowed to enter one or more keywords to describe a content item. Resources that share one or more identical tags can be linked together easily—the more overlap between tags, the more the resources are likely to have in common.

Figure 1.2. Tags on flickr.com

![Screenshot of Popular Tags on Flickr Photo Sharing showing a tag cloud with terms such as amsterdam, animal, animals, april, architecture, art, australia, baby, barcelona, beach, berlin, birthday, black, blackandwhite, blue, boston, bw, california, cameraphone, camping, canada, canon, car, cat, cats, chicago, china, christmas, church, city, clouds, color, concert, day, dc, dog, dogs, england, europe, family, festival, film, florida, flower, flowers, food, france, friends, fun, garden, geotagged, germany, girl, graduation, graffiti, green, halloween, hawaii, hiking, holiday, home, honeymoon, hongkong, house, india, ireland, island, italy, japan, july, june, kids, lake, landscape, light, london, losangeles, macro, march, may, me, mexico, moblog, mountain, mountains, museum, music, nature, new, newyork, newyorkcity, newzealand, night, nikon, nyc, ocean, paris, park, party, people, photo, portrait, red, river, roadtrip, rock, rome, san, sanfrancisco, school, scotland, sea, seattle, show, sky, snow, spain, spring, street, summer, sun, sunset, sydney, taiwan, texas, thailand, tokyo, toronto, travel, tree, trees, trip, uk, urban, usa, vacation, vancouver, washington, water, wedding, white, winter, yellow, york, zoo]

Instead of displaying a hierarchical category tree, the tags used in an application are commonly displayed as a "tag cloud" in which each of the tags is represented in a font-size that corresponds to how often that tag has been applied to content items within the system.

Tags are used extensively on sites such as the Flickr photo-sharing web site shown in Figure 1.2,[9] the del.icio.us bookmark-sharing site,[10] and the Technorati weblog search engine.[11]

Summary

We've explored a bit of history in this chapter. Along the way, we learned where both the Ruby language and the Rails framework have come from, and looked in some detail at the niche that they've carved out for themselves in the web development world. I also explained the philosophy behind the Ruby programming language and showed you a snippet of Ruby code. We'll cover much more of Ruby's inner workings in Chapter 3.

We also talked briefly about some of the basic principles that drive Rails development, and saw how Rails supports Agile development methods. Now that you're aware of the possibilities, perhaps some of these ideas and principles will influence your own work with Rails.

Finally, we created a brief specification for the web application we're going to build throughout this book. We described what our application will do, and identified the list of features that we're going to implement. We'll develop a clone of the story-sharing web site digg.com iteratively, taking advantage of some of the Agile development practices that Rails supports.

In the next chapter, we'll install Ruby, Rails, and the MySQL database server software in order to set up a development environment for the upcoming development tasks.

Are you ready to join the fun? If so, turn the page.

---

[9] http://flickr.com/
[10] http://del.icio.us/
[11] http://www.technorati.com/

Getting Started

To get started with Ruby on Rails, we first need to install some development software on our systems. The packages we'll be installing are:

the Ruby language interpreter

The Ruby interpreter translates our Ruby code (or any Ruby code, for that matter, including Rails itself) into something the computer can understand and execute. When this book was being written, Ruby 1.8.4 was recommended for use with Rails, so that's what I've used here.

the Ruby on Rails framework

Once we've downloaded Ruby, we can install the Rails framework itself. As I mentioned in Chapter 1, Rails is written in Ruby. At the time of writing, version 1.2 Release Candidate 2 had been released, and a stable 1.2 release was imminent.

the MySQL database server

The MySQL database server is developed by a company called MySQL AB.[1] MySQL is one of several cross-platform, open-source database servers that are available. While Rails supports plenty of other database servers (such as PostgreSQL, Microsoft SQL Server, and Oracle, to name a few), MySQL is easy to install and set up, sports many advanced features, and is basically the

---

[1] http://www.mysql.com/

only database server you can use with Rails without installing further database connection adapter software. Oh, and it's free!

At the time of writing, the most recent stable release of the MySQL General Release was version 5.0.27.

Instructions for installing Rails differ ever so slightly between operating systems. You may also need to install some additional tools as part of the process, depending on the platform that you use. Here, I'll provide installation instructions for Windows, Mac OS X, and Linux.

Watch your Version Numbers!

It's possible that by the time you read this, a more recent version of Ruby, MySQL, or one of the other packages mentioned here will have been released. Beware! Don't just assume that because a package is newer, it can reliably be used for Rails development. While, in theory, everything should be compatible and these instructions should still apply, sometimes the latest is *not* the greatest.

If you download a more recent version of one of the components listed here, there's a chance that it may not have been as thoroughly tested for compatibility as you might hope. For example, if you choose to use Ruby 1.8.5 rather than 1.8.4, you'll find that elements of the section covering breakpoints in Chapter 11 simply *won't work*! The problem is caused by the fact that the proper working of the `breakpoint` library packaged with Rails is reliant on a bug in Ruby. This bug was patched in Ruby 1.8.5, so `breakpoint` stopped working. We hope that the problem will be resolved soon, but in the meantime you'll be fine if you stick with Ruby 1.8.4.

Feel free to skip the sections that relate to operating systems other than yours, and to focus on those that address your specific needs.

What Does All this Cost?

Everything we need is available for download from the Web, and is licensed under free software licenses. This basically means that everything you'll be installing is free for you to use in both personal and commercial applications. Please refer to the individual license file for each package (they're included in the downloads) if you're curious about the differences between each license.

Installing on Windows

For some reason, the Windows folks have the easiest install procedure. A very helpful fellow by the name of Curt Hibbs sat down and packaged everything required to develop Rails applications on a Windows machine.[2] He now offers the package as an easy-to-install, easy-to-run, single file download called InstantRails. InstantRails ships with the following software:

❑ the Ruby interpreter

❑ the MySQL database server

❑ the Apache web server (although we won't be using it in this book)

❑ Ruby on Rails

That's everything we need in one handy package—how convenient!

To install InstantRails, download the InstantRails 1.3a zip[3] archive from the InstantRails project file list[4] on RubyForge and extract its contents to a folder of your choice.[5] Be careful, though—InstantRails doesn't support folders whose names contain spaces, so unfortunately the obvious choice of `C:\Program Files\` is not a good one. I'd recommend using `C:\InstantRails\` instead.

After you've extracted the `.zip` file (it has approximately 18,000 items in packaged documentation, so if you're using the Windows built-in file compression tool, it could take up to an hour to unzip everything), navigate to the `InstantRails` folder and double-click the `InstantRails.exe` file. You'll be prompted with a dialog like the one shown in Figure 2.1—click OK to continue.

---

[2] Hibbs also published the very early ONLamp.com series of tutorials for Rails entitled *Rolling with Ruby on Rails* [http://www.onlamp.com/pub/a/onlamp/2005/01/20/rails.html].

[3] http://rubyforge.org/frs/download.php/9957/InstantRails-1.3a-win.zip

[4] http://rubyforge.org/frs/?group_id=904

[5] I'm recommending you use InstantRails 1.3a, rather than 1.4 or newer, due to the previously mentioned problem with Ruby 1.8.5 and Rails's included breakpoint library. The newer versions of InstantRails ship with Ruby 1.8.5, and the Ruby on Rails download page recommends Ruby 1.8.5. However, if you choose to install Ruby 1.8.5, you won't be able to use the breakpoint client introduced in Chapter 11 of this book.

Figure 2.1. Configuring InstantRails doesn't get much easier ...

If you're on Windows XP Service Pack 2 or later, you'll also be greeted with the alert message in Figure 2.2 from the Windows internal firewall (or any additional personal firewall software that you might have installed). Of course, the Apache web server isn't trying to do anything malicious—InstantRails just fires it up as part of its initialization process. Go ahead and click Unblock to allow it to start.

Figure 2.2. Allowing Apache to run

You should now see the InstantRails control panel, which, as Figure 2.3 illustrates, should report that everything has started up successfully.

Figure 2.3. The InstantRails control panel

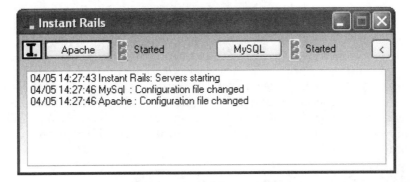

The final step is to update Rails. To do that, right-click on the red I icon in the System Tray to bring up the InstantRails menu. From this menu, select Rails Applications > Open Ruby Console. Once the console opens, enter the following command:

```
C:\InstantRails> gem install rails --include-dependencies
```

Don't Use Other Installations of MySQL

Be careful if you already have MySQL installed and running on your machine—it's not safe to assume that the version you have is compatible with InstantRails. I'd recommend shutting down your existing instance and letting InstantRails start its own version of MySQL instead.

That's it! Everything you need is installed and configured. Feel free to skip the instructions for Mac and Linux, and start building your application!

Installing on Mac OS X

Okay, so the Windows guys had it easy. For the rest of us, though, things aren't quite so simple. While Mac OS X isn't a platform that makes life unnecessarily difficult, installing Rails on OS X is just a tad harder than installing a regular Mac application.[6]

---

[6] There is an all-in-one installer available for Mac OS X, called Locomotive [http://locomotive.raaum.org/]. Unfortunately, it ships with the SQLite database server, instead of MySQL. It's not that I have anything against SQLite as a database, but in a book that's already covering all operating systems, there's only so far one can go to cater for possible combinations of technologies. For this reason, I don't recommend that you use Locomotive to work through this book.

Mac OS X 10.5 (Leopard)

If your Mac is a relatively recent purchase, you may be running OS X version 10.5 (Leopard) or later. If this is the case, then you've got much less to do, because your machine comes pre-installed with both Ruby *and* Rails—congratulations!

Unfortunately, this doesn't mean you can skip the rest of these installation instructions: you still need to install MySQL, so tread carefully if you decide to skip any steps. In fact, it wouldn't do you any harm to work through all of the steps anyway, just to make sure that you're running the appropriate versions of everything.

Mac OS X 10.4 (Tiger) and Earlier

"But wait!" I hear you cry. "My (slightly older) Mac comes with Ruby preinstalled!" Yes, that may indeed be true. However, the version of Ruby that shipped with OS X prior to version 10.5 is a slimmed-down version that's incompatible with Rails, and is therefore unsuited to our needs. Packages like MacPorts[7] do make the installation of Ruby easier, but unfortunately MacPorts currently installs Ruby 1.8.5, which at the time of writing, was incompatible with the Rails breakpoint client (despite the Rails Core team advocating Ruby 1.8.5 as the preferred version to use with Rails).

For the purposes of this book, we'll need to build Ruby on our machine from scratch.[8] Don't worry. I know it sounds intimidating, but it's actually relatively painless—and you'll only need to do it once!

Let's get installing then, shall we?

Installing Xcode

The first step in the process is to make sure we have everything we need for the installation to go smoothly. The only prerequisite for this process is Xcode, the Apple Developer Tools that come on a separate CD with Mac OS X. If you haven't installed the tools yet, and don't have your installation CD handy, you

---

[7] http://www.macports.org/
[8] A tip of the hat is in order for Dan Benjamin, who did a lot of the heavy lifting in the early days of documenting the installation of Rails on OS X. Parts of these installation instructions are heavily influenced by his article "Building Ruby, Rails, LightTPD, and MySQL on Tiger" [http://hivelogic.com/articles/2005/12/01/ruby_rails_lighttpd_mysql_tiger/].

can download the Xcode package for free from http://developer.apple.com/ (although at more than 900MB, it's a hefty download!).

To install Xcode, run the packaged installer by clicking on the XcodeTools.mpkg icon and following the on-screen instructions illustrated in Figure 2.4. The installation tool is a simple wizard that will require you to click Continue a few times, agree to some fairly standard terms and conditions, and hit the Install button.

Figure 2.4. Installing the Xcode developer tools

Introducing the Command Line

For the next few steps, we're going to leave the comfort and security of our pretty graphical user interface and tackle the much geekier UNIX command line. If this is the first time you've used the command line on your Mac, don't worry—we'll be doing a lot more of it throughout this book, so you'll get plenty of practice! Let's dive in.

First, open up a UNIX session in OS X using the Terminal utility. Launch Terminal by selecting Go > Utilities from the Finder menu bar, and double-clicking the Terminal icon. Your Terminal window should look something like Figure 2.5.

Figure 2.5. A Terminal window on Mac OS X

Let's dissect these crazy command line shenanigans. The collection of characters to the left of the cursor is called the **prompt**. By default, it displays:

❑ the name of your Mac

❑ the current directory

❑ the name of the user who's currently logged in

In my case, this is:

```
Core:~ scoop$
```

So, what's what here?

❑ `Core` is the name of my Mac

❑ `scoop` is the name of the user who is currently logged in.

But what the heck is this sign: ~? It's called a **tilde**, and it's shorthand notation for the path to the current user's home directory. Take another look at Figure 2.5, and you'll see I've used the pwd command to *print* the *working* *directory*. The result is /Users/scoop, which just happens to be my home directory. For future command line instructions, though, I'll simply display the prompt as $, to avoid taking up valuable real estate on the page.

Setting the Path

The next thing we need to make sure of is that Mac OS X can locate all of the command line tools that we'll be using during this installation. The PATH environment variable stores the list of folders to which OS X has access; we'll store the changes we make to this variable in a file in our home directory.

The name of the file we'll use is .profile. (On UNIX-based systems such as Mac OS X, files that start with a period are usually hidden files.) It might look slightly intimidating, but if you type out the following command exactly, your PATH environment variable will be set correctly every time you open a new Terminal window. As it's quite long, I've split the command over two lines using the \ character, but you can type it out on one line if you like:

```
$ echo 'export PATH="/usr/local/bin:/usr/local/sbin:$PATH"' >> \
    ~/.profile
```

To activate this change (without having to open and close the Terminal window), type the following command:

```
$ . ~/.profile
```

Yes, that's a single period at the beginning of the line. Note that these commands don't produce any feedback, as Figure 2.6 shows, but they're still taking effect.

Figure 2.6. Setting the correct path

It would be a shame to clutter up this home directory—or our desktop—with a huge number of files, so let's go about this installation business in an organized fashion.

Staying Organized

The process of extracting, configuring, and compiling the source code for all of the packages that we'll be downloading will take up a decent amount of space on your hard drive. To keep things organized, we'll operate within a single folder rather than making a mess of our desktop.

The desktop on your Mac is actually a subfolder of your home directory. Change to the Desktop folder using the cd command (short for *change directory*). Once you're there, you can use mkdir to *make* a *dir*ectory in which to store our downloads and other assorted files. Let's call this directory build:

```
$ cd Desktop
$ mkdir build
$ cd build
```

The result is that we have on the desktop a new directory, which is now our current working directory. This is also reflected by our prompt. As Figure 2.7 shows, mine now reads:

```
Core:~/Desktop/build scoop$
```

Figure 2.7. Creating a temporary working directory

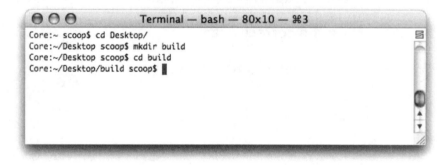

Now the fun begins!

Installing Ruby on a Mac

Before installing Ruby itself, we need to install another library on which Ruby depends: Readline.

Here's the sequence of (somewhat convoluted) commands for installing the Readline library. It's a fairly small library, so the installation shouldn't take too long:

```
$ curl ftp://ftp.gnu.org/gnu/readline/readline-5.1.tar.gz | tar xz
$ cd readline-5.1
$ ./configure --prefix=/usr/local
$ make
$ sudo make install
$ cd ..
```

With Readline in place, we're now able to install Ruby itself. Type out the following series of commands, exactly as you see them here. It's not important that you understand every line, but it is important that you don't make any typos. This step might also test your patience somewhat, as the configuration step may take half an hour or more to complete, depending on the speed of your system and your network connection.

```
$ curl ftp://ftp.ruby-lang.org/pub/ruby/1.8/ruby-1.8.4.tar.gz \
    | tar xz
$ cd ruby-1.8.4
$ ./configure --prefix=/usr/local --enable-pthread \
    --with-readline-dir=/usr/local
$ make
$ sudo make install
$ sudo make install-doc
$ cd ..
```

How did you go? It might be prudent at this point to run some checks, to determine whether our installation is on track so far. The simplest and safest way to tell whether our Ruby installation is working is to type the following command into the Terminal window:

```
$ ruby -v
```

The version that you should see displayed is ruby 1.8.4 (2005-12-24), as shown in Figure 2.8. If anything else is displayed here (such as ruby 1.8.2 (2004-12-25)), something has gone wrong. You should carefully repeat the instructions up to this point.[9]

---

[9] Remember—if you get stuck, you can always try asking for help on SitePoint's Ruby forum [http://www.sitepoint.com/launch/rubyforum/].

> **Be a Super User for a Day**
>
> sudo is a way for "regular" computer users to perform system-wide installations that are normally reserved for system administrators. You'll need to enter your account password before you'll be allowed to execute this command. To use sudo, the user account must have Allow user to administer this computer setting checked. This can be changed in the Accounts section of the Apple System Preferences window.

Figure 2.8. Checking the Ruby version

Next up is the installation of RubyGems.

Installing RubyGems on a Mac

"What is RubyGems?" I hear you ask. RubyGems is a utility for managing the additions to the Ruby programming language that other people have developed and made available as free downloads. Think of it as pre-packaged functionality that you can install on your machine so you don't have to reinvent the wheel over and over again while you're working on your own projects.[10] Rails is released and published through the RubyGems system.

The following sequence of commands will download and install RubyGems on your Mac. It should be a relatively quick procedure:

```
$ curl -L \
  http://rubyforge.org/frs/download.php/11289/rubygems-0.9.0.tgz \
  | tar xz
$ cd rubygems-0.9.0
```

---

[10] The RubyGems web site [http://gems.rubyforge.org/] has additional documentation for the gem command that we'll use in this section.

```
$ sudo ruby setup.rb
$ cd ..
```

Figure 2.9. Confirmation of a successful RubyGems installation

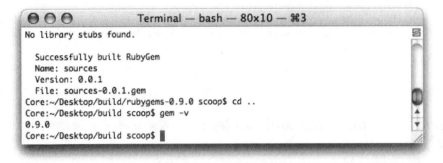

Are you getting the hang of this command line thing? Good! We now have *another* new command at our fingertips: gem. The gem command is used to install and manage Ruby packages on your machine—enter the following to check that RubyGems is working properly:

```
$ gem -v
```

The output should identify the version of RubyGems that you installed, as Figure 2.9 shows. We'll use the gem command to install Rails.

Installing Rails on a Mac

Whew! After eight pages of installation instructions, we're finally here: the installation of the Rails framework. Don't despair—it's all been worth it. Plus, in contrast to the Windows users, you'll have a much easier upgrade path the next time a new version of Ruby or Rails is released (which I'll explain later).

Without further ado, enter this command to install Rails:

```
$ sudo gem install rails --include-dependencies
```

What's happening here is that RubyGems system is downloading Rails and the packages on which it depends, before installing the necessary files and documentation. This process may take ten minutes or more to complete, but it'll get there in the end.

While you're waiting for Rails to install, I'll let you in on a little secret: the command that we just entered is the *same* command that you can use to stay up-to-date with future Rails releases. Whenever you want to upgrade Rails, just enter that command again, and your system will be updated. Cool, huh?

Once the installation has finished, you can verify the version of Rails you just installed by running the following command in your Terminal window.

```
$ rails -v
```

This should give you the version number of Rails, as illustrated in Figure 2.10.

Figure 2.10. Installing Rails on Mac OS X via RubyGems

```
● ● ●            Terminal — bash — 80x24
Core:~ scoop$ sudo gem install rails --include-dependencies
Password:
Bulk updating Gem source index for: http://gems.rubyforge.org
Successfully installed rails-1.1.6
Successfully installed rake-0.7.1
Successfully installed activesupport-1.3.1
Successfully installed activerecord-1.14.4
Successfully installed actionpack-1.12.5
Successfully installed actionmailer-1.2.5
Successfully installed actionwebservice-1.1.6
Installing ri documentation for rake-0.7.1...
Installing ri documentation for activesupport-1.3.1...
Installing ri documentation for activerecord-1.14.4...
Installing ri documentation for actionpack-1.12.5...
Installing ri documentation for actionmailer-1.2.5...
Installing ri documentation for actionwebservice-1.1.6...
Installing RDoc documentation for rake-0.7.1...
Installing RDoc documentation for activesupport-1.3.1...
Installing RDoc documentation for activerecord-1.14.4...
Installing RDoc documentation for actionpack-1.12.5...
Installing RDoc documentation for actionmailer-1.2.5...
Installing RDoc documentation for actionwebservice-1.1.6...
Core:~ scoop$ rails -v
Rails 1.1.6
Core:~ scoop$ ▋
```

Phew, we got there in the end. Don't break out the champagne just yet, though—we still need a database server!

Installing MySQL on a Mac

If you've been feeling nervous about all of these command line instructions, then you can breathe easily for a moment. We're going to head back into familiar territory for a moment—close your Terminal window, point your browser at http://dev.mysql.com/downloads/, and download the `mysql-standard-version-osxversion-platform`.dmg (at the time of writing, the current stable version of MySQL was 5.0.24). Double-click the disk image to mount it, double-click the installer, and get installing!

The MySQL installer is shown in Figure 2.11. You've clicked your way through a few of these wizards now, so it should be second nature to you!

Figure 2.11. Installing MySQL on Mac OS X

Excellent. Next, we need to start the server—we'll do this manually for now. Open a Terminal window and enter the following command:

```
$ sudo /usr/local/bin/mysqld_safe5
```

Once MySQL is running, you can tell it to run in the background by hitting Ctrl-Z, then entering this command:

```
$ bg
```

You can now close the Terminal window; MySQL will continue to run as a server on your system. Now, all that's left to do is confirm that the MySQL server is indeed running as expected. In your Terminal window, type the following:

```
$ ps -ax | grep mysql
```

This command should return a few processes that relate to MySQL, as Figure 2.12 illustrates. If it does, you can try to connect to your database with the following command:

```
$ mysql5
```

This should present you with a mysql> prompt like the one shown in Figure 2.12. If this all seems a little confusing, don't worry—we won't operate this way when we're developing our application. Just knowing that we can connect to the database server from the client is reassuring!

Figure 2.12. Confirming MySQL installation on Mac OS X

Type exit to leave the MySQL client.

The last thing you might consider doing is to set the database server to start automatically when your computer boots. The MySQLStartupItem.pkg installer that came with the MySQL download will set this up for you. Once this package has been installed, you can safely remove the mounted disk image by dragging it to the Trash, and delete the .dmg file.

Congratulations, you're all done!

Installing on Linux

I bet you Linux folks smirked when the Mac OS X guys had to use the command line (possibly for the first time), didn't you?

Well, if you're running Linux, I'm going to assume that you're used to the command line, so I won't feel bad throwing you an archaic series of commands to install all the software you need to get up and running with Rails.

One Size Fits All?

There are literally thousands of different distributions of Linux—more than any other operating system. Each distribution has its own quirks and pitfalls, its own package manager, and different permissions settings, and installations are often tweaked and customized over time. So while I've put every effort into ensuring that these instructions are sound, it would be impossible to offer an absolute guarantee that they will work on any possible installation of Linux without individual tweaking.

If you do run into any problems installing Rails or its constituents on your machine, I'd recommend you ask for assistance on the friendly SitePoint Ruby forum.[11] Chances are that someone else has experienced the same problem, and will be happy to help you out.

Using a Package Manager

As I mentioned, many Linux distributions come with their own package managers, including apt-get , yum, and rpm, among others.

Of course, you're free to use the package manager that's bundled with your Linux distribution to install Ruby, and if you get stuck with these instructions for whatever reason, it might be a good option for you. However, I'm afraid you're on your own if you go down that path.

---

[11] http://www.sitepoint.com/launch/rubyforum/

Rather than attempt to cover all of the different package managers that are available, I'll show you how to install Ruby the manual way.

Prerequisites

The only prerequisite for installing Ruby on Linux is that you have the gcc compiler installed on your machine. gcc ships with most Linux distributions by default, but if it's not on your system, you'll either need to use your system's package management system to install it (look for "build essential" or "basic compiler"), or to download a native binary for your system.[12]

Enter the following instructions at the command line to confirm that your compiler is in place:

```
$ gcc -v
```

If the version number for the compiler is displayed, as shown in Figure 2.13, then you're ready to install Ruby.

Figure 2.13. Confirming the gcc compiler is installed

---

[12] http://gcc.gnu.org/install/binaries.html

Installing Ruby on Linux

Ruby is available for download from the Ruby ftp site.[13] As I mentioned earlier in this chapter, I recommend the use of version 1.8.4 of the Ruby interpreter.

Download the appropriate `tar` file for Ruby (this will be called something like `ruby-1.8.4.tar.gz`), and extract the archive using the `gunzip` and `tar` commands, as shown below. Then change into the new directory that was created, as illustrated in Figure 2.14.

```
$ gunzip ruby-1.8.4.tar.gz
$ tar xvf ruby-1.8.4.tar
$ cd ruby-1.8.4
```

Figure 2.14. Extracting the Ruby archive on Linux

From this directory, run the following command to compile and install Ruby in `/usr/local`:

```
$ sudo ./configure && make && make install
```

---

[13] ftp://ftp.ruby-lang.org/pub/ruby/1.8/ruby-1.8.4.tar.gz

This process may take 20 minutes or more, so be patient.

Once it's completed, you should add `/usr/local/bin` to your PATH environment variable. I'll assume that, being a Linux user, you know how to do that. Once that environment variable is set, you can now enter the following command to check which version of Ruby you installed:

```
$ ruby -v
```

The message that's displayed should confirm that you're running version 1.8.4, as Figure 2.15 illustrates.

Figure 2.15. Installing Ruby on Linux

```
scoop@Core: ~/ruby-1.8.4

File  Edit  View  Terminal  Tabs  Help

install -c -p -m 0644 dln.h /usr/local/lib/ruby/1.8/i686-linux
install -c -p -m 0644 env.h /usr/local/lib/ruby/1.8/i686-linux
install -c -p -m 0644 intern.h /usr/local/lib/ruby/1.8/i686-linux
install -c -p -m 0644 missing.h /usr/local/lib/ruby/1.8/i686-linux
install -c -p -m 0644 node.h /usr/local/lib/ruby/1.8/i686-linux
install -c -p -m 0644 re.h /usr/local/lib/ruby/1.8/i686-linux
install -c -p -m 0644 regex.h /usr/local/lib/ruby/1.8/i686-linux
install -c -p -m 0644 ruby.h /usr/local/lib/ruby/1.8/i686-linux
install -c -p -m 0644 rubyio.h /usr/local/lib/ruby/1.8/i686-linux
install -c -p -m 0644 rubysig.h /usr/local/lib/ruby/1.8/i686-linux
install -c -p -m 0644 st.h /usr/local/lib/ruby/1.8/i686-linux
install -c -p -m 0644 util.h /usr/local/lib/ruby/1.8/i686-linux
install -c -p -m 0644 version.h /usr/local/lib/ruby/1.8/i686-linux
install -c -p -m 0644 config.h /usr/local/lib/ruby/1.8/i686-linux
mkdir -p -m 755 /usr/local/man/man1
install -c -p -m 0644 ruby.1 /usr/local/man/man1/ruby.1
./miniruby ./ext/extmk.rb --dest-dir="" --make="make" --mflags="" --make-flags="
" --extout=".ext" --extension --extstatic -- install
cp -r ./.ext/. /usr/local/lib/ruby/1.8
scoop@Core: ~/ruby-1.8.4$ ruby -v
ruby 1.8.4 (2005-12-24) [i686-linux]
scoop@Core: ~/ruby-1.8.4$
```

Now, on to the next step: installing RubyGems.

Installing RubyGems on Linux

Next up is the installation of RubyGems, the package manager for Ruby-related software. RubyGems works much like the package manager that your operating system uses to manage the various Linux utilities that you have installed on your machine. RubyGems makes it easy to install all sorts of additional software and extensions for Ruby.

RubyGems is available for download from http://rubyforge.org/projects/rubygems/. Once you've downloaded and extracted it, change to the `rubygems` directory and run the following command:

```
$ sudo ruby setup.rb
```

This will setup and install RubyGems for use on your system, and also make the `gem` command available for you to use—the `gem` command is what we'll use to install Rails itself. It shouldn't take long, and once it completes, you can execute the `gem` command to confirm that your installation was successful. The output should look something like that in Figure 2.16.

Figure 2.16. Installing RubyGems on Linux

We have successfully installed RubyGems. Now we can finally install the Rails framework!

Installing Rails on Linux

Using RubyGems, the installation of Rails itself is a breeze. To install Rails, type the following input at the command prompt as the `root` user (or using `sudo` if it's installed on your system):

```
$ sudo gem install rails --include-dependencies
```

The process may take ten minutes or so, depending on your Internet connection, but that's all you need to do! And as an added bonus, RubyGems gives us an easy way to stay up-to-date with future Rails releases—whenever we want to up-grade Rails, we just need to type this command!

To confirm that your Rails installation was successful, type the following command to display the version of Rails that was installed:

```
$ rails -v
```

The result that you see should be the same as that shown in Figure 2.17.

Figure 2.17. Installing Rails via RubyGems on Linux

All that's left now is to install a database—then we can get to work!

Installing MySQL on Linux

Although it's not quite as crucial as it was with the installation of Ruby, I'd still recommended that you use the official MySQL binaries that are available for download from http://dev.mysql.com/ instead of the pre-packaged versions that may already have been installed with your version of Linux.

1. Download and extract the file.

   Download the current stable release of MySQL from http://dev.mysql.com/downloads/. There are a number of packages for each flavor of Linux, but the one you're after is the Standard version for Linux (x86, glibc-2.2, "standard is static", gcc) under the Linux (non RPM package) downloads heading. I used version 5.0.24a, which was about 44MB.

   Once you've downloaded the file, log in as the `root` user to ensure that you have sufficient permissions to install it on your machine. Extract the downloaded file to `/usr/local`, which will create a directory called `mysql-standard-version-linux-i686`.

   ```
   $ cd /usr/local
   $ tar xvf mysql-standard-version-linux-i686.tar.gz
   ```

2. Create symbolic links.

   It's a good idea to create a symbolic link called `mysql` in the `/usr/local` directory. This will make accessing the directory containing the database server much easier.

   ```
   $ ln -s mysql-standard-version-linux-i686 mysql
   $ cd mysql
   ```

   There are also a few command line tools that it's convenient for us to be able to access readily. Let's create a few links for those as well, so we have easy access to them when we need them.

   ```
   $ ln -s /usr/local/mysql/bin/mysql /usr/local/bin/mysql
   $ ln -s /usr/local/mysql/bin/mysqladmin
   /usr/local/bin/mysqladmin
   $ ln -s /usr/local/mysql/bin/mysqldump
   /usr/local/bin/mysqldump
   $ ln -s /usr/local/mysql/bin/mysqld_safe
   /usr/local/bin/mysqld_safe
   ```

3. Set groups and permissions.

   It's possible to run the MySQL database server as the root user, but for security reasons you're better off creating a special user that is dedicated to running this process. We'll name the user `mysql`.

To create this user, enter the following commands:

```
$ groupadd mysql
$ useradd -g mysql mysql
```

From the mysql directory, run the following script, which will install the default databases for MySQL to use:

```
$ scripts/mysql_install_db --user=mysql
```

Finally, we should secure the data directory in which our precious database information will reside. It's best to make it only accessible to our new mysql user; the following instructions will achieve this for us:

```
$ chown -R root .
$ chown -R mysql data
$ chgrp -R mysql
```

The database server has now been installed. Let's start it up!

4. Start the server.

    Everything's in place, so let's see what happens when we launch our server. Enter the following command:

```
$ mysqld_safe --user=mysql &
```

If the MySQL server started without throwing any errors, everything has worked as planned. Good job! If it didn't, check the hostname.err file that is created whenever an error occurs—it should give you some insight as to what went wrong.

You can now try connecting to your database! Log in to the mysql client using the following command:

```
$ mysql
```

You should see a mysql> prompt, like the one shown in Figure 2.18. If this all seems a little confusing, don't worry—we won't operate this way when developing our application. Just knowing that we can log in to the database server is reassuring enough.

Figure 2.18. Starting the MySQL database server on Linux

```
scoop@Core: ~
File  Edit  View  Terminal  Tabs  Help
Please report any problems with the ./bin/mysqlbug script!

The latest information about MySQL is available on the web at
http://www.mysql.com
Support MySQL by buying support/licenses at http://shop.mysql.com
$ chown -R root .
$ chown -R mysql data
$ chgrp -R mysql .
$ bin/mysqld_safe --user=mysql &
[1] 28193
scoop@Core:/usr/local/mysql$ Starting mysqld daemon with databases from
 /usr/local/mysql/data
$ mysql
Welcome to the MySQL monitor.  Commands end with ; or \g.
Your MySQL connection id is 8 to server version: 5.0.24a-standard

Type 'help;' or '\h' for help. Type '\c' to clear the buffer.

mysql> exit
Bye
$ █
```

That's it—you're done. Incidentally, the command to execute whenever you
want to stop the server is:

```
$ mysqladmin -u root shutdown
```

5. Launch the server on startup.

    You might like to configure your machine so that the database server will
    launch whenever your machine boots. However, the process to achieve this
    differs wildly between variants of Linux, so if you run into problems, you
    might consider asking for help at the SitePoint Forums.[14] The following
    procedure should work in most cases.

    First, locate the file called my.cnf, which resides in the support-files dir-
    ectory of the MySQL installation, and open it in a text editor. Add the fol-
    lowing lines:

```
[mysqld]
user=mysql
```

---

[14] http://www.sitepoint.com/forums/

This will ensure that the user that launches the process will be our special `mysql` user. Now start the server again, but this time use the following command:

```
$ support-files/mysql.server start
```

Login to the `mysql` client to check that you are able to establish a connection. If so, you're in good shape to add that startup command to your launch sequence. Here are the commands to do that:

```
$ cp /usr/local/mysql/support-files/mysql.server /etc/init.d/
$ cd /etc/rc2.d
$ ln -s ../init.d/mysql.server S99mysql
$ cd /etc/rc3.d
$ ln -s ../init.d/mysql.server S99mysql
$ cd /etc/rc5.d
$ ln -s ../init.d/mysql.server S99mysql
$ cd /etc/rc0.d
$ ln -s ../init.d/mysql.server K01mysql
```

Once you've completed these steps, reboot your machine. Then connect to the database server using the `mysql` client, as before, to confirm that the server started up as expected.

Building a Foundation

Is everyone prepared? Good! Now that you've put your workstation on Rails, let's do something with it. In this section, we'll build the foundations of the application that we'll develop throughout the rest of this book.

One Directory Structure to Rule them All

In Chapter 1, I mentioned that Rails applications follow certain conventions. One of these conventions is that an application that's written in Rails always has the same directory structure—one in which everything has its designated place. By gently forcing this directory structure upon developers, Rails ensures that your work is semi-automatically organized "the Rails way."

Figure 2.19 shows what the structure looks like. We'll create this directory structure for our application in just a moment.

Figure 2.19. The default directory structure for a Rails application

As you can see, this standard directory structure consists of quite a few subdirectories (and I'm not even showing *their* subdirectories yet!). This wealth of subdirectories can be overwhelming at first, but we'll explore them one by one. A lot of thought has gone into establishing and naming the folders, and the result is an application whose file system is well structured.

Before you go and manually create all these directories yourself, let me show you how to set up that pretty directory structure using just one command—I told you that Rails allows us to do *less* typing!

Creating the Standard Directory Structure

It's easy to generate the default directory structure shown in Figure 2.19 for a new Rails application using the `rails` command.

Before we start, I'd like to introduce you to the secret, under-the-hood project name we'll give to our digg clone: *Shovell*. Yes, it's cheeky, but it'll work.

Now, let's go ahead and create the directory structure to hold our application.

A Regular Console Window Just Won't Do!

If you're a Windows user, you might be tempted to fire up a regular DOS console for your command line work. This won't do, I'm afraid—instead, launch a Ruby console by starting InstantRails, then clicking on the I button in the top-left of the control panel. From the menu that appears, select Rails Applications > Open Ruby Console Window, as Figure 2.20 illustrates.

The Ruby console must be used because InstantRails doesn't modify anything in your regular Windows environment when it installs; by launching a console from the InstantRails control panel, your console will be loaded with all of the environment settings that Rails needs. The Windows Ruby console is depicted in Figure 2.21.

Figure 2.20. Launching a console window from InstantRails

Figure 2.21. The Ruby Console under Windows

```
C:\WINDOWS\system32\cmd.exe                                    _ □ ×

C:\INSTAN~1>CD C:\InstantRails

C:\InstantRails>PATH C:\InstantRails\ruby\bin;C:\InstantRails\mysql\bin;C:\WINDO
WS\system32;C:\WINDOWS\System32\Wbem;C:\INSTAN~1\ruby\bin;C:\INSTAN~1
\Apache;C:\INSTAN~1\PHP

C:\InstantRails>cd rails_apps

C:\InstantRails\rails_apps>dir
 Volume in drive C is Local Disk
 Volume Serial Number is E421-05AB

 Directory of C:\InstantRails\rails_apps

10/08/2006  11:28 AM    <DIR>          .
10/08/2006  11:28 AM    <DIR>          ..
10/08/2006  11:28 AM    <DIR>          cookbook
10/08/2006  11:28 AM    <DIR>          typo-2.6.0
               0 File(s)              0 bytes
               4 Dir(s)  29,575,213,056 bytes free

C:\InstantRails\rails_apps>_
```

The `rails` command takes a single parameter: the directory in which you'd like to store your application. You can, and are encouraged to, execute it from the parent directory in which you want your new Rails application to live. I'll do this right in my home directory:

```
$ rails shovell
create
create app/controllers
create app/helpers
create app/models
create app/views/layouts
```

```
create config/environments
create components
create db
create log/server.log
create log/production.log
create log/development.log
create log/test.log
```

Congratulations, your directory structure has been created!

Starting our Application

Even before we write any code, it's possible to start up our application environment to check that our setup is working correctly. This should give us a nice boost of confidence before we progress any further.

What we'll do is launch **WEBrick**, a small web server written in Ruby. WEBrick is included with the Ruby installation that we stepped through earlier in this chapter, so it's installed on our machine and ready to use.

To start up WEBrick—and the rest of the Rails environment for our application—we return once again to the command line. Change into the Shovell subdirectory that was created when we executed the rails command in the previous section. From the Shovell directory, enter the command ruby script/server.

This will fire up the WEBrick web server, which will then begin listening for requests on TCP port 3000 of your local machine.

```
$ cd shovell
$ ruby script/server
=> Booting WEBrick…
=> Rails application started on http://0.0.0.0:3000
=> Ctrl-C to shutdown server; call with --help for options
[2006-05-07 14:29:51] INFO WEBrick 1.3.1
[2006-05-07 14:29:51] INFO ruby 1.8.4 (2005-12-24) [i686-darwin8.6
[2006-05-07 14:29:51] INFO WEBrick::HTTPServer#start: pid=468 port
```

Well done—you just started up your application for the first time! Okay, so it's not going to be doing a whole lot (we haven't written any lines of code yet, after all), but you can now connect to your application by entering http://localhost:3000/ into your web browser's address bar; you should see something similar to Figure 2.22.

Figure 2.22. Welcome aboard: the Rails welcome screen

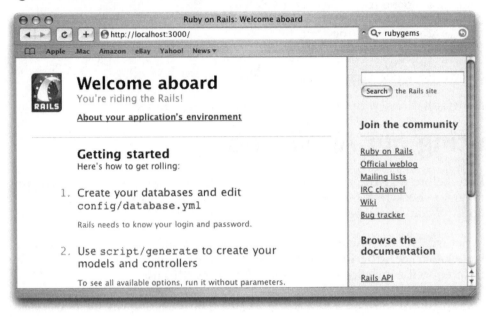

This welcome screen provides us with a few items, including some steps for getting started with Rails application development. Don't mind these just yet; we'll get there soon enough. You'll also notice in the sidebar some links to sites such as the Rails wiki and the mailing list archives, which you can browse through at your leisure. And there are some links to documentation for Rails and for Ruby; you'll find these resources useful once you've progressed further with Rails development.

If you're interested to see the version numbers of each of the components we've installed, click on the link labeled About your application's environment. You'll see a nicely animated information box, like the one in Figure 2.23. This dialog contains all the version information you should ever need. If you've followed the installation instructions in this book, you should have the latest versions of everything.

Figure 2.23. Viewing version information

Okay, so you're finally ready to write some code. But wait! Which text editor will you be using?

Which Text Editor?

The question of which text editor is best for web development has spawned arguments that border on religious fanaticism. However, while it's certainly possible to develop Rails applications using the default text editor that comes bundled with your operating system, I wouldn't recommend it—the benefits provided by a specifically designed programmer's editor can prevent typing errors and increase your productivity immeasurably.

In this section, I've suggested a couple of alternatives for each operating system, and I'll let you make a choice that suits your personal preferences and budget.

Windows Text Editors

UltraEdit

The most popular option for editing Rails code on Windows seems to be Ultra-Edit,[15] which is shown in Figure 2.24. UltraEdit is available for download as a free trial, and may be purchased online for US$39.95. It offers syntax highlighting, code completion, and proper Unicode support (for international characters), as well as providing the facility to jump quickly between several files (this is a huge plus for Rails applications, which usually consist of several dozen files).

Figure 2.24. UltraEdit: a seriously powerful Windows editor

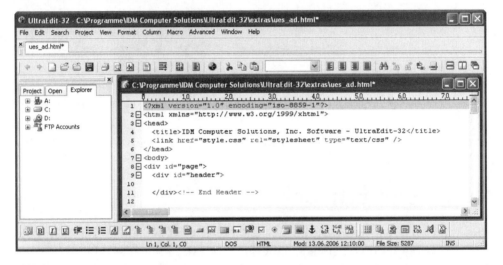

ConTEXT

A free alternative is ConTEXT,[16] shown in Figure 2.25, which holds its own in the features department. It also supports syntax highlighting for Ruby (which is available as a separate download[17]), the ability to open multiple documents in tabs, and a host of other features to make your development experience more enjoyable. I especially like the fact that ConTEXT is quite lightweight, so it loads very quickly. Oh, and that price tag is pretty attractive, too!

---

[15] http://www.ultraedit.com/
[16] http://context.cx/
[17] http://www.context.cx/component/option,com_docman/task,cat_view/gid,76/Itemid,48/

Figure 2.25. ConTEXT: a free, feature-rich text editor for Windows

Mac OS X Text Editors

TextMate

For Mac OS X users, the hands-down winner in the Rails code editor popularity contest is TextMate,[18] which is shown in Figure 2.26. TextMate is the editor you can see in action in numerous screen casts[19] available from the Rails web site. It's available for download as a free, 30-day trial, and the full version of the product costs €39.

TextMate boasts terrific project management support, amazing macro recording/code completion functionality, and one of the most complete syntax highlighting implementations for Rails code. As you can probably tell, I'm a big fan, and recommend it heartily. But this is beginning to sound like a television commercial, so I'll leave it at that.

---

[18] http://www.macromates.com/
[19] http://www.rubyonrails.org/screencasts/

Figure 2.26. TextMate running under Mac OS X

TextWrangler

TextWrangler is a free, simple text editor made by BareBones Software. As with the other editors listed here, TextWrangler tidies up your workspace by allowing you to have several files open at the same time. The documents are listed in a pull-out "drawer" to one side of the interface, rather than as tabs.

If you can live without syntax highlighting (it's now only supported by BBEdit, TextWrangler's big brother[20]), you can download TextWrangler from the Bare-Bones Software web site.[21] Figure 2.27 shows TextWrangler in action.

---

[20] http://barebones.com/products/bbedit/
[21] http://barebones.com/products/textwrangler/

Figure 2.27. TextWrangler, a free text editor for Mac OS X

Linux and Cross-platform Editors

A number of development-centric text editors that run on a variety of platforms are available for free download. The following editors have loyal followings, and all run equally well on Linux as on Microsoft Windows and Mac OS X:

❏ Emacs, http://www.emacswiki.org/

❏ jEdit, http://www.jedit.org/

❏ RadRails, http://www.radrails.org/

❏ Vim, http://www.vim.org/

A more comprehensive (non-alphabetical) list of text editors can be found in the Rails Wiki.[22] This page also covers potential enhancement modules for other editors.

Summary

In this chapter, I showed you how to install all of the software that you need to develop a web application in Ruby on Rails.

---

[22] http://wiki.rubyonrails.org/rails/pages/Editors/

We installed Ruby, Rails, and MySQL, and set up the standard directory structure for our application, which we've named "Shovell." We even launched the application for the first time, which enabled us to check which versions we were running of the components involved. And finally, I gave you some options for text editors you can use to build the application.

All this work has been completed in preparation for Chapter 4, where we'll begin to write our first lines of application code. But first, we've got some theory to get through—hold on tight, we'll get coding soon enough!

Introducing Ruby

While it certainly makes no attempt to constitute a complete guide to the Ruby language, this chapter will introduce you to some of the basics of Ruby. We'll power through a crash-course in object oriented programming, covering the more common features of the language along the way, and leaving the more obscure aspects of Ruby for a dedicated reference guide.[1] I'll also point out some of the advantages that Ruby has over other languages when it comes to developing applications for the Web.

Some Rails developers suggest that it's possible to learn and use Rails without learning the Ruby basics first, but as far as I'm concerned, it's extremely beneficial to know even a *little* Ruby before diving into the guts of Rails. In fact, if you take the time to learn the Ruby basics first, you'll automatically become a better Rails programmer.

Ruby is a Scripting Language

In general, programming languages fall into one of two categories: they're either compiled languages or scripting languages. Let's explore what each of those terms means, and understand the differences between them.

---

[1] http://www.ruby-doc.org/stdlib/

Compiled Languages

The language in which you write an application is not actually something that your computer understands. Your code needs to be translated into bits and bytes that can be executed by your computer. This process of translation is called **compilation**, and any language that requires compilation is referred to as a **compiled language**. Examples of compiled languages include C, C#, and Java.

For a compiled language, the actual compilation is the final step in the development process. You invoke a **compiler**—the software program that translates your final hand-written, human-readable code into machine-readable code—and the compiler creates an executable file. This final product is then able to execute independently of the original source code.

Thus, if you make changes to your code, and you want those changes to be incorporated into the application, you must stop the running application, recompile it, then start the application again.

Scripting Languages

On the other hand, a scripting language such as Ruby, PHP, or Python, relies upon an application's source code all of the time. **Scripting languages** don't have a compiler or a compilation phase per se; instead, they use an **interpreter**—a program that runs on the web server—to translate hand-written code into machine-executable code on the fly. The link between the running application and your hand-crafted code is never severed, because that scripting code is translated every time it is invoked—in other words, for every web page that your application renders.

As you might have gathered from the name, the use of an interpreter rather than a compiler is the major difference between a scripting language and a compiled language.

The Great Performance Debate

If you've come from a compiled-language background, you might be concerned by all this talk of translating code on the fly—how does it affect the application's performance?

These concerns are valid—translating code on the web server every time it's needed is certainly more expensive, performance-wise, than executing pre-compiled code, as it requires more effort on the part of your machine's processor. The good news is that there are ways to speed up scripted languages, including techniques such as code caching and persistent interpreters. However, both topics are beyond the scope of this book.

There's also an upside to scripted languages in terms of performance—namely, *your* performance while developing an application.

Imagine that you've just compiled a shiny new Java application, and launched it for the first time ... and then you notice a typo on the welcome screen. To fix it, you have to stop your application, go back to the source code, fix the typo, wait for the code to recompile, and restart your application to confirm that it is fixed. And if you find another typo, you'll need to repeat that process *again*. Lather, rinse, repeat.

In a scripting language, you can fix the typo and just reload the page in your browser—no restart, no recompile, no nothing. It's as simple as that.

Ruby is an Object Oriented Language

Ruby, from its very beginnings, was built as a programming language that adheres to the principles of **object oriented programming** (OOP). Before getting into Ruby specifics, I'd like to introduce you to some fundamental concepts of OOP. Now I know that theory can seem a bit dry to those who are itching to start coding, but we'll cover a lot of ground in this short section, so don't skip it. This discussion will hold you in good stead—trust me.

OOP is a programming paradigm that first surfaced in the 1960s, but didn't gain traction until the 1980s with C++. The core idea behind it is that programs should be composed of individual entities, or **objects**, each of which has the ability to communicate with other objects around it. Additionally, each object may have the facility to store data internally, as depicted in Figure 3.1.

Figure 3.1. Communication between objects

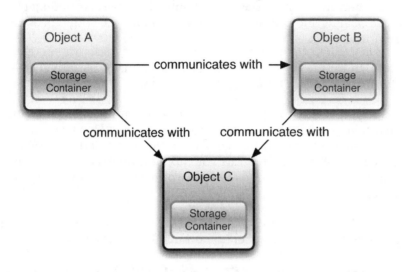

Objects in an OOP application are often modeled on real-world objects, so even non-programmers can usually recognize the basic role that an object plays.

And, just like the real world, OOP defines objects with similar characteristics as belonging to the same **class**. A class is a construct for defining properties for objects that are alike, and equipping them with functionality. For example, a class named `Car` might define the attributes `color` and `mileage` for its objects, and assign them functionality—actions such as "open the trunk," "start the engine," and "change gears." These different actions are known as **methods**, although you'll often see Rails enthusiasts refer to the methods of a controller as "actions"—you can safely consider the two terms to be interchangeable.

Understanding the relationship between a class and its objects is integral to understanding how OOP works. For instance, one object can invoke functionality on another object, and can do so without affecting other objects of the same class. So, if one car object was instructed to open its trunk (think of KITT, the talking car from the classic 80s television show "Knight Rider," if it helps with the metaphor),[2] then its trunk would open, but the trunk of other cars would remain

---

[2] "Knight Rider" [http://en.wikipedia.org/wiki/Knight_rider/] was a popular series in the 1980s that featured modern-day cowboy Michael Knight (played by David Hasselhoff) and his opinionated, talking, black Pontiac Firebird named KITT. Having seen the show is not critical to understanding object oriented programming—just knowing that the car could talk will suffice!

closed. Similarly, if our high-tech talking car were instructed to change color to red, then it would do so, but other cars would not.

When we create a new object in OOP, we base it on an existing class. The process of creating new objects from a class is called **instantiation**. Figure 3.2 illustrates the concept.

Figure 3.2. Classes and objects

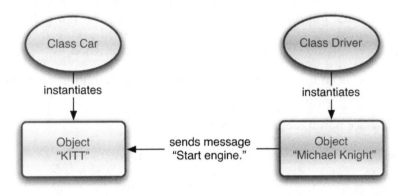

As I mentioned, objects can communicate with each other and invoke functionality (methods) on other objects. Invoking an object's methods can be thought of as asking the object a question, and getting an answer in return.

Consider the example of our famous talking car again. Let's say we ask the talking car object to report its current mileage. This question is not ambiguous—the answer that the object gives is called a **return value**, and is shown in Figure 3.3.

Figure 3.3. Asking a simple question

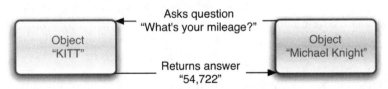

In some cases, the question and answer analogy doesn't quite fit. In these situations, we might rephrase the analogy to consider the question to be an instruction, and the answer a status report indicating whether or not the instruction was executed successfully. This might look something like the diagram in Figure 3.4.

Figure 3.4. Sending instructions

Sometimes we need a bit more flexibility with our instructions. For example, if we wanted to tell our car to change gear, we need to tell it not only to change gear, but also which gear to change to. The process of asking these kinds of questions is referred to as passing an argument to the method.

An **argument** is an input value that's provided to a method. An argument can be used in two ways:

❏ to influence how a method operates

❏ to influence which object a method operates on

An example is shown in Figure 3.5, where the method is "change gear," and the number of the gear to which the car must change (two) is the argument.

Figure 3.5. Passing arguments

A more general view of all of these different types of communication between objects is this: invoking an object's methods is accomplished by sending messages to it. As one might expect, the object sending the message is called the **sender**, and the object receiving the message is called the **receiver**.

Armed with this basic knowledge about object oriented programming, let's look at some Ruby specifics.

Reading and Writing Ruby Code

Learning the syntax of a new language has the potential to induce the occasional yawn. So, to make things more interesting, I'll present it to you in a practical way that lets you play along at home: we'll use the interactive Ruby shell.

The Interactive Ruby Shell (irb)

You can fire up the interactive Ruby shell by entering irb into a terminal window.

Not the Standard DOS Box!

Windows users, don't forget to use the Open Ruby Console option from the Instant Rails control panel, to make sure the environment you're using contains the right settings.

irb allows you to issue Ruby commands interactively, one line at a time. This is great for playing with the language, and it's also great for debugging, as we'll see in Chapter 11.

A couple of points about the irb output you'll see in this chapter:

❑ Lines beginning with the Ruby shell prompt (irb>) are typed in by you (and me).

❑ Lines beginning with => show the return value of the command that has been entered.

We'll start with a *really* brief example:

```
irb> 1
=> 1
```

In this example, I've simply thrown the number 1 at the Ruby shell, and got back what appears to be the very same number.

Looks can be deceiving, though—it's actually *not* the very same number. What we were handed back is in fact a fully-featured Ruby object.

Remember our discussion about object oriented programming in the previous section? Well, in Ruby, absolutely everything is treated as an object with which we can interact—each object belongs to a certain class, therefore each object is able to store data and functionality in the form of methods.

To find the class to which our number belongs, we call the number's `class` method:

```
irb> 1.class
=> Fixnum
```

We touched on senders and receivers earlier. In this example, we've sent the `class` message to the 1 object, so the 1 object is the receiver (there's no sender, as we're sending the message from the interactive command line rather than from another object). The value that's returned by the method we've invoked is `Fixnum`, which is the Ruby class that represents integer values.

Since everything in Ruby (*including* a class) is an object, we can actually send the very same message to the `Fixnum` class. The result is different, as we'd expect:

```
irb> Fixnum.class
=> Class
```

This time, the return value is `Class`, which is somewhat reassuring—we did invoke it on a class name, after all.

Note that the method `class` is all lowercase, yet the return value `Class` begins with a capital letter. A method in Ruby is always written in lowercase, whereas the first letter of a class is always capitalized.

Interacting with Ruby Objects

Getting used to thinking in terms of objects can take some time. Let's look at a few different types of objects, and see how we can interact with them.

Literal Objects

Literal objects are character strings or numbers that appear directly in the code, as did the number 1 that was returned in the previous section. We've seen numbers in action; next, let's look at a string literal.

A **string literal** is an object that contains a string of characters, such as a name, an address, or an especially witty phrase. In the same way that we created the 1 literal object in the previous example, we can easily create a new string literal object, then send it a message. A string literal is created by enclosing the characters that make up the string in single or double quotes, like this:

```
irb> "The quick brown fox"
=> "The quick brown fox"
```

First, we'll confirm that our string literal indeed belongs to class String:

```
irb> "The quick brown fox".class
=> String
```

This String object has a wealth of embedded functionality. For example, we can ascertain the number of characters that our string literal comprises by sending it the length message:

```
irb> "The quick brown fox".length
=> 19
```

Easy stuff, eh?

Variables and Constants

Every application needs a way to store information. Enter: variables and constants. As their names imply, these two data containers have their own unique roles to play.

A **constant** is an object that's assigned a value once, and once only (usually when the application starts up). Constants are therefore used to store information that doesn't need to change within a running application. As an example, a constant might be used to store the version number for an application. Constants in Ruby are always written using uppercase letters, as shown below:

```
irb> CONSTANT = "The quick brown fox in a constant"
=> "The quick brown fox in a constant"
irb> APP_VERSION = 5.04
=> 5.04
```

Variables, in contrast, are objects that are able to change at any time. They can even be reset to nothing, which frees up the memory space that they previously occupied. Variables in Ruby always start with a lowercase character:

```
irb> variable = "The quick brown fox in a variable"
=> "The quick brown fox in a variable"
```

There's one more special (and, one might say, *evil*) thing about a variable—its scope. The **scope** of a variable is the part of the program to which a variable is visible. If you try to access a variable from outside its scope (i.e. from a part of an application to which that variable is not visible), you generally won't be able to.

The notable exception to the rules defining a variable's scope are global variables. As the name implies, a **global variable** is accessible from any part of the program. While this might sound convenient at first, usage of global variables is discouraged—the fact that they can be written to and read from any part of the program introduces security concerns.

Let's return to the string literal example we saw earlier. Assigning a `String` to a variable allows us to invoke on that variable the same methods we invoked on the string literal earlier:

```
irb> fox = "The quick brown fox"
=> "The quick brown fox"
irb> fox.class
=> String
irb> fox.length
=> 19
```

Punctuation in Ruby

The use of punctuation in Ruby code differs greatly from other languages such as Perl and PHP, so it can seem confusing at first if you're used to programming in those languages. However, once you have a few basics under your belt, punctuation in Ruby begins to feel quite intuitive and can greatly enhance the readability of your code.

Dot Notation

One of the most common punctuation characters in Ruby is the period (.). As we've seen, Ruby uses the period to separate the receiver from the message that's being sent to it, in the form *Object.receiver*.

If you need to comment a line, either for documentation purposes or to temporarily take a line of code out of the program flow, use a hash mark (#). Comments may start at the beginning of a line, or they may appear further along, after some Ruby code:

```
irb> # This is a comment. It doesn't actually do anything.
irb> 1 # So is this, but this one comes after a statement.
=> 1
irb> fox = "The quick brown fox"    # Assign to a variable
=> "The quick brown fox"
irb> fox.class                      # Display a variable's class
=> String
irb> fox.length                     # Display a variable's length
=> 19
```

Chaining Statements Together

Ruby doesn't require us to use any character to separate commands, unless we want to chain multiple statements together on a single line. In this case, a semicolon (;) is used as the separator. However, if you put every statement on its own line (as we've been doing until now), the semicolon is completely optional.

If you chain multiple statements together in the interactive shell, only the output of the last command that was executed will be displayed to the screen:

```
irb> fox.class; fox.length; fox.upcase
=> "THE QUICK BROWN FOX"
```

Use of Parentheses

If you've ever delved into the source code of one of the many JavaScript libraries out there, you might have run screaming from your computer when you saw all the parentheses that are involved in the passing of arguments to methods.[3]

In Ruby, the use of parentheses for method calls is optional in cases in which no arguments are passed to the method. The following statements are therefore equal:

```
irb> fox.class()
=> String
irb> fox.class
=> String
```

It's common practice to include parentheses for method calls with multiple arguments, such as the insert method of the String class:

---

[3] http://www.sitepoint.com/article/javascript-library/

```
irb> "jumps over the lazy dog".insert(0, 'The quick brown fox ')
=> "The quick brown fox jumps over the lazy dog"
```

This call inserts the second argument passed to the insert object ("The quick brown fox ") at position 0 of the receiving String object ("jumps over the lazy dog"). Position 0 refers to the very beginning of the string.

Method Notation

Until now, we've looked at cases where Ruby uses *less* punctuation than its competitors. In fact, Ruby makes heavy use of expressive punctuation when it comes to the naming of methods.

A regular method name, as we've seen, is a simple, alphanumeric string of characters. If a method has a potentially destructive nature (for example, it directly modifies the receiving object rather than changing a copy of it), it's commonly suffixed with an exclamation mark (!).

The following example uses the upcase method to illustrate this point:

```
irb> fox.upcase
=> "THE QUICK BROWN FOX"
irb> fox
=> "The quick brown fox"
irb> fox.upcase!
=> "THE QUICK BROWN FOX"
irb> fox
=> "THE QUICK BROWN FOX"
```

Here, the contents of the fox variable have been modified by the upcase! method.

Punctuation is also used in the names of methods that return **boolean values**. A boolean value is a value that's either true or false; these values are commonly used as return values for methods that ask yes/no questions. Such methods end in a question mark, which nicely reflects the fact that they have yes/no answers:

```
irb> fox.empty?
=> false
irb> fox.is_a? String
=> true
```

These naming conventions make it easy to recognize methods that are destructive, and those that return boolean values, making your Ruby code more readable.

Object Oriented Programming in Ruby

Let's build on the theory that we covered at the start of this chapter as we take a look at Ruby's implementation of OOP.

As we already know, the structure of an application based on OOP principles is focused on interaction with objects. These objects are often representations of real-world objects, like a `Car`. Interaction with an object occurs when we send it a message or ask it a question. If we really did have a `Car` object called `kitt` (we don't—yet), starting the car might be as simple as:

```
irb> kitt.start
```

This short line of Ruby code sends the message `start` to the object `kitt`. Using OOP terminology, we would say that this code statement calls the `start` method of the `kitt` object.

As I mentioned before, in contrast to other object oriented programming languages such as Python and PHP, in Ruby, *everything* is an object. Especially when compared with PHP, Ruby's OOP doesn't feel like a "tacked-on" afterthought—it was clearly intended to be a core feature of the language from the beginning, which makes using the OOP features in Ruby a real pleasure.

As we saw in the previous section, even the simplest of elements in Ruby (like literal strings and numbers) are objects to which you can send messages.

Classes and Objects

As in any other OOP language, in Ruby, each object belongs to a certain class (for example, `PontiacFirebird` might be an object of class `Car`). As we saw in the discussion at the beginning of this chapter, a class can group objects of a certain kind, and equip those objects with common functionality. This functionality comes in the form of methods, and in the object's ability to store information. For example, a `PontiacFirebird` object might need to store its mileage, as might any other object of the class `Car`.

In Ruby, the instantiation of a new object that's based on an existing class is accomplished by sending that class the `new` message. The result is a new object of that class. The following few lines of code show an extremely basic class definition into Ruby—the third line is where we create an instance of the class that we just defined.

```
irb> class Car
irb> end
=> nil
irb> kitt = Car.new
=> #<Car:0x75e54>
```

Another basic principle in OOP is **encapsulation**. According to this principle, objects should be treated as independent entities, each taking care of its own internal data and functionality. If we need to access an object's information—for instance, its internal variables—we make use of the object's **interface**, which is the subset of the object's methods that are made available for other objects to call.

Ruby provides objects with functionality at two levels—the object level, and class level—and it adheres to the principle of encapsulation while it's at it! Let's dig deeper.

Object-level Functionality

At the object level, data storage is handled by **instance variables** (a name that's derived from the instantiation process mentioned above). Think of instance variables as storage containers that are attached to the object, but to which other objects do not have direct access.

To store or retrieve data from these variables, another object must call an **accessor method** on the object. An accessor method has the ability to set (and get) the value of the object's instance variables.

Let's look at how instance variables and accessor methods relate to each other, and how they're implemented in Ruby.

Instance Variables

Instance variables are bound to an object, and contain values for that object only.

Revisiting our cars example, the mileage values for a number of different Car objects are likely to differ, as each car will have a different mileage. Therefore, mileage is held in an instance variable.

An instance variable can be recognized by its prefix: a single "at" sign (@). To redefine the Car class we saw earlier, exit from the Ruby shell, then enter a new shell—this will give us a "clean slate."

```
irb> exit
$ irb
irb>
```

Then, type out the following class definition:

```
irb> class Car
irb>   @mileage = 0
irb> end
=> nil
irb> kitt = Car.new
=> #<Car:0x75e54>
```

Our kitt object now has the ability to store mileage! There's only one problem: we don't have any way to retrieve or change that value. This is where instance methods come into play.

Instance Methods

Data storage and retrieval is not the only capability that can be bound to a specific object—functionality, too, can be bound to objects. We achieve this binding through the use of **instance methods**, which are specific to an object. Invoking an instance method (in other words, sending a message that contains the method name to an object) will invoke that functionality on the receiving object only.

Instance methods are defined using the def keyword, and end with the end keyword. Enter the following example into a new Ruby shell:

```
$ irb
irb> class Car
irb>   def open_trunk
irb>     # code to open trunk goes here
irb>   end
irb> end
=> nil
irb> kitt = Car.new
=> #<Car:0x75e54>
```

Indenting your Code

While the indentation of code is a key element of the syntax of languages such as Python, in Ruby, indentation is purely cosmetic—it aids readability, but does not affect the code in any way. In fact, while we're experimenting with the Ruby shell, you needn't be too worried about indenting any of the code. However, when we're saving files that will be edited later, you'll want the readability benefits that come from indenting nested lines.

The Ruby community has agreed upon two spaces as being optimum for indenting blocks of code such as class or method definitions. We'll adhere to this indentation scheme throughout this book.

What you've done is define a class called Car, which has an instance method with the name open_trunk. A Car object instantiated from this class will (possibly using some fancy robotics connected to our Ruby program) open its trunk when its open_trunk method is called. (Ignore that nil return value for the moment; we'll look at nil values in the next section.)

With our class in place, we can make use of this method:

```
irb> kitt.open_trunk
=> nil
```

Since we don't want the trunks of all cars to open at once, we've made this functionality available as an instance method.

I know, I know: we *still* haven't modified any data. We use accessor variables for this task.

Accessor Methods

An accessor method is a special type of instance method, and is used to read or write to an instance variable. There are two types: **readers** (sometimes called "getters") and **writers** (or "setters").

A reader method will look inside the object, fetch the value of an instance variable, and hand this value back to us. A writer method, on the other hand, will look inside the object, find an instance variable, and assign the variable the value that it was passed.

Let's add some methods for getting and setting the @mileage attribute of our Car objects. Once again, exit from the Ruby shell so that we can create an entirely new Car class definition. Our class definition is getting a bit longer now, so enter each line carefully. If you make a typing mistake, exit the shell and start over.

```
$ irb
irb> class Car
irb>   @mileage = 0
irb>   def set_mileage(x)
```

```
irb>     @mileage = x
irb>   end
irb>   def get_mileage
irb>     @mileage
irb>   end
irb> end
=> nil
irb> kitt = Car.new
=> #<Car:0x75e54>
```

Now, we can finally modify and retrieve the mileage of our `Car` objects!

```
irb> kitt.set_mileage(5667)
=> 5667
irb> kitt.get_mileage
=> 5667
```

This is still a bit awkward. Wouldn't it be nice if we could give our accessor methods exactly the same names as the attributes that they read from or write to? Luckily, Ruby contains shorthand notation for this very task. We can rewrite our class definition as follows:

```
$ irb
irb> class Car
irb>   @mileage = 0
irb>   def mileage=(x)
irb>     @mileage = x
irb>   end
irb>   def mileage
irb>     @mileage
irb>   end
irb> end
=> nil
irb> kitt = Car.new
=> #<Car:0x75e54>
```

With these accessor methods in place, we can read to and write from our instance variable as if it were available from outside the object.

```
irb> kitt.mileage = 6032
=> 6032
irb> kitt.mileage
=> 6032
```

These accessor methods form part of the object's interface.

Class-level Functionality

At the class level, **class variables** handle data storage. They're commonly used to store state information, or as a means of configuring default values for new objects. Class variables are typically set in the body of a class, and can be recognized by their prefix: a double "at" sign (@@).

First, enter the following class definition into a new Ruby shell.

```
$ irb
irb> class Car
irb>   @@number_of_cars = 0
irb>   def initialize
irb>     @@number_of_cars = @@number_of_cars + 1
irb>   end
irb> end
=> nil
```

The class definition for the class Car above has an internal counter for the total number of Car objects that have been created. Using the special instance method initialize, which is invoked automatically every time an object is instantiated, this counter is incremented for each new Car object.

By the way, we have actually already used a class method. Do you like how I snuck it in there? The new method is an example of a class method that ships with Ruby and is available to all classes—whether they're defined by you, or form part of the Ruby Standard Library.[4]

Custom class methods are commonly used to create objects with special properties (such as a default color for our Car objects), or to gather statistics about the class's usage.

Extending the earlier example, we could use a class method called count to return the value of the @@number_of_cars class variable. Remember that this is a variable that's incremented for every new Car object that's created. Class methods are defined identically to instance methods: using the def and end keywords. The only difference is that class method names are prefixed with self. Enter this code into a new Ruby shell:

---

[4] The Ruby Standard Library is a large collection of classes that's included with every Ruby installation. The classes facilitate a wide range of common functionality, such as accessing web sites, date calculations, file operations, and more.

```
$ irb
irb> class Car
irb>    @@number_of_cars = 0
irb>    def self.count
irb>       @@number_of_cars
irb>    end
irb>    def initialize
irb>       @@number_of_cars+=1
irb>    end
irb> end
=> nil
```

The following code instantiates some new `Car` objects, then makes use of our new class method:

```
irb> kitt = Car.new          # Michael Knight's talking car
=> #<0xba8c>
irb> herbie = Car.new        # The famous VolksWagen love bug!
=> #<0x8cd20>
irb> batmobile = Car.new     # Batman's sleek automobile
=> #<0x872e4>
irb> Car.count
=> 3
```

The method tells us that two instances of the `Car` class have been created. Note that we can't call a class method on an object:[5]

```
irb> kitt.count
NoMethodError: undefined method 'count' for #<Car:0x89da0>
```

As implied by the name, the `count` class method is available only to the `Car` class, not to any objects instantiated from that class.

I sneakily introduced something else in there. Did you spot it? In many languages, including PHP and Java, the ++ and -- operators are used to increment a variable by one. Ruby doesn't support this notation; instead, when working with Ruby, we need to use the += operator. Therefore, the shorthand notation for incrementing our counter in the class definition is:

```
irb>     @@number_of_cars+=1
```

This code is identical to the following:

---

[5] Ruby actually does provide a way to invoke *some* class methods on an object, using the : : operator, but we won't worry about that for now. We'll see the : : operator in use in Chapter 4.

```
irb>     @@number_of_cars = @@number of cars + 1
```

Both of these lines can be read as "my_variable becomes equal to my_variable plus one."

Inheritance

If your application deals with more than the flat hierarchy we've explored so far, you might want to construct a scenario whereby some classes inherit from other classes. Continuing with the car analogy, let's suppose that we had a green limousine named Larry (this assigning of names to cars might feel a bit strange, but it's important for this example, so bear with me). In Ruby, the larry object would probably descend from a StretchLimo class, which could in turn descend from the class Car. Let's implement that, to see how it works:

```
$ irb
irb> class Car
irb>    @@wheels = 4
irb> end
=> nil
irb> class StretchLimo < Car
irb>    @@wheels = 6
irb>    def turn_on_television
irb>      # Invoke code for switching on on-board TV here
irb>    end
irb> end
=> nil
```

Now, if we were to instantiate an object of class StretchLimo, we'd end up with a different kind of car. Instead of the regular four wheels that standard Car objects have, this one would have six wheels (stored in the class variable @@wheels). It would also have extra functionality, made possible by an extra method—turn_on_television— which would be available to be called by other objects.

However, if we were to instantiate a regular Car object, the car would have only four wheels, and there would be no instance method for turning on an on-board television. Think of inheritance as a way for the functionality of a class to become more specialized the further we move down the inheritance path.

Don't worry if you're struggling to wrap your head around all the aspects of OOP—you'll automatically become accustomed to them as you work through this book. You might find it useful to come back to this section, though, especially if you need a reminder about a certain term later on.

Return Values

It's always great to receive feedback. Remember our talk about passing arguments to methods? Well, regardless of whether or not a method accepts arguments, invoking a method in Ruby *always* results in feedback—it comes in the form of a return value, which is returned either explicitly or implicitly.

To return a value explicitly, use the `return` statement in the body of a method:

```
irb> def toot_horn
irb>    return "toooot!"
irb> end
=> nil
```

Calling the `toot_horn` method in this case would produce the following:

```
irb> toot_horn
=> "toooot!"
```

However, if no return statement is used, the result of the last statement that was executed is used as the return value. This behavior is quite unique to Ruby:

```
irb> def toot_loud_horn
irb>    "toooot!".upcase
irb> end
=> nil
```

Calling the `toot_loud_horn` method in this case would produce:

```
irb> toot_loud_horn
=> "TOOOOT!"
```

Standard Output

When you need to show output to the users of your application, use the `print` and `puts` ("put string") statements. Both methods will display the arguments passed to them as `Strings`; `puts` also inserts a carriage return at the end of its output. Therefore, in a Ruby program the following lines:

```
print "The quick "
print "brown fox"
```

would produce this output:

```
The quick brown fox
```

However, using `puts` like so:

```
puts "jumps over"
puts "the lazy dog"
```

would produce this output:

```
jumps over
the lazy dog
```

At this stage, you might be wondering why *all* of the trial-and-error code snippets that we've typed into the Ruby shell actually produced output, given that we haven't been making use of the `print` or `puts` methods. The reason is that `irb` automatically writes the return value of the last statement it executes to the screen before displaying the `irb` prompt. This means that using a `print` or `puts` from within the Ruby shell might in fact produce two lines of output—the output that you specify should be displayed, and the return value of the last command that was executed, as in the following example:

```
irb> puts "The quick brown fox"
"The quick brown fox"
=> nil
```

Here, `nil` is actually the return value of the `puts` statement. Looking back at previous examples, you will have encountered `nil` as the return value for class and method definitions, and you'll have received a hexadecimal address, such as `<#Car:0x89da0>`, as the return value for object definitions. This hexadecimal value showed the location in memory that the object we instantiated occupied, but luckily we won't need to bother with such geeky details any further.

Having met the `print` and `puts` statements, you should be aware that a Rails application actually has a completely different approach to displaying output, called templates. We'll look at templates in Chapter 4.

Ruby Core Classes

We've already talked briefly about the `String` and `Fixnum` classes in the previous sections, but Ruby has a lot more under its hood. Let's explore!

Arrays

We use Ruby's Arrays to store collections of objects. Each individual object that's stored in an Array has a unique numeric key, which we can use to reference it. As with many languages, the first element in an Array is stored at position 0 (zero).

To create a new Array, simply instantiate a new object of class Array (using the Array.new construct). You can also use a shortcut approach, which is to enclose the objects you want to place inside the Array in square brackets.

For example, an Array containing the mileage at which a car is due for its regular service might look something like this:

```
irb> service_mileage = [5000, 15000, 30000, 60000, 100000]
=> [5000, 15000, 30000, 60000, 100000]
```

To retrieve individual elements from an Array, we specify the numeric key in square brackets.

```
irb> service_mileage[0]
=> 5000
irb> service_mileage[2]
=> 30000
```

Ruby has another shortcut, which allows us to create an Array from a list of Strings: the %w( ) syntax. Using this shortcut saves us from having to type a lot of double-quote characters:

```
irb> available_colors = %w( red green blue black )
=> ["red", "green", "blue", "black"]
irb> available_colors[0]
=> "red"
irb> available_colors[3]
=> "black"
```

In addition to facilitating simple element retrieval, Arrays come with an extensive set of class methods and instance methods that ease data management tasks tremendously.

❏ empty? returns true if the receiving Array doesn't contain any elements:

```
irb> available_colors.empty?
=> false
```

- ❑ `size` returns the number of elements in an `Array`:

```
irb> available_colors.size
=> 4
```

- ❑ `first` and `last` return an `Array`'s first and last elements, respectively:

```
irb> available_colors.first
=> "red"
irb> available_colors.last
=> "black"
```

- ❑ `delete` removes the named element from the `Array` and returns it:

```
irb> available_colors.delete "red"
=> "red"
irb> available_colors
=> ["green", "blue", "black"]
```

The complete list of class methods and instance methods provided by the `Array` class is available via the Ruby reference documentation, which you can access by entering the `ri` command into the terminal window (for your operating system, *not* the Ruby shell), followed by the class name you'd like to look up:

```
$ ri Array
```

Oh, and `ri` stands for ruby interactive, in case you're wondering. Don't confuse it with `irb`.

Hashes

A `Hash` is another kind of data storage container. `Hashes` are similar, conceptually, to dictionaries: they map one object (the `key`—for example, a word) to another object (the `value`—for example, a word's definition) in a one-to-one relationship.

New `Hashes` can be created either by instantiating a new object of class `Hash` (using the `Hash.new` construct) or by using the curly brace shortcut shown below. When we define a `Hash`, we must specify each entry using the `key => value` syntax.

For example, the following `Hash` maps car names to a color:

```
irb> car_colors = {
irb>    'kitt' => 'black',
irb>    'herbie' => 'white',
irb>    'batmobile' => 'black',
irb>    'larry' => 'green'
irb> }
=> {"kitt"=>"black", "herbie"=>"white", "batmobile"=>"black",
   "larry"=>"green"}
```

To query this newly built Hash, we pass the key of the entry we want to look up in square brackets, like so:

```
irb> car_colors['kitt']
=> "black"
```

All sorts of useful functionality is built into Hashes, including the following methods:

❑ empty? returns true if the receiving Hash doesn't contain any elements:

```
irb> car_colors.empty?
=> false
```

❑ size returns the number of elements in a Hash:

```
irb> car_colors.size
=> 4
```

❑ keys returns all keys of a Hash as an Array:

```
irb> car_colors.keys
=> ["kitt", "herbie", "larry", "batmobile"]
```

❑ values returns all values of a Hash as an Array, although care should be taken with regards to the order of the elements (keys in a Hash are ordered for optimal storage and retrieval; this order does not necessarily reflect the order in which they were entered):

```
irb> car_colors.values
=> ["black", "white", "green", "black"]
```

There are lots more—for the complete list of class methods and instance methods provided by the Hash class, consult the Ruby reference documentation.

Strings

The typical Ruby `String` object—yep, that very object we've been using in the past few sections—holds and manipulates sequences of characters. Most of the time, new `String` objects are created using string literals that are enclosed in single or double quotes. The literal can then be stored in a variable for later use:

```
irb> a_phrase = "The quick brown fox"
=> "The quick brown fox"
irb> a_phrase.class
=> String
```

If the string literal includes the quote character used to enclose the string itself, it must be escaped with a backslash character (\):

```
irb> 'I\'m a quick brown fox'
=> "I'm a quick brown fox"
irb> "Arnie said, \"I'm back!\""
=> "Arnie said, \"I'm back!\""
```

An easier way to specify string literals that contain quotes is to use the `%Q` shortcut, like this:

```
irb> %Q(Arnie said, "I'm back!")
=> "Arnie said, \"I'm back!\""
```

`String` objects also support the substitution of Ruby code into a string literal via the Ruby expression `#{}`:

```
irb> "The current time is: #{Time.now}"
=> "The current time is: Wed Aug 02 21:15:19 CEST 2006"
```

The `String` class also has rich embedded functionality for modifying `String` objects. Here are some of the most useful methods:

❑ gsub substitutes a given pattern within a `String`:

```
irb> "The quick brown fox".gsub('fox', 'dog')
=> "The quick brown dog"
```

❑ include? returns true if a `String` contains another specific `String`:

```
irb> "The quick brown fox".include?('fox')
=> true
```

❑ length returns the length of a String in characters:

```
irb> "The quick brown fox".length
=> 19
```

❑ slice returns a portion of a String:

```
irb> "The quick brown fox".slice(0, 3)
=> "The"
```

The complete method reference is available using the ri command-line tool:

```
$ ri String
```

Numerics

Since there are so many different types of numbers, Ruby has a separate class for each, the popular Float, Fixnum, and Bignum classes among them. In fact, they're all subclasses of Numeric, which provides the basic functionality.

Just like Strings, numbers are usually created from literals:

```
irb> 123.class
=> Fixnum
irb> 12.5.class
=> Float
```

Each of the specific Numeric subclasses comes with features that are relevant to the type of number it's designed to deal with. However, the following functionality is shared between all Numeric subclasses:

❑ integer? returns true if the object is a whole integer:

```
irb> 123.integer?
=> true
irb> 12.5.integer?
=> false
```

❑ round rounds a number to the nearest integer:

```
irb> 12.3.round
=> 12
```

```
irb> 38.8.round
=> 39
```

❑ zero? returns true if the number is equal to zero:

```
irb> 0.zero?
=> true
irb> 8.zero?
=> false
```

Additionally, there are ways to convert numbers between the Numeric subclasses. to_f converts a value to a Float, and to_i converts a value to an Integer:

```
irb> 12.to_f
=> 12.0
irb> 11.3.to_i
=> 11
```

Symbols

In Ruby, a Symbol is a simple textual identifier. Like a String, a Symbol is created using literals; the difference is that a Symbol is prefixed with a colon:

```
irb> :fox
=> :fox
irb> :fox.class
=> Symbol
```

The main benefit of using a Symbol instead of a String is that a Symbol contains less functionality. This can be an advantage in certain situations. For example, the car_colors Hash that we looked at earlier could be rewritten as follows:

```
car_colors =
  :kitt => 'black',
  :herbie => 'white',
  :larry => 'green',
  :batmobile => 'black'
}
```

Objects of class String can be converted to Symbols, and vice-versa:

```
irb> "fox".to_sym
=> :fox
```

```
irb> :fox.to_s
=> "fox"
```

We'll use Symbols frequently as we deal with Rails functionality in successive chapters of this book.

nil

I promised earlier that I'd explain nil values—now's the time!

All programming languages have a value that they can use when they actually mean *nothing*. Some use undef; others use NULL. Ruby uses nil. A nil value, like everything in Ruby, is also an object. It therefore has its own class: NilClass.

Basically, if a method doesn't return anything, it is, in fact, returning the value nil. And if you assign nil to a variable, you effectively make it empty. nil shows up in a couple of additional places, but we'll cross those bridges when we come to them.

Running Ruby Files

For the simple Ruby basics that we've experimented with so far, the interactive Ruby shell (irb) has been our tool of choice. I'm sure you'll agree that experimenting in a shell-like environment, where we can see immediate results, is a great way to learn the language.

However, we're going to be talking about control structures next, and for tasks of such complexity, you'll want to work in a text editor. This environment will allow you to run a chunk of code many times without having to retype it.

In general, Ruby scripts are simple text files containing Ruby code and have a .rb extension. These files are passed to the Ruby interpreter, which executes your code, like this:

```
$ ruby myscript.rb
```

To work with the examples that follow, I'd recommend that you open a new text file in your favorite text editor (which might be one of those I recommended back in Chapter 2) and type the code out as you go—this really is the best way to learn. However, I acknowledge that some people aren't interested in typing everything out, and just want to cut to the chase. These more impatient readers can download the code archive for this book, which contains all of these examples.[6] You can execute this code in the Ruby interpreter straight away.

As demonstrated above, to run the files from the command line, you simply need to type **ruby**, followed by the filename.

Control Structures

Ruby has a rich set of features for controlling the flow of your application. **Conditionals** are key words that are used to decide whether or not certain statements are executed based on the evaluation of one or more conditions; **loops** are constructs that execute statements more than once; **blocks** are a means of encapsulating functionality (for example, to be executed in a loop).

To demonstrate these control structures, let's utilize some of the Car classes that we defined earlier. Type out the following class definition and save the file (or load it from the code archive); we'll build on it in this section as we explore some control structures.

File: **01-car-classes.rb**

```ruby
class Car
  @@wheels = 4               # class variable
  @@number_of_cars = 0       # class variable
  @mileage = 0               # instance variable
  def initialize
    @@number_of_cars = @@number_of_cars + 1
  end
  def self.count
    @@number_of_cars
  end
  def mileage=(x)            # mileage writer
    @mileage = x
  end
  def mileage                # mileage reader
    @mileage
  end
end

class StretchLimo < Car
  @@wheels = 6               # class variable
  @@televisions = 1          # class variable
  def turn_on_television
```

---

[6] http://www.sitepoint.com/books/rails1/code.php

```
      # Invoke code for switching on on-board TV here
   end
end

class PontiacFirebird < Car
end

class VolksWagen < Car
end
```

Conditionals

There are two basic conditional constructs in Ruby: `if` and `unless`. Each of these constructs can be used to execute a group of statements on the basis of a given condition.

The `if` Construct

An `if` construct wraps statements that are to be executed only if a certain condition is met. The keyword `end` defines the end of the `if` construct. The statements contained between the condition and the `end` keyword are executed only if the condition is met.

File: **02-if-construct.rb (excerpt)**

```
if Car.count.zero?
  puts "No cars have been produced yet."
end
```

You can provide a second condition by adding an `else` block: when the condition is met, the first block is executed; otherwise, the `else` block is executed. This kind of control flow will probably be familiar to you. Here it is in action:

File: **03-if-else-construct.rb (excerpt)**

```
if Car.count.zero?
  puts "No cars have been produced yet."
else
  puts "New cars can still be produced."
end
```

The most complicated example involves an alternative condition. If the first condition is not met, then a second condition is evaluated. If neither conditions are met, the `else` block is executed:

File: **04-if-elsif-else.rb** (excerpt)

```
if Car.count.zero?
  puts "No cars have been produced yet."
elsif Car.count >= 10
  puts "Production capacity has been reached."
else
  puts "New cars can still be produced."
end
```

If the count method returned 5, the code above would produce the following output:

```
New cars can still be produced.
```

An alternative to the traditional if condition is the if **statement modifier**. A statement modifier does just that—it modifies the statement of which it is part. The if statement modifier works exactly like a regular if condition, but it sits at the *end* of the line that's affected, rather than before a block of code:

File: **05-if-statement-modifier.rb** (excerpt)

```
puts "No cars have been produced yet." if Car.count.zero?
```

This version of the if condition is often used when the code that's to be executed conditionally comprises just a single line. Having the ability to create conditions like this results in code that's a lot more like English than other programming languages with more rigid structures.

The unless Construct

The unless condition is a negative version of the if condition. It's useful for situations in which you want to execute a group of statements when a certain condition is *not* met.

Let's create a few instances to work with:[7]

File: **06-unless-construct.rb** (excerpt)

```
kitt = PontiacFirebird.new
kitt.mileage = 5667
```

---

[7] Aficionados of comics will notice that I've created the BatMobile as a Pontiac Firebird—in fact, the caped crusader's choice of transport has varied over the years, taking in many of the automobile industry's less common innovations, and including everything from a 1966 Lincoln Futura to an amphibious tank. But we'll stick with a Pontiac for this example.

```
herbie = VolksWagen.new
herbie.mileage = 33014

batmobile = PontiacFirebird.new
batmobile.mileage = 4623

larry = StretchLimo.new
larry.mileage = 20140
```

Now if we wanted to find out how many Knight Rider fans KITT could take for a joy-ride, we could check which class the kitt object was. As with the if expression, the end keyword defines the end of the statement.

File: **06-unless-construct.rb (excerpt)**

```
unless kitt.is_a?(StretchLimo)
  puts "This car is only licensed to seat two people."
end
```

Like the if condition, the unless condition may have an optional else block of statements, which is executed when the condition is met:

File: **07-unless-else.rb (excerpt)**

```
unless kitt.is_a?(StretchLimo)
  puts "This car only has room for two people."
else
  puts "This car is licensed to carry up to 10 passengers."
end
```

Since KITT is definitely *not* a stretch limousine, this code would return:

```
This car only has room for two people.
```

Unlike if conditions, unless conditions do *not* support a second condition. However, like the if condition, the unless condition is also available as a statement modifier. The following code shows an example of this. Here, the message will not display if KITT's mileage is less than 25000:

File: **08-unless-statement-modifier.rb (excerpt)**

```
puts "Service due!" unless kitt.mileage < 25000
```

Loops

Ruby provides the while and for constructs for looping through code (i.e. executing a group of statements a specified number of times, or until a certain condition is met). Also, a number of instance methods are available for looping over the elements of an `Array` or `Hash`; we'll cover these in the next section.

while and until Loops

A `while` loop executes the statements it encloses repeatedly, as long as the specified condition is met.

File: **09-while-loop.rb (excerpt)**

```
while Car.count < 10
  Car.new
  puts "A new car instance was created."
end
```

This simple `while` loop executes the `Car.new` statement repeatedly, as long as the total number of cars is below ten. It exits the loop when the number reaches ten.

Like the relationship between `if` and `unless`, the `while` loop also has a complement: the `until` construct. If we use `until`, the code within the loop is executed *until* the condition is met. We could rewrite the loop above using `until` like so:

File: **10-until-loop.rb (excerpt)**

```
until Car.count == 10
  Car.new
  puts "A new car instance was created."
end
```

The Difference Between = and ==

It's important to note the difference between the **assignment operator** (a single equal sign) and the **equation operator** (a double equal sign) when using them within a condition.

If you're comparing two values, use the equation operator:

```
if Car.count == 10
  ...
end
```

If you're assigning a value to a variable, use the assignment operator:

```
my_new_car = Car.new
```

If you confuse the two, you might modify a value that you were hoping only to inspect, with potentially disastrous consequences!

for Loops

for loops allow us to iterate over the elements of a collection—such as an Array—and execute a group of statements once for each element. Here's an example:

File: **11-for-loop.rb** (excerpt)

```
for car in [ kitt, herbie, batmobile, larry ]
  puts car.mileage
end
```

The code above would produce the following output:

```
5667
33014
4623
20140
```

This simple for loop iterates over an Array of Car objects and outputs the mileage for each car. For each iteration, the car variable is set to the current element of the Array. The first iteration has car set to the equivalent of lincoln_towncar, the second iteration has it set to chrysler_voyager, and so forth.

In practice, the traditional while and for loops covered here are little used. Instead, most people tend to use the instance methods provided by the Array and Hash classes, which we'll cover next.

Blocks

Blocks are probably the single most attractive feature of Ruby. However, they're also one of those things that take a while to "click" for Ruby newcomers. Before we dig deeper into creating blocks, let's take a look at some of the core features of Ruby that use blocks.

We looked at some loop constructs in the previous section, and this was a useful way to explore the tools that are available to us. However, you'll probably never actually come across many of these constructs in your work with other Ruby scripts, simply because it's almost always much easier to use a block to perform the same task. A block, in conjunction with the `each` method that is provided by the `Array` and `Hash` classes, is a very powerful way to loop through your data.

Let me illustrate this point with an example. Consider the `for` loop we used a moment ago. We could rewrite that code to use the `each` method, which is an instance method of the `Array` class, like so:

File: **12-simple-block.rb** (excerpt)

```
[ kitt, herbie, batmobile, larry ].each do |car_name|
  puts car_name.mileage
end
```

Let's analyze this: the block comprises the code between the `do` and `end` keywords. A block is able to receive parameters, which are placed between vertical bars (`|`) at the beginning of the block. Multiple parameters are separated by commas. Therefore, this code performs an identical operation to the `for` loop we saw before, but in a much more succinct manner.

Let's take another example. To loop through the elements of a `Hash`, we use the `each` method, and pass two parameters to the block—the key (`car_name`) and the value (`color`)—like this:

File: **13-block-with-params.rb** (excerpt)

```
car_colors = {
  'kitt' => 'black',
  'herbie' => 'white',
  'batmobile' => 'black',
  'larry' => 'green'
}
car_colors.each do |car_name, color|
  puts "#{car_name} is #{color}"
end
```

This code produces the following output:

```
kitt is black
herbie is white
batmobile is black
larry is green
```

The `Integer` class also sports a number of methods that use blocks. The `times` method of an `Integer` object, for example, executes a block exactly *n* times, where *n* is the value of the object.

File: **14-block-integer.rb (excerpt)**

```
10.times { Car.new }
puts "#{Car.count} cars have been produced."
```

The code above produces this output:

```
10 cars have been produced.
```

One final point to note here is the alternate block syntax of curly braces. Instead of the do…end keywords that we used in previous examples, curly braces are the preferred syntax for blocks that are very short, as in the previous example.

Here's another method of the Integer class—in the spirit of times, the upto method counts from the value of the object up to the argument passed to the method.

File: **15-block-upto.rb**

```
5.upto(7) { |i| puts i }
```

This code produces the output shown here:

```
5
6
7
```

In Ruby parlance, the object i is a parameter of the block. Parameters for blocks are enclosed in vertical bars, and are usually available only from within the block. If we have more than one parameter, we separate them using commas, like so: |parameter1, parameter2|. In the example above, we would no longer have access to i once the block had finished executing.

As we work through this book, we'll explore many more uses of blocks in combination with the Rails core classes.

Summary

Wow, we covered a *lot* in this chapter! First, we swept through a stack of object oriented programming theory—probably the equivalent of an introductory computer science course! This gave us a good grounding for exploring the basics of the Ruby programming language, and the Interactive Ruby Shell (irb) was a fun way to do this exploration.

We also investigated many of the Ruby core classes, such as `String`, `Array`, and `Hash`, from within the Ruby shell. We then moved from the shell to create and save proper Ruby files, and using these files, we experimented with control structures such as conditionals, loops, and blocks.

In the next chapter, we'll look at the major cornerstones that make up the Rails framework—the integrated testing facilities—as well as the roles that the development, testing, and production environments play.

Rails Revealed

As you might have gathered from Chapter 1, quite a bit of thought has been put into the code base that makes up the Rails framework. Over time, many of the internals have been rewritten, which has improved their speed and efficiency, and allowed the implementation of additional features, but the original architecture remains largely unchanged. This chapter will shed some light on the inner workings of Rails.

Three Environments

Rails encourages the use of a different environment for each of the stages in an application's lifecycle—development, testing, and production. If you've been developing Web applications for a while, this is probably how you operate anyway; Rails just formalizes these environments.

development   In the development environment, changes to an application's source code are immediately visible; all we need to do is reload the corresponding page in a web browser. Speed is not a critical factor in this environment; instead, the focus is on providing the developer with as much insight as possible into the components involved in displaying each page. When an error occurs in the development environment, the developer is able to tell at a glance which line of code is responsible for the error, and how that particular line was invoked. This capability is provided by the **stack trace** (a comprehensive list of all the method calls leading up to the error), which is displayed when an unexpected error occurs.

test   In testing, we usually refresh the database with a baseline of dummy data each time a test is repeated—this ensures that the results of the tests are consistent, and that behavior is reproducible. Unit and functional testing procedures are fully automated in Rails.

When we test a Rails application, we don't view it using a traditional web browser. Instead, tests are invoked from the command line, and can be run as background processes. The testing environment provides a dedicated environment in which these processes can operate.

production   By the time your application finally goes live, it should be well tested, so that all (or at least most) of the bugs have been eliminated. As a result, updates to the code base should be infrequent, which means that the production environments can be optimized to focus on performance. Tasks such as writing extensive logs for debugging purposes should be unnecessary at this stage. Besides, if an error does occur, you don't want to scare your visitors away with a cryptic stack trace—that's best kept for the development environment.

As the requirements of each of the three environments are quite different, Rails stores the data for each environment in entirely separate databases. So at any given time, you might have:

❑ live data with which real users are interacting in the production environment

❑ a partial copy of this live data that you're using to debug an error or develop new features in the development environment

❑ a set of testing data that's constantly being reloaded into the testing environment

Let's look at how we can configure our database for each of these environments.

Database Configuration

Configuring the database for a Rails application is frighteningly easy—all of the critical information is contained in just one file. We'll take a look at it now, then create some databases for our application to use.

The Database Configuration File

The separation of environments is reflected in the Rails database configuration file database.yml. We saw a sample of this file back in Chapter 1, and in fact we created our very own configuration file in Chapter 2, when we used the rails command. Go take a look! It lives in the config subdirectory of our Shovell application.

With the comments removed, the file should look like this:[1]

File: **01-database.yml**

```
development:
  adapter: mysql
  database: shovell_development
  username: root
  password:
  host: localhost
test:
  adapter: mysql
  database: shovell_test
  username: root
  password:
  host: localhost
production:
  adapter: mysql
  database: shovell_production
  username: root
  password:
  host: localhost
```

This file lists the minimum amount of information we need in order to connect to the database server for each of our environments (development, test, and production). With the default setup of MySQL that we installed in Chapter 2, we can be confident to proceed with our development using the root user and

---

[1] Depending on your MySQL configuration, you may need to use **127.0.0.1** as your host value, instead of localhost.

an empty password for the time being—all of our development should take place on a local machine, so we needn't be concerned about someone accessing our super-secret Shovell application.

The parameter `database` sets the name of the database that's to be used in each environment. As the configuration file suggests, Rails is able to support multiple databases in parallel. Note that we're actually talking about different *databases* here, not just different tables—each database can host an arbitrary number of different tables in parallel. Figure 4.1 shows a graphical representation of this architecture.

Figure 4.1. The database architecture of a Rails application

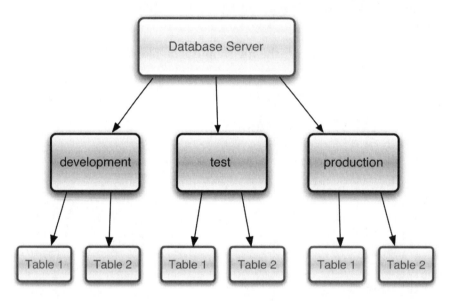

However, there's one vital aspect missing from our current configuration: the databases referenced in our configuration file don't exist yet! Let's create them now.

We can create these databases using one of the many graphical front ends that are available for MySQL, or we can just jump into the command line. Because the commands are fairly simple, let's create the databases from the command line for now; we'll look at graphical database clients later in this chapter.

Creating the Databases

To launch the MySQL command line interface, type `mysql -u root` at the command prompt. (On a Mac, the command is called `mysql5` instead of `mysql`—Mac users like to be different.)

```
$ mysql -u root
mysql>
```

The command to create a new database is simple enough: `create database` *newdatabasename*.

We'll use it to create three databases—one for each of our environments—as shown in Figure 4.2.

File: **02-create-databases.sql**

```
CREATE DATABASE shovell_development;
CREATE DATABASE shovell_test;
CREATE DATABASE shovell_production;
```

Database Security and the root User

If you have any experience with databases, you might be feeling a little uncomfortable that we're developing our application using the `root` user, without even setting a password. The reasoning behind this advice is as follows:

1. The default configuration of MySQL is such that connections to the database server can only be made from the same machine. This means that nobody—whether they're sitting next to you, or working from the other side of the world—will be able to wreak havoc in your Rails development environment.

2. The MySQL command line and permissions system are complex and powerful tools, and database security is a topic that's definitely beyond the scope of this book.

Of course, this is not a configuration that I would recommend for your production environment, but we'll get into that in Chapter 12. If you're interested in securing the database in your development environment, the MySQL manual contains some post-installation instructions that should serve you well.[2]

---

[2] http://dev.mysql.com/doc/refman/5.0/en/post-installation.html

Figure 4.2. Creating a database for each environment

```
Core:~ scoop$ mysql5 -u root
Welcome to the MySQL monitor.  Commands end with ; or \g.
Your MySQL connection id is 10 to server version: 5.0.24

Type 'help;' or '\h' for help. Type '\c' to clear the buffer.

mysql> create database shovell_development;
Query OK, 1 row affected (0.04 sec)

mysql> create database shovell_test;
Query OK, 1 row affected (0.01 sec)

mysql> create database shovell_production;
Query OK, 1 row affected (0.11 sec)

mysql> quit
Bye
Core:~ scoop$ ▊
```

Now that our databases exist, we can use them to store data for our application!

development is the Default Database

By default, all Rails applications use the development environment unless specified otherwise. So any Rails commands that you execute from the command line will, for the time being, only affect the data in the development database. In Chapter 12, we'll learn how to switch to the production environment.

The Model-view-controller Architecture

The model-view-controller (MVC) architecture that we first encountered in Chapter 1 is not unique to Rails. In fact, it pre-dates both Rails and the Ruby language by many years. However, Rails really takes the idea of separating an application's data, user interface, and control logic to a whole new level.

Let's take a look at the concepts behind building an application using the MVC architecture. Once we have the theory in place, we'll see how it translates to our Rails code.

MVC in Theory

MVC is a pattern for the architecture of a software application. It separates an application into the following three components:

❑ **models**, for handling data and business logic

❑ **controllers**, for handling the user interface and application logic

❑ **views**, for handling graphical user interface objects and presentation logic

This separation results in user requests being processed as follows:

1. The browser, on the client, sends a request for a page to the controller on the server.

2. The controller retrieves the data it needs from the model in order to respond to the request.

3. The controller renders the page and sends it to the view.

4. The view sends the page back to the client for the browser to display.

This process is illustrated in Figure 4.3.

Figure 4.3. Processing a page request in an MVC architecture

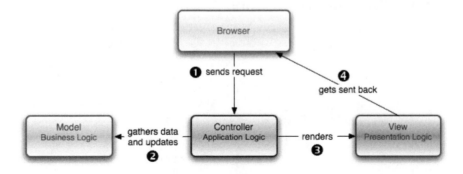

Separating a software application into these three distinct components is a good idea for a number of reasons, including the following:

□ It improves **scalability** (the ability for an application to grow): if your application begins experiencing performance issues because database access is slow, for example, you can upgrade the hardware running the database without other components being affected.

□ It makes maintenance easier: because the components have a low dependency on each other, making changes to one (to fix bugs or change functionality) does not affect another.

□ It promotes reuse: a model may be reused by multiple views, and vice versa.

□ It makes the application distributable: a distinct separation of code between components means that each of them could potentially reside on a separate machine, if necessary.

If you haven't quite got your head around the concept of MVC yet, don't worry. For now, the important thing is to remember that your Rails application is separated into three distinct components. Jump back to Figure 4.3 if you need to refer to it later on.

MVC the Rails Way

Rails implements the concept that models, views, and controllers should be kept quite separate by storing the code for each of these elements as separate files, in separate directories.

Figure 4.4. The app subdirectory

This is where the Rails directory structure that we created back in Chapter 2 comes into play. The time has come for us to poke around a bit within that structure. If you take a look inside the `app` directory, which is depicted in Figure 4.4, you'll see some folders whose names might be starting to sound familiar.

As you can see, each component of the model-view-controller architecture has its place within the `app` subdirectory—the `models`, `views`, and `controllers` subdirectories, respectively. (We'll talk about that `helpers` directory in Chapter 6.)

This separation continues within the code that comprises the framework itself. The classes that form the core functionality of Rails reside within the following modules:

ActiveRecord

ActiveRecord is the module for handling business logic and database communication. It plays the role of *model* in our MVC architecture.[3]

ActionController

ActionController is the component that handles browser requests and facilitates communication between the model and the view. Your *controllers* will inherit from this class. It forms part of the `ActionPack` library, a collection of Rails components that we'll explore in depth in Chapter 5.

ActionView

ActionView is the component that handles the presentation of pages returned to the client. *Views* inherit from this class, which is also part of the `ActionPack` library.

Let's take a closer look at each of these components in turn.

ActiveRecord (the Model)

ActiveRecord is designed to handle all of an application's tasks that relate to the database, including:

❑ establishing a connection to the database server

---

[3] While it might seem odd that **ActiveRecord** doesn't have the word "model" in its name, there is a reason for this: Active Record is also the name of a famous design pattern—one that this component implements in order to perform its role in the MVC world. Besides, if it had been called **ActionModel** then it would have sounded more like an overpaid Hollywood star than a software component …

❏ retrieving data from a table

❏ storing new data in the database

It also has a few other neat tricks up its sleeve. Let's look at some of them now.

Database Abstraction

`ActiveRecord` ships with a large number of database adapters to connect to a variety of popular database server packages, such as MySQL, PostgreSQL, Oracle, and Microsoft SQL Server.

The `ActiveRecord` module is based on the concept of database abstraction. As we mentioned in Chapter 1, database abstraction is a way of coding an application so that it isn't dependent upon any one database. Code that's specific to a particular database server is hidden safely in `ActiveRecord`, and invoked as needed. The result is that a Rails application is not bound to any specific database server software. Should you need to change the underlying database server at a later time, no changes to your application code should be required.

Examples of code that differs greatly between vendors, and which `ActiveRecord` abstracts, include:

❏ the process of logging into the database server

❏ date calculations

❏ handling of boolean (`true`/`false`) data

Before I can show you the magic of `ActiveRecord` in action, though, we need to do a little housekeeping.

Database Tables

We've already created a database for each of our environments (development, testing, production), but there aren't any **tables** in those databases yet. Tables are the containers within a database that store our data in a structured manner, and they're made up of rows and columns. The rows map to individual objects, and the columns map to the attributes of those objects. The collection of all the tables in a database, and the relationships between those tables, is called the database **schema**.

Figure 4.5. The structure of a typical database table, including rows and columns

An example of a table is shown in Figure 4.5.

In Rails, the naming of Ruby classes and database tables follows an intuitive pattern: if we have a table called `stories` that consists of five rows, then that table will store the data for five `Story` objects. The nice thing about the mapping between classes and tables is that it's not something that you need to write code to achieve—it just happens, because `ActiveRecord` infers the name of the table from the name of the class. Note that the name of our class in Ruby is a singular noun (`Story`), but the name of the table is plural (`stories`).

This relationship makes sense if you think about it: when we refer to a `Story` object in Ruby, we're dealing with a single story. But the MySQL table holds a multitude of stories, so its name should be plural. While it's possible to override these conventions (as is sometimes necessary when dealing with legacy databases), it's much easier to adhere to them.

The close relationship between tables and objects extends even further: if our `stories` table were to have a `link` column, as our example in Figure 4.5 does, then the data in this column would automatically be mapped to the `link` attribute in a `Story` object. And adding a new column to a table would cause an attribute of the same name to become available in all of that table's corresponding objects.

So, let's create some tables to hold the stories we create.

For the time being, we'll create a table using the old-fashioned approach of entering SQL into the MySQL command line. You could type out the following SQL commands, although I acknowledge that typing out SQL isn't much fun. Instead, I'd encourage you to download the following script from the code archive, and copy and paste it straight into your MySQL console.

File: **03-create-stories-table.sql**

```
USE shovell_development;
CREATE TABLE `stories` (
  `id` int(11) NOT NULL auto_increment,
  `name` varchar(255) default NULL,
  `link` varchar(255) default NULL,
  PRIMARY KEY (`id`)
);
```

You needn't worry about remembering these SQL commands to use in your own projects; instead, take heart in knowing that in Chapter 5 we'll look at something called **migrations**, which are special Ruby classes that we can write to create database tables for our application without using any SQL at all.

Using the Rails Console

Now that we have our `stories` table in place, let's exit the MySQL console and open up a Rails console. A Rails console is just like the interactive Ruby console (irb) that we used in Chapter 3, but with one key difference: in a Rails console, you have access to all of the environment variables and classes that are available to your application while it is running. These are not available from within a standard irb console.

To enter a Rails console, change to your `shovell` folder, and enter the command `ruby script/console`, as shown below. The `>>` prompt is ready to accept your commands:

```
$ cd shovell
$ ruby script/console
Loading development environment.
>>
```

Saving an Object

To start using `ActiveRecord`, simply define a class that inherits from the `ActiveRecord::Base` class. (We touched on the `::` operator very briefly in Chapter 3, where we used it to refer to constants. It can also be used to refer to classes that exist within a module, which is what we're doing here.) Flip back to the section on object oriented programming (OOP) in Chapter 3 if you need a refresher on inheritance.

Consider the following code snippet:

```
class Story < ActiveRecord::Base
end
```

These two lines of code define a seemingly empty class called Story. However, this class is far from empty, as we'll soon see.

From the Rails console, let's create this Story class, and an instance of the class called story, by entering these commands:

```
>> class Story < ActiveRecord::Base; end
=> nil
>> story = Story.new
=> #<Story:0x2642900 @attributes={"link"=>nil, "name"=>nil},
@new_record=true>
>> story.class
=> Story
```

As you can see, the syntax for creating a new ActiveRecord object is identical to the syntax we used to create other Ruby objects in Chapter 3. At this point, we've created a new Story object. However, this object exists in memory only—we haven't stored it in our database yet.

We can confirm the fact that it hasn't been saved yet by checking the value of the new_record attribute, using the object's accessor method:

```
>> story.new_record?
=> true
```

Because the object has not been saved yet, it will be lost when we exit the Rails console. To save it to the database, we need to invoke the object's save method:

```
>> story.save
=> true
```

Now that we've saved our object (a return value of true indicates that the save method was successful) our story is no longer a new record. It's even been assigned a unique ID, as shown below:

```
>> story.new_record?
=> false
>> story.id
=> 1
```

Defining Relationships Between Objects

As well as the basic functionality that we've just seen, `ActiveRecord` makes the process of defining relationships (or associations) between objects as easy as possible. Of course, it's possible with some database servers to define such relationships entirely within the database schema. However, in order to put `ActiveRecord` through its paces, let's look at the way it defines these relationships within Rails.

Object relationships can be defined in a variety of ways; the main difference between these relationships is the number of records that are specified in the relationship. The primary types of database associations are:

❑ one-to-one associations

❑ one-to-many associations

❑ many-to-many associations

Let's look at some examples of each of these associations. Feel free to type them into the Rails console if you like, for practice. Remember that your class definitions won't be saved, though—I'll show you how to define associations in a file later.

Suppose our application has the following associations:

❑ An `Author` can have one `Weblog`:

```
class Author < ActiveRecord::Base
  has_one :weblog
end
```

❑ An `Author` can submit many `Stories`:

```
class Author < ActiveRecord::Base
  has_many :stories
end
```

❑ A `Story` belongs to an `Author`:

```
class Story < ActiveRecord::Base
  belongs_to :author
end
```

❏ A Story has, and belongs to, many different Topics:

```
class Story < ActiveRecord::Base
  has_and_belongs_to_many :topics
end
class Topic < ActiveRecord::Base
  has_and_belongs_to_many :stories
end
```

You're no doubt growing tired of typing class definitions into a console, only to have them disappear the moment you exit the console. For this reason, we won't go any further with the associations between our objects—we'll delve into the ActiveRecord module in more detail in Chapter 5.

The ActionPack Module

ActionPack is the name of the library that contains the view and controller parts of the MVC architecture. Unlike the ActiveRecord module, these modules are a little more intuitively named: ActionController and ActionView.

Exploring application logic and presentation logic on the command line doesn't make a whole lot of sense (views and controllers *are* designed to interact with a web browser, after all!). Instead, I'll just give you a brief overview of the Action-Pack components, and we'll cover the hands-on stuff in Chapter 5.

ActionController (the Controller)

The controller handles the application logic of your program, acting as a glue between the application's data, the presentation layer, and the web browser. In this role, a controller performs a number of tasks, including:

❏ deciding how to handle a particular request (for example, whether to render a full page or just one part of it)

❏ retrieving data from the model to be passed to the view

❏ gathering information from a browser request, and using it to create or update data in the model

When we introduced the MVC diagram in Figure 4.3 earlier in this chapter, it might not have occurred to you that a Rails application can consist of a number of different controllers. Well, it can! Each controller is responsible for a specific part of the application.

For our Shovell application, we'll create:

❑ one controller for displaying story links, which we'll name `StoryController`

❑ another controller for handling user authentication, called `AccountController`

Both controllers will inherit from the `ActionController::Base` class,[4] but they'll have different functionality, implemented as instance methods. Here's a sample class definition for the `StoryController` class:

```
class StoryController < ActionController::Base
  def index
  end
  def show
  end
end
```

This simple class definition sets up our `StoryController` with two empty methods—the `index` method, and the `show` method—both of which we'll expand upon in later chapters.

Each controller resides in its own Ruby file (with a `.rb` extension), which lives within the `app/controllers` directory. The `StoryController` class that we just defined, for example, would live in the file `app/controllers/story_controller.rb`.

IMPORTANT

Naming Classes and Files

You'll have noticed by now that the names of classes and files follow different conventions:

❑ Class names are written in **CamelCase** (each word beginning with a capital letter, with no spaces between words).

❑ Filenames are written in lowercase, with underscores separating each word.

---

[4] There will actually be an intermediate class between this class and the `ActionController::Base` class; we'll cover the creation of the `StoryController` class in more detail in Chapter 5. However, this doesn't change the fact that `ActionController::Base` is the base class from which every controller inherits.

This is important! If this convention is *not* followed, Rails will have a hard time locating your files. Luckily, you won't need to name your files manually very often, if ever, as you'll see when we look at generated code in Chapter 5.

ActionView (the View)

As we discussed earlier, one of the principles of MVC is that a view should contain **presentation logic** only. This means that the code in a view should only perform actions that relate to displaying pages in the application—none of the code in a view should perform any complicated application logic, nor should it store or retrieve any data from the database. In Rails, everything that is sent to the web browser is handled by a view.

Predictably, views are stored in the `app/views` folder of our application.

A view need not actually contain any Ruby code at all—it may be that one of your views is a simple HTML file. However, it's more likely that your views will contain a combination of HTML and Ruby code, making the page more dynamic. The Ruby code is embedded in HTML using **embedded Ruby** (ERb) syntax.

ERb is similar to PHP or JSP, in that it allows server-side code to be scattered throughout an HTML file by wrapping that code in special tags. For example, in PHP you might do something like this:

```
<strong><?php echo 'Hello World from PHP!' ?></strong>
```

The equivalent in ERb would be the following:

```
<strong><%= 'Hello World from Ruby!' %></strong>
```

There are two forms of the ERb tag pair: one that includes the equal sign, and one that does not:

`<%= ... %>`
> This tag pair is for regular output. The output of a Ruby expression between these tags will be displayed in the browser.

`<% ... %>`
> This tag pair is for code that is not intended to be displayed, such as calculations, loops, or variable assignments.

An example of each is shown below:

```
<%= 'This line is displayed in the browser' %>
<% 'This line executes silently, without displaying any output' %>
```

You can place any Ruby code—be it simple or complex—between these tags.

Creating an instance of a view is a little different to that of a model or a controller. While ActionView::Base (the parent class for all views) is one of the base classes for views in Rails, the instantiation of a view is handled completely by the Action-View module. The only thing a Rails developer needs to modify is the **template**, which is the file that contains the presentation code for the view. As you might have guessed, these templates are stored in the app/views folder.

As with most things in Rails, a strict convention applies to the naming and storage of template files:

❑ A template has a one-to-one mapping to the action (method) of a controller. The name of the template file matches the name of the action to which it maps.

❑ The folder that stores the template is named after the controller.

❑ The extension of the template file varies on the basis of the template's type. By default there are three types of template in Rails:

rhtml
   This is the extension for standard HTML templates that are sprinkled with ERb tags.

rxml
   This extension is used for templates that output XML (for example, to generate RSS feeds for your application).

rjs
   This extension is used for templates that return JavaScript instructions. This type of template might be used, for example, to modify an existing page (via Ajax) to update the contents of a <div> tag.

This convention may sound complicated, but it's actually quite intuitive. For example, consider the StoryController class that we defined earlier. Invoking the read method for this controller would, by default, attempt to display the ActionView template that lived in the app/views/story directory. Assuming the page was a standard HTML page (containing some ERb code), the name of this template would be read.rhtml.

Rails also comes with special templates such as **layouts** and **partials**. Layouts are templates that control the global layout of an application, such as structures that remain unchanged between pages (the primary navigation menu, for instance). Partials are special subtemplates (the result of a template being split into separate files, such as a secondary navigation menu or a form) that can be used multiple times within the application. We'll cover both layouts and partials in Chapter 7.

Communication between controllers and views occurs via instance variables that are populated from within the controller's action. Let's expand upon our sample `StoryController` class to illustrate this point (there's no need to type any of this out just yet):

```
class StoryController < ActionController::Base
  def index
    @variable = 'Value being passed to a view'
  end
end
```

As you can see, the instance variable `@variable` is being assigned a string value within the controller's action. Through the magic of `ActionView`, this variable can now be referenced directly from the corresponding view, as shown in the code below:

```
<p>The instance variable @variable contains: <%= @variable %></p>
```

This approach allows more complex computations to be performed outside the view (remember, it should only contain presentational logic), leaving the view to display just the end result of the computation.

Rails also provides access to special containers, such as the `params` and `session` hashes. These contain information including the current page request and the user's session. We'll make use of these hashes in the chapters that follow.

Code Generation

Rather than having us create all of our application code from scratch, Rails gives us the facility to generate an application's basic structure with considerable ease. In the same way that we created our application's entire directory structure, we can create new models, controllers, and views using a single command.

To generate code in Rails, we use the `generate` script, which lives in the `script` folder. Give it a try now: type `ruby generate` without any command line parameters. Rails displays an overview of the available parameters for the command, and lists the generators from which we can choose, as Figure 4.6 illustrates.

Figure 4.6. Sample output from `script/generate`

```
Core:~ scoop$ cd shovell
Core:~/shovell scoop$ cd script
Core:~/shovell/script scoop$ ruby generate
Usage: generate generator [options] [args]

General Options:
    -p, --pretend          Run but do not make any changes.
    -f, --force            Overwrite files that already exist.
    -s, --skip             Skip files that already exist.
    -q, --quiet            Suppress normal output.
    -t, --backtrace        Debugging: show backtrace on errors.
    -h, --help             Show this help message.
    -c, --svn              Modify files with subversion. (Note: svn mu
st be in path)


Installed Generators
   Builtin: controller, integration_test, mailer, migration, model, plugin, scaff
old, session_migration, web_service

More are available at http://rubyonrails.org/show/Generators
   1. Download, for example, login_generator.zip
   2. Unzip to directory /Users/mattymcg/.rails/generators/login
       to use the generator with all your Rails apps
       or to /Users/mattymcg/shovell/generators/login
       to use with this app only.
   3. Run generate with no arguments for usage information
        generate login

Generator gems are also available:
   1. gem search -r generator
   2. gem install login_generator
   3. generate login

Core:~/shovell/script scoop$
```

Rails can generate code of varying complexity. At its simplest, creating a new controller causes a template file to be placed in the appropriate subdirectory of your application. The template itself consists of a mainly empty class definition, similar to the Story and Author classes that we looked at earlier in this chapter.

However, code generation can also be a very powerful tool for automating complex, repetitive tasks; for instance, you might generate a foundation for handling user authentication. We'll launch straight into generating code in Chapter 5, when we begin generating our models and controllers.

Another example is the generation of a basic web-based interface to a model, referred to as **scaffolding**. We'll also look at scaffolding in Chapter 5, as we make a start on building our views.

`ActionMailer`

While not strictly part of the Web, email is a big part of our online experience, and Rails's integrated support for email is worth a mention. Web applications frequently make use of email for tasks like sending sign-up confirmations to new users and resetting a user's password.

`ActionMailer` is the Rails component that makes it easy to incorporate the sending and receiving of email into your application. `ActionMailer` is structured in a similar way to `ActionPack` in that it consists of controllers and actions with templates.

While the creation of emails, and the processing of incoming email, are complex tasks, `ActionMailer` hides these complexities and handles the tasks for you. This means that creating an outgoing email is simply a matter of supplying the subject, body, and recipients of the email using templates and a little Ruby code. Likewise, `ActionMailer` processes incoming email for you, providing you with a Ruby object that encapsulates the entire message in a way that's easy to access.

Adding email functionality to a web application is beyond the scope of this book, but you can read more about `ActionMailer` on the Ruby on Rails wiki.[5]

Testing and Debugging

Testing

A number of different types of testing are supported by Rails, including automated and integration testing.

Automated Testing

The concept of automated testing isn't new to the world traditional software development, but it's fairly uncommon in web application development. While most Java-based web applications make use of comprehensive testing facilities,

---

[5] http://wiki.rubyonrails.com/rails/pages/ActionMailer/

a large number of PHP and Perl web applications go live after only some manual tests have been performed (and sometimes without any testing at all!). Although performing automated tests may be an option, developers may decide not to use them for reasons ranging from the complexity of the task to time constraints.

We touched on this briefly in Chapter 1, but it's worth stressing again: the fact that comprehensive automated testing is built into Rails, and is dead easy to implement, means there's no longer a question about whether or not you should test your apps: *just do it!*

The `generate` command that we introduced a moment ago can automatically create testing templates that you can use with your controllers, views, and models. (Note that Rails just assists you in doing your job, it's not replacing you—yet!)

The extent to which you want to implement automated testing is up to you. It may suit your needs to wait until something breaks, then write a test that proves the problem exists. Once you've fixed the problem so that the test no longer fails, you'll never get a bug report for that particular problem again.

If, on the other hand, you'd like to embrace automated testing completely, you can write tests to ensure that a specific HTML tag exists at a precise position within a page's hierarchy.[6] Yes, automated tests *can* be that precise.

Integration Testing

Rails's testing capabilities also include **integration testing**.

Integration testing refers to the testing of several web site components in succession—typically, the order of the components resembles the path that a user would follow when using the application. You could, for example, construct an integration test that reconstructs the actions of a user clicking on a link, registering for a user account, confirming the registration email you send, and visiting a page that's restricted to registered users.

We'll look at both automated testing and integration testing in more detail in later chapters.

---

[6] The hierarchy referred to here is the Document Object Model (DOM), a W3C standard for describing the hierarchy of an (X)HTML page.

Debugging

When you're fixing problems, the first step is to identify the source of the problem. Like many languages, Rails assists this process by providing the developer (that's you!) with a full stack trace of the code. As we saw earlier, a stack trace is a list of all of the methods that were called up to the point at which an exception was raised. The list includes not only the name of each method, but also the classes to which those methods belong, and the names of the files in which they reside.

Using the information contained in the stack trace, you can go back to your code to determine the problem. There are a few different ways to approach this, depending on the nature of the problem itself:

❑ If you have a rough idea of what the problem might be, and are able to isolate it to your application's model (either a particular class or aspect of your data), your best bet is to use the Rails console that we looked at earlier in this chapter. Type `console` from the `script` directory to launch the console. Once inside, you can load the particular model that you're interested in, and poke at it to reproduce and fix the problem.

❑ If the problem leans more towards something related to the user's browser or session, you can add a `breakpoint` statement around the spot at which the problem occurs. With this in place, you can reload the browser and step through your application's code using the `breakpointer` command line tool to explore variable content or to execute Ruby statements manually.

We'll be covering all the gory details of debugging in Chapter 11.

A GUI Tool for MySQL

The MySQL command line that we've been using in this chapter is one way to maintain your database structure and the data that it contains. But working in a command line client can definitely be overwhelming, complex, and tedious—especially when you're just taking your first steps with databases and don't know your way around!

A GUI tool available for use with MySQL that's worth a mention is the MySQL Query Browser. Published by MySQL AB (the makers of MySQL), the MySQL

Query Browser is a free, cross-platform tool that is currently available for Windows, Linux, and Mac OS X.[7]

Installing MySQL Query Browser is a straightforward process on most platforms:

Windows
A binary installer exists for Windows—launch the installer and select the default options for each step in the wizard.

Mac OS X
A binary installer exists for the Mac as well. Mount the disk image and drag the application icon to your `Applications` folder.

Linux
A package exists for most distributions of Linux; install the application using your distribution's package manager.

Figure 4.7. The MySQL Query Browser connection screen

---

[7] The MySQL Query Browser is available for download from
http://dev.mysql.com/downloads/query-browser/. Unfortunately there is no binary install package for
OS X 10.3 or earlier; CocoaMySQL [http://cocoamysql.sourceforge.net/] is a good alternative.

The MySQL Query Browser can be used to perform queries against your database. You can also use it to alter your database structure by creating and modifying databases and tables. Figure 4.7 shows the connection screen.

The connection details to use are identical to the ones we used earlier, when we configured Rails to connect to our database in the `config/database.yml` file. Assuming that you haven't changed your MySQL configuration since then, enter `localhost` into the Hostname field and `root` for the Username. Now hit Connect.

Once you're connected, you should be greeted by a window similar to the one shown in Figure 4.8.

Figure 4.8. MySQL Query Browser's Query window

At the top of the main window is a text field in which you can type database queries. The pull-out tab on the right-hand side lists the databases to which you can connect. There's even a function and syntax reference.

The MySQL Query Browser displays the table schema of the `stories` table exactly as we've created it, with the added benefit that we can alter it with just a mouse click. By clicking the + button at the bottom of the column list, you can add a column; clicking the - button removes the currently selected column. Pretty simple, isn't it?

Exploring every feature of the query browser is definitely beyond the scope of this book, but there is one more thing I'd like to show you: the Table Editor, which is shown in Figure 4.9.

To launch the Table Editor, first expand the `shovell_development` database by clicking on the triangle next to the database's name. This will list all of the tables in the database. Currently, there should only be one: the `stories` table that we created earlier. Now right-click (Control-click on a Mac) on the table that you want to edit, and select Edit Table from the menu that appears.

Figure 4.9. The MySQL Table Editor

The Table Editor allows you to edit existing tables and add new tables, all using a nice GUI interface. I'm sure you'll agree this is a much friendlier experience than having to battle with the cryptic command line tool.

That's it for the MySQL Query Browser—we'll revisit it briefly in Chapter 5, but feel free to close the application now.

Summary

In this chapter, we peeled back some of the layers that comprise the Ruby on Rails framework. By now you should have a good understanding of which parts of Rails perform particular roles in the context of an MVC architecture. It should also be reasonably clear how a request that's made by a web browser is processed by a Rails application.

We looked at the different environments that Rails provides to address the different stages in the lifecycle of an application, and we created databases to support these environments. We also provided Rails with the necessary details to connect to our database.

We also had our first contact with real code, as we looked at the `ActiveRecord` models, `ActionController` controllers, and `ActionView` templates for our Shovell application. We explored the topics of code generation, testing, and debugging, and we took a brief look at a GUI client that makes interacting with our MySQL database more convenient.

In the next chapter, we'll build on all of this knowledge as we use the code generation tools to create actual models, controllers, and views for our Shovell application. It's going to be a big one!

Models, Views, and Controllers

In Chapter 4, we introduced the principles behind the model-view-controller architectural pattern, and saw how each of the components is implemented within the Rails framework. In this chapter, we'll put this knowledge to good use as we use Rails's code generation techniques to create these components for our Shovell application.

Generating a Model

As our application will be used to share links to *stories* on the Web, a `Story` is the fundamental object around which our application should evolve. Here, we'll use the Rails model generator to create a `Story` model, and then build everything else around it.

The Model Generator

The model generator is actually driven by a command line script that we encountered back in Chapter 4: the `generate` script. It lives in the `script` directory, and makes generating a `Story` model very simple.

Running the generate Script

generate can be called from the command line and takes several parameters. The first parameter is the type of component that's to be generated. You can probably guess which value I'm going to suggest you use for this parameter. We're creating a model, so the parameter to pass is simply model. Let's take a look at what happens when we pass that to the script:

```
$ cd shovell
$ ruby script/generate model
```

Figure 5.1 shows the resulting output.

Figure 5.1. Sample output from the model generator

```
000                    Terminal — bash — 94x37
Core:~ scoop$ cd shovell
Core:~/shovell scoop$ ruby script/generate model
Usage: script/generate model ModelName [options]

Options:
        --skip-migration          Don't generate a migration file for this model

General Options:
    -p, --pretend                 Run but do not make any changes.
    -f, --force                   Overwrite files that already exist.
    -s, --skip                    Skip files that already exist.
    -q, --quiet                   Suppress normal output.
    -t, --backtrace               Debugging: show backtrace on errors.
    -h, --help                    Show this help message.
    -c, --svn                     Modify files with subversion. (Note: svn must be in path)

Description:
    The model generator creates stubs for a new model.

    The generator takes a model name as its argument.  The model name may be
    given in CamelCase or under_score and should not be suffixed with 'Model'.

    The generator creates a model class in app/models, a test suite in
    test/unit, test fixtures in test/fixtures/singular_name.yml, and a migration
    in db/migrate.

Example:
    ./script/generate model Account

    This will create an Account model:
        Model:      app/models/account.rb
        Test:       test/unit/account_test.rb
        Fixtures:   test/fixtures/accounts.yml
        Migration:  db/migrate/XXX_add_accounts.rb

Core:~/shovell scoop$ ▊
```

On reading this output, we can deduce that using `generate` to create a new model for our application won't actually do very much—some "stubs" (empty files) will be created in the appropriate directories, but that's about it.

Let's go ahead and try it anyway. We'll create a `Story` model, then we'll examine each of the generated files in turn.

From the `shovell` folder, enter the following:

```
$ ruby script/generate model Story
```

The output of this command will list exactly what has been done; it's shown in Figure 5.2.

Figure 5.2. Generating a `Story` model

Let's take a closer look at what the `generate` script has done here.

Understanding the Output

To begin with, `generate` skipped over three folders that already exist. The script indicates that it's skipping a folder by displaying the word exists, followed by the name of the folder. The folders that were skipped in Figure 5.2 were those that were generated when we ran the `rails` command back in Chapter 2.

Next, `generate` actually created some files (indicated by the word create, followed by the name of the file that was created) and a folder. Let's look at each of the files in turn:

story.rb

This file contains the actual class definition for the `Story` model. Locate the file (it's in the `app/models` folder) and examine its contents in your text editor—the class definition is absolutely identical to the one that we typed out in Chapter 4:

File: **01-story.rb**

```
class Story < ActiveRecord::Base
end
```

Okay, being able to generate these two lines of code isn't exactly ground-breaking. But stay with me here!

story_test.rb

This file is much more exciting; it's an automatically generated unit test for our model. We'll look at it in detail in Chapter 6, but briefly, by building up the contents of this file, we can ensure that all of the code in our model is covered by a unit test. As we mentioned back in Chapter 1, once we have all our unit tests in place, we can automate the process of checking that our code behaves as intended.

stories.yml

To help with our unit test, a file called `stories.yml` is created. This file is referred to as a **fixture**. Fixtures are files that contain sample data for unit testing purposes—when we run the test suite, Rails will wipe the database and populate our tables using the fixtures. In this way, fixtures allow us to ensure that every unit test of a given application is run against a consistent baseline.

By default, the `stories.yml` fixture file will insert two rows in our `stories` table. The `.yml` extension for that file indicates that it is a YAML file. We'll look at what this means in the next section.

001_create_stories.rb

This file is what's known as a migration file. We'll be exploring migrations in a moment.

What's YAML?

YAML (a tongue-in-cheek recursive acronym that stands for YAML Ain't Markup Language) is a lightweight format for representing data. YAML files have the extension .yml. As they employ none of the confusing tags that XML uses, YAML files are much easier for humans to read, and are just as efficiently read by computers.

Rails uses YAML files extensively to specify fixtures. We've seen a couple of examples of YAML files so far: the database.yml file that we used to configure our database connection was one; the stories.yml file that we just created with the generate script is another.

Let's dissect the stories.yml file—open it up in a text editor (it's in the test/fixtures directory), and you'll see the following code:

File: **02-stories.yml**

```
first:
  id: 1
another:
  id: 2
```

This YAML file represents two separate records (first, and another). Each record contains a single data field: a column called id. This id field maps to the id column of our stories table.

Let's expand on each of these records by adding name and link fields. Edit the file so that it looks like this:

File: **03-stories.yml**

```
first:
  id: 1
  name: My shiny weblog
  link: http://poocs.net/
another:
  id: 2
  name: SitePoint Forums
  link: http://www.sitepoint.com/forums/
```

As you can see, each record in a YAML file begins with a unique name, which is *not* indented. This name is not the name of the record, or of any of the fields in the database; it's simply used to identify the record within the file. (It's also utilized in testing, as we'll see in Chapter 11.) In our expanded `stories.yml` file, `first` and `another` are these identifying names.

After the unique name, we see a series of key/value pairs, each of which is indented by one or more spaces (we'll use two spaces, to keep consistent with our convention for Rails code). In each case, the key is separated from its value by a colon.

Now, let's take a look at the last file that was generated—the migration file. If your experience with modifying databases has been limited to writing SQL, then this next section is sure to be an eye-opener, so buckle up! This is going to be an exciting ride.

Modifying the Schema Using Migrations

As we mentioned earlier, the last of the four files that our `generate` script created—`001_create_stories.rb`—is a **migration file**. A migration file is a special file that can be used to adjust the database schema in a variety of ways (each change that's defined in the file is referred to as a **migration**).

Migrations can be a handy way to make alterations to your database as your application evolves. Not only do they provide you with a means to change your database schema in an iterative manner, but they let you do so using Ruby code, rather than SQL. As you may have gathered by now, I'm not a big fan of writing lots of SQL, and migrations are a great way to avoid it.

Migration files are numbered so that they can be executed sequentially. In our case, the file for creating stories is the first migration file, so our migration file has the number `001` in its name.

Like SQL scripts, migrations can be built on top of each other, which reinforces the need for these files to be executed in order. Sequential execution removes the possibility that, for example, an attempt is made to add a new column to a table that does not yet exist.

Let's examine the migration file that was generated for us.

Creating a Skeleton Migration File

Open the file `001_create_stories.rb` in your text editor (it lives in `db/migrate`). It should look like this:

File: **04-001_create_stories.rb**

```ruby
class CreateStories < ActiveRecord::Migration
  def self.up
    create_table :stories do |t|
      # t.column :name, :string
    end
  end

  def self.down
    drop_table :stories
    end
  end
end
```

As you can see, a migration file contains a class definition that inherits from the ActiveRecord::Migration class. The class that's defined in the migration file is assigned a name by the generate script, based on the parameters that are passed to it. In this case, our migration has been given the name CreateStories, which is a fairly accurate description of the task that it will perform—we're generating a new model (a Story), so the code in the migration file creates a stories table in which to store our stories.

The class contains two class methods:

❏ self.up is called when the migration is applied (when we're setting *up* our schema).

❏ self.down is called when the migration is reversed (when we're tearing it *down*).

These methods are complementary—the task performed by the down method in a migration file should be the exact opposite of that performed by the up method.

Luckily, our down method is complete and needs no tweaking. Its purpose is to undo the changes that are applied in the up method; all it needs to do to achieve that is to drop the database table, which is exactly what this method does.

The up method, on the other hand, needs some work. It doesn't achieve an awful lot at the moment—it creates a table for us, but that table has no fields (yet). It also contains a block (jump back to Chapter 3 if you need a refresher on blocks), but the only line of code inside that block is commented out! The code in this comment gives us a hint about what we need to add—Rails has provided us with a skeleton, and it's up to us to flesh out the detail. Let's do that now!

Filling in the Gaps

What's missing from our migration file is code that specifies the details of the columns that our **stories** table should contain. Like an SQL script, each column in our migration file should have a *name* and a *type* of data storage (such as a string, number, or date).

In addition to creating completely new tables, migrations can be used to alter existing tables. If you were to decide tomorrow that your **stories** table needed to store the time and date at which each story is added, it would be a painful task to have to recreate the whole table just to add the extra column. Once again, good old SQL can be used to perform this job efficiently, but to use it, we'd have to learn yet *another* awkward SQL command. Using migrations, you can add this column to an existing table without losing any of the data that the table contains.

We'll use migrations to alter the **stories** table in Chapter 6. For now, let's expand the up method as follows:[1]

File: **05-001_create_stories.rb (excerpt)**

```
def self.up
  create_table :stories, :force => true do |t|
    t.column :name, :string
    t.column :link, :string
  end
end
```

This code will create a **stories** table that has three columns:

❏ name, for storing the name of the story, of type **string**

❏ link, for storing the URL of the story, of type **string**

❏ id, an automatically generated column that will serve as the primary identifier for each row in the table

This approach reflects the "pure" Rails method of creating and altering database tables that we talked about back in Chapter 4.

---

[1] The **:force => true** at the beginning of the block isn't usually required—we've included it in this case to counter the fact that we created a table for this model back in Chapter 4, using raw SQL. Without it, our **create_table** call would fail, because the table already exists.

Now that we have a migration file complete with methods for setting up and tearing down our schema, we just need to make the migration take place. We use the `rake` tool to achieve this task.

Using `rake` to Migrate our Data

`rake` is a tool for executing a set of tasks that are specific to your project.

If you've ever written or compiled a C program, you'll have come across the `make` tool. Well, `rake` is to Ruby code as `make` is to C code. Written by Jim Weirich, the `rake` package borrows its naming conventions and basic functionality from `make`, but that's where the similarities end.[2]

You can define the tasks that you want `rake` to execute in a file named `Rakefile`, which is written purely in Ruby code. In fact, Rails itself uses its own `Rakefile` to supply you with a number of handy tasks (check your `shovell` folder—you'll find it there). Alternatively, you can access the entire list of tasks available to a Rails application by typing `rake --tasks` from the application's root folder (in our case, the `shovell` directory). Some of those tasks are shown in Figure 5.3.

Figure 5.3. Some of the tasks that are available using `rake`

A `rake` task can also accept a **namespace**, which is a conceptual container that allows us to group related tasks together.

---

[2] Jim maintains a blog about Ruby and Rails at http://onestepback.org/.

One example is the db namespace, which groups all tasks that are related to the database. Namespaces are designated by the use of a colon, so tasks within the db namespace are addressed using the prefix db:.

Common tasks that you might use in your day-to-day Rails work include:

❏ db:migrate, for applying new migrations

❏ db:test:clone_structure, for recreating your test database using the structure in your development environment

❏ test, for running your test suite

As the last of these examples demonstrates, not every task belongs to a namespace—some tasks stand alone.

As we saw in Figure 5.3, the default Rakefile for our application comes with a boatload of predefined tasks, each of which offers unique functionality. For now, we're only interested in the db:migrate task (that is, the migrate task from the db namespace). We'll explore some other rake tasks in later chapters.

The rake command accepts a number of options (type rake --help to see them all). At its simplest, it takes the following format:

```
$ rake namespace:task
```

For example, to apply the migrations in the migration file that we created earlier, we'd type the following:

```
$ rake db:migrate
```

When executed without any other arguments, this command achieves the following tasks:

1. It checks the database for the unique number of the migration that was most recently applied.

2. It steps through the migrations that have not yet been applied, one by one.

3. For each migration, it executes the up method for that migration class, to bring the database in line with the structure specified in the migration files.

Go ahead and execute our database migration task from the shovell folder now. Figure 5.4 shows the output you should receive.

Figure 5.4. Database migration using `rake`

```
Terminal — bash — 79x15
Core:~/shovell scoop$ rake db:migrate
(in /Users/mattymcg/shovell)
== CreateStories: migrating ============================================
-- create_table(:stories)
   -> 0.0118s
== CreateStories: migrated (0.0132s) ===================================

Core:~/shovell scoop$ █
```

As the output indicates, running this task has caused the `CreateStories` migration that we created to be applied to our database. Assuming it was applied successfully, you should now (once again) have a `stories` table within your `shovell_development` database—take a look using the MySQL Query Browser to check that it worked, if you like.

With this table in place, we can create some data about stories!

Rolling Back is Easy, Too!

As our database schema evolves, so do the migration files that represent it. Rolling back to a previous version of the schema is incredibly easy with migrations. Simply type the following to revert to a previous version of the database (*n* represents the version number that you want to restore):

```
$ rake db:migrate -VERSION=n
```

For example, the following command would undo the `stories` table that we just created, resulting in the blank database that we began with:

```
$ rake db:migrate -VERSION=0
```

Managing Data Using the Rails Console

While we've developed a solid architecture for our application, and created a table to store data, we don't yet have a nice front-end interface for managing that data. We'll start to build that interface in Chapter 6, but in the meantime, we need to find a way to add stories to our table.

That's right—it's the Rails console to the rescue once again!

Creating Records

We can use two approaches to create records from the console. The long-winded approach is to create the object, then populate each of its attributes one by one, as follows:

```
$ ruby script/console
Loading development environment.
>> s = Story.new
=> #<Story:0x285718c @new_record=true,
@attributes={"name"=>nil, "link"=>nil}>
>> s.name = 'My shiny weblog'
=> "My shiny weblog"
>> s.link = 'http://poocs.net/'
=> "http://poocs.net/"
>> s.save
=> true
```

Let's step through what we've done here.

After loading the Rails console, we created a new Story object. We assigned this object to a variable named s (the s is for Story—I know, it won't win any awards for creativity). We then assigned values to each of the columns that exist on a Story object. Finally, we called the save method, and our Story was stored in the database.

How can we be sure that the data was written successfully? We could look at the raw data using our trusty MySQL Query Browser, but we're trying to keep our distance from SQL. Instead, we can confirm that our story saved correctly by checking its id (the unique identifier that the database generates automatically when an object is saved). We can do so from within the Rails console:

```
>> s.id
=> 1
```

Our object's id is not nil, so we know that the save was successful. Of course, there's another way to ensure that the data was written successfully, and that is to use the new_record? method, which you may remember from Chapter 4.

```
>> s.new_record?
=> false
```

Hooray! As this method returns `false`, we know for certain that the object was written to the database. Just in case you need even more convincing, there's one more check that we can use: the `count` class method of the `Story` class. This method allows us to query the database for the number of stories it currently contains.

```
>> Story.count
=> 1
```

Okay, that makes sense. Let's create another `Story` now, this time using a shortcut technique:

```
>> Story.create(
  :name => 'SitePoint Forums',
  :link => 'http://www.sitepoint.com/forums/')
=> #<Story:0x279d474 @new_record=false, @errors=#<ActiveRecord::Er
rors:0x279c72c @errors={}, @base=#<Story:0x279d474 …>>, @attribu
tes={"name"=>"SitePoint Forums", "id"=>2, "link"=>"http://www.site
point.com/forums/"}>
```

The `create` class method achieves the same task as the long-winded approach we just saw, but it only uses one line (not counting word wrapping). This method also (very conveniently) saves the record to the database once the object has been created. And it allows us to assign values to the columns of the record (in this case, in the columns `name` and `link`) at the same time as the record is created.

Hang on—we forgot to assign the object to a variable! How can we query it for additional information?

Retrieving Records

It's all very well to be able to create and save new information, but what good is that information if we can't retrieve it? One approach to retrieving a story from our database would be to guess its `id`—the `id`s are auto-incremented, so we could anticipate the number of the record that we're after. We could then use the `find` class method to retrieve a row based on its `id`:

```
>> Story.find(2)
=> #<Story:0x2796ca0 @attributes={"name"=>"SitePoint Forums",
   "id"=>"2", "link"=>"http://www.sitepoint.com/forums/"}>
```

This approach might be fine for our testing setup, but once our application has deleted and created more than a handful of records, it won't work.

Another approach is to retrieve every row in the table. We can do this by passing `:all` as the argument to the `find` method:

```
>> Story.find(:all)
=> [#<Story:0x2788f9c @attributes={"name"=>"My shiny weblog",
   "id"=>"1", "link"=>"http://poocs.net/"}>, #<Story:0x2788e70
   @attributes={"name"=>"SitePoint Forums", "id"=>"2",
   "link"=>"http://www.sitepoint.com/forums/"}>]
```

This returns an object of class `Array` containing all rows of the `stories` table.

Arrays also have `first` and `last` methods to retrieve (surprise!) the first and last elements of the array:

```
>> Story.find(:all).last
=> #<Story:0x277f80c @attributes={"name"=>"SitePoint Forums",
   "id"=>"2", "link"=>"http://www.sitepoint.com/forums/"}>
```

Making use of the `:all` argument and the `first` and `last` methods gives us some additional flexibility, but this approach isn't exactly resource-friendly—especially if we're working with larger sets of data. As its name suggests, using `:all` has the effect of transferring *all* database records from the database into Ruby's memory. This may not be the most efficient solution—especially if your application is only looking for a single record.

A better approach would be to let the record selection process be handled by the database itself. To facilitate this goal, we can pass two arguments to the `find` method:

`:first`
  This argument retrieves the first element from the set of retrieved records.

`:order`
  This argument allows us to specify the sort order of the returned objects.

The `:order` argument should contain a tiny bit of SQL that tells the database how the records should be ordered. To get the last element, for example, we would assign `:order` a value of `id DESC`, which specifies that the records should be sorted by the `id` column in descending order.

```
>> Story.find(:first, :order => 'id DESC')
=> #<Story:0x2779100 @attributes={"name"=>"SitePoint Forums",
   "id"=>"2", "link"=>"http://www.sitepoint.com/forums/"}>
```

The object that's returned is identical to the one we retrieved using :all in conjunction with our object's last attribute, but this approach is much more resource-friendly.

Now, while all of these retrieval techniques have worked for us so far, any approach that retrieves an object on the basis of its id is fundamentally flawed. It assumes that no-one else is using the database, which certainly will not be a valid assumption when our social news application goes live!

What we need is a more reliable method of retrieving records—one that retrieves objects based on a column other than the id. What if we were to retrieve a Story by its name? That's easy:

```
>> Story.find_by_name('My shiny weblog')
=> #<Story:0x2773bd8 @attributes={"name"=>"My shiny weblog",
   "id"=>"1", "link"=>"http://poocs.net/"}>
```

In fact, we can even query by the link column, or any other column in our stories table! Rails automatically creates these **dynamic finder** methods by prefixing the column name in question with find_by_. In this case, the Story class has the dynamic finders find_by_name and find_by_link (find_by_id would be redundant, as a simple find does the same thing).

Pretty cool, huh?

Updating Records

We know how to add stories to our database, but what happens when someone submits to our Shovell application a story riddled with typos or (gasp!) factual errors? We need to be able to update existing stories, to ensure the integrity and quality of the information on Shovell, and the continuation of the site's glowing reputation.

Before we can update an object, we need to retrieve it. For this example, we'll retrieve a Story from the database using its name, but any of the techniques outlined in the previous section would suffice.

```
>> s = Story.find_by_name('My shiny weblog')
=> #<Story:0x272965c …>
>> s.name
```

```
=> "My shiny weblog"
>> s.name = 'A weblog about Ruby on Rails'
=> "A weblog about Ruby on Rails"
```

As you can see, the task of changing the value of an attribute (name, in this case) is as straightforward as assigning a new value to it. Of course, this change is not yet permanent—we've simply changed the attribute of an object in memory. To save the change to the database, we need to call the save method, just as we did when we learned how to create new objects earlier in this chapter.

```
>> s.save
=> true
```

Once again, there's a shortcut—update_attribute—that allows us to update the attribute and save the object to the database in one fell swoop:

```
>> s.update_attribute :name, 'A weblog about Ruby on Rails'
=> true
```

This is straightforward stuff. Just one more command, then we'll leave the console for good. (Well, for this chapter, anyway!)

Deleting Records

To destroy a database record, simply call the destroy method of the ActiveRecord object. This will remove the record from the database *immediately*:

```
>> s.destroy
=> #<Story:0x272965c …>
```

If you try to use the find method to locate an object that has been destroyed (or didn't exist in the first place), Rails will throw an error:

```
>> Story.find(1)
=> ActiveRecord::RecordNotFound: Couldn't find Story with ID=1
```

As you can see, deleting records is a cinch—at least, for Rails developers! In fact, SQL is doing a good deal of work behind the scenes. Let's pull back the curtain and take a closer look at the SQL statements that result from our commands.

Where's the SQL?

For all of the creating, updating, and deleting of records that we've done in this section, we haven't seen a lot of SQL.

If you'd like to peek at the SQL statements that Rails has saved you from having to type, take a look at the log files located in the `log` folder. In it, you'll find files named after each of the environments. We've been working in the development environment, so have a look at `development.log`. Figure 5.5 shows the contents of the log file on my computer.

Figure 5.5. The log file for the development environment

The contents of the log file vary greatly between environments, and for good reason: the development log file contains *every* SQL statement that's sent to the database server, including the details of how long it took to process each statement. This information can be very useful if you're debugging an error or looking for some additional insight into what is going on. However, it's not appropriate in a production environment—a large number of queries might be executing at any one time, which would result in an enormous log file.

We'll revisit these log files in Chapter 6, when we examine the entries written to them by the `ActionController` and `ActionView` modules.

Generating a Controller

Now that we have our model in place, let's build a controller. In the same way that we generated a model, we generate a controller by running the `script/generate` script from our application's root folder.

Running the generate Script

Run the `generate` script from the command line again, but this time, pass `controller` as the first parameter:

```
$ ruby script/generate controller
```

The output of this command is depicted in Figure 5.7.

As you might have deduced from the output, calling the `generate` script to generate a controller requires us to pass as a parameter the name of the controller that we want to generate. Other parameters that we can pass include any actions that we would like to generate.

Let's try it out. Type in the following:

```
$ ruby script/generate controller Story index
```

The output of the `generate` script, shown in Figure 5.6, tells us exactly what it's doing. Let's analyze each of these lines of output.

Figure 5.6. Generating a Story controller

```
Core:~ scoop$ cd shovell
Core:~/shovell scoop$ ruby script/generate controller Story index
      exists  app/controllers/
      exists  app/helpers/
      create  app/views/story
      exists  test/functional/
      create  app/controllers/story_controller.rb
      create  test/functional/story_controller_test.rb
      create  app/helpers/story_helper.rb
      create  app/views/story/index.rhtml
Core:~/shovell scoop$
```

Figure 5.7. Sample output from the controller generator

```
Terminal — bash — 78x43

Usage: script/generate controller ControllerName [options]

General Options:
    -p, --pretend           Run but do not make any changes.
    -f, --force             Overwrite files that already exist.
    -s, --skip              Skip files that already exist.
    -q, --quiet             Suppress normal output.
    -t, --backtrace         Debugging: show backtrace on errors.
    -h, --help              Show this help message.
    -c, --svn               Modify files with subversion. (Note: svn
must be in path)

Description:
    The controller generator creates stubs for a new controller and its views.

    The generator takes a controller name and a list of views as arguments.
    The controller name may be given in CamelCase or under_score and should
    not be suffixed with 'Controller'.  To create a controller within a
    module, specify the controller name as 'module/controller'.

    The generator creates a controller class in app/controllers with view
    templates in app/views/controller_name, a helper class in app/helpers,
    and a functional test suite in test/functional.

Example:
    ./script/generate controller CreditCard open debit credit close

    Credit card controller with URLs like /credit_card/debit.
        Controller: app/controllers/credit_card_controller.rb
        Views:      app/views/credit_card/debit.rhtml [...]
        Helper:     app/helpers/credit_card_helper.rb
        Test:       test/functional/credit_card_controller_test.rb

Modules Example:
    ./script/generate controller 'admin/credit_card' suspend late_fee

    Credit card admin controller with URLs /admin/credit_card/suspend.
        Controller: app/controllers/admin/credit_card_controller.rb
        Views:      app/views/admin/credit_card/debit.rhtml [...]
        Helper:     app/helpers/admin/credit_card_helper.rb
        Test:       test/functional/admin/credit_card_controller_test.rb

Core:~/shovell scoop$ █
```

Understanding the Output

The meaning of the messages the controller generator output should be quite familiar to you by now.

❑ First, the `generate` script skipped over the creation of a couple of folders, because they already exist in our project.

❑ Next, the `app/views/story` folder was created. As I mentioned when we first looked at `ActionView` in Chapter 4, the templates for our newly-created `StoryController` will be stored in this folder.

❑ After skipping over one more folder, `generate` created four new files:

story_controller.rb

This file houses the actual class definition for our `StoryController`. It's mostly empty, though—all it comes with is a method definition for the `index` action, which, admittedly, is empty as well. Don't worry—we'll expand it soon!

File: **06-story_controller.rb**

```
class StoryController < ApplicationController
  def index
  end
end
```

More astute readers will notice that our `StoryController` doesn't inherit from the `ActionController::Base` class in the way we'd expect. The `ApplicationController` class that we see here is actually an empty class that inherits directly from `ActionController::Base`. The class is defined in the `application.rb` file, which lives in the `app/controllers` folder, if you're curious. The resulting `StoryController` has exactly the same attributes and methods as if it had inherited directly from `ActionController::Base`. Using an intermediary class like this provides a location for storing variables and pieces of functionality that are common to all controllers.

story_controller_test.rb

This file contains the functional test for our controller. We'll skip over it for now, but we'll expand the test cases that this file contains in the section called "Testing the StoryController" in Chapter 9.

story_helper.rb

> This is the empty **helper** class for the controller (helpers are chunks of code that can be reused throughout your application). We'll look at helpers in more detail in Chapter 6.

index.rhtml

> This file is the template that corresponds to the index action that we passed as a parameter to the generate script. For the moment, it's the only one in the app/views/story directory, but as we create others, they'll be stored alongside index.rhtml and given names that match their actions (for example, the read action will end up with a template named read.rhtml).

With this knowledge under our belts, we're finally in a position to breathe life into our little Rails monster, in the true spirit of Frankenstein.

Watch your Controller Class Names!

You'll notice the controller class that was created by the generate script is called StoryController, though the first parameter that we specified on the command line was simply Story. If our parameter had been StoryController, we'd have ended up with a class name of StoryControllerController!

Starting our Application ... Again

It's time to fire up our application again. While our previous experience with WEBrick was somewhat uneventful, this time, our application should do a little more.

Start up the web server using the following command:

```
$ ruby script/server
```

Once the server has completed its startup sequence, type the following address into your web browser: http://localhost:3000/story

If everything goes to plan, you should be looking at a page similar to the one in Figure 5.8.

Figure 5.8. Accessing our `StoryController` from a browser

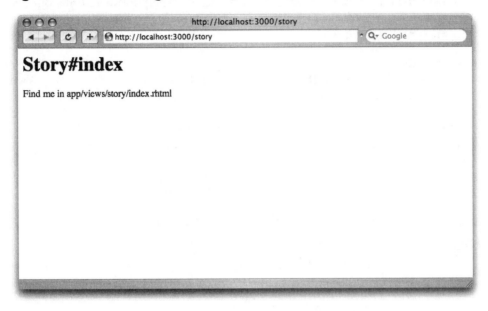

What does this display tell us? Well, this simple (and not especially pretty) page confirms that:

1. The routing between controllers and views is working correctly—Rails has found and instantiated our `StoryController` class, based on the story model that we asked it to retrieve.

2. The `index` action is the default action that's called when no explicit action is specified in the URL (all that we specified was a controller name, using the path `/story`). When you consider that most web servers usually load a file called `index` by default (`index.html`, `index.php`, `index.jsp`, `index.aspx` etc.), this seems like a sensible default.

3. Our controller is able to locate its views—the HTML for the page we see rendered in the browser is contained in the file that's mentioned on screen (`app/views/story/index.rhtml`).

If you think about it, this is actually quite an accomplishment, given that we've really only executed two commands for generating code from the command line.

So that we can complete the picture, let's pull some data from our model into our `index` action.

Creating a View

We can use two approaches to build views for our Rails application. One is to make use of scaffolding; the other is to "go it alone."

We'll look at scaffolding very briefly, but we won't be using it much in the development of our Shovell application. I'll introduce just enough to give you a taste of this topic, then leave it up to you to decide whether or not you find it worthwhile in your own projects.

After that, we'll roll up our sleeves and build some views from scratch.

Generating Views with Scaffolding

In the early days of Rails, scaffolding was one of the features that the Rails community used as a selling point when promoting the framework. Ironically, this feature also received a considerable amount of criticism, though this was largely due to critics failing to understand fully the intended uses of scaffolding.

So what is scaffolding, anyway?

Scaffolding is a tool that quickly creates a web interface for interacting with your model data. The interface lists the existing data in a table, and provides an easy way to add new records and manipulate or delete existing ones.

There are two approaches to using scaffolding:

temporary scaffolding
Temporary scaffolding, which is simply a one-line addition to one of your controllers, is a technique for generating code that's not intended to be built upon. Much like its construction namesake, temporary scaffolding is intended to support a primary structure, not form part of it. Once the primary structure has been completed, the scaffolding is taken away.

We'll be utilizing this type of scaffolding to interact with the data for our Shovell application.

permanent scaffolding

Permanent scaffolding, as you might have guessed, *is* intended to be extended, modified, and built upon. It uses the `generate` script which we've experimented with in this chapter to create fully working template code that can be modified over time. Features provided by the template code can then be tweaked or implemented in a different manner, and code that doesn't suit your project can be removed.

We won't be generating any permanent scaffolding in this project, but I do encourage you to experiment with this approach in your own projects, as there may be cases in which you'll find it useful.

Regardless of which approach you use, you should keep in mind that scaffolding is a tool designed for quick interaction with models, and should only be used as such. It is by no means intended to be a fully automated tool for generating web applications (or even administration interfaces).

Let's return to our example. Edit the `story_controller.rb` file, which lives in the `app/controllers` folder, so that it looks like this:

File: **07-story_controller.rb**

```
class StoryController < ApplicationController
  scaffold :story
end
```

These edits will *temporarily* remove our precious `index` action, which so faithfully served up the page in the previous section. Don't worry, we'll add that action back later.

For now, the command `scaffold :story` provides a hook for Rails to equip our `StoryController` with the functionality necessary to create, update, and delete stories. Reload the page located at http://localhost:3000/story, and this time you should see something similar to the display shown in Figure 5.9.

Figure 5.9. Scaffolding provides a quick administration interface

Feel free to play with the interface—edit the existing story, create some new stories using the New story link at the bottom of the page, and then destroy the newly created story. You get the idea.

As you can see, scaffolding can be a fast track to working with model data. You can also take advantage of the interface to create some dummy records in your database, to make further development easier.

However, scaffolding does have its limits, as I mentioned earlier. For example, it can't cope with `ActiveRecord` associations such as "a `Story` belongs to a `User`," which we saw in Chapter 4. Additionally, since most applications end up requiring a fully fledged administrative interface, you're often better off just creating the real thing rather than fiddling around with a dummy interface.

Scaffolding is certainly a powerful feature of Rails, and it's rewarding to get the instant visual feedback that comes with having some views created for us. However, it's now time for us to create some views of our own.

Creating Static Pages

Back in Chapter 4, we looked briefly at the `ActionView` module, but only from the command line. Let's create some custom views that we can actually view using a web browser.

As a quick refresher, `ActionView` represents the view part of the model-view-controller architecture. Files that are used to render views are called templates, and they usually consist of HTML code interspersed with Ruby code. These files are referred to as **ERb templates**.

One of these templates (albeit a boring one) has already been created for us—it's the `index.rhtml` file that's located in `app/views/story`:

File: **08-index.rhtml**

```
<h1>Story#index</h1>
<p>Find me in app/views/story/index.rhtml</p>
```

It looks familiar, doesn't it? This is the HTML code that we viewed in our web browser earlier in this chapter. As you can see, it's a **static** page (meaning that it doesn't contain any Ruby code). **Dynamic** pages (pages that pull in data from a database, or from some other source) are much more interesting! Let's have a closer look at them now.

Creating Dynamic Pages

Let's begin our adventure in building dynamic pages. We'll add the current date and time to the HTML output of our view a value. Although simple, this value is considered to be dynamic.

Open the template file in your text editor and delete everything that's there. In its place add the following line:

File: **09-index.rhtml**

```
<%= Time.now %>
```

Here, we call the `now` class method that lives on the `Time` class, which is part of the Ruby standard library. This method call is wrapped in ERb tags (beginning with `<%=` and ending with `%>`).

You may remember from Chapter 4 that the equal sign attached to the opening ERb tag will cause the return value of `Time.now` to be output to the web page (rather than executing silently).

As we altered our controller code to use scaffolding in the last section, we need to reverse this change so that Rails renders regular views once more. Open the file `app/controllers/story_controller.rb`, and change it to the following:

File: **10-story_controller.rb**

```
class StoryController < ApplicationController
  def index
  end
end
```

If you refresh your browser now, the page should display the current time, as shown in Figure 5.10. Just to confirm that this value is indeed dynamic, reload your page a few times—you'll notice that the value does indeed change.

Figure 5.10. Our first dynamic page: displaying the current time

Passing Data Back and Forth

There's one fundamental problem with what we've done here. Can you spot it?

In order to adhere to the model-view-controller architecture, we want to avoid performing any hefty calculations from within any of our views—that's the job of the controller. Strictly speaking, our call to `Time.now` is one such calculation, so it should really occur within the controller. But what good is the result of a calculation if we can't display it?

We introduced the concept of passing variables between controllers and views briefly in Chapter 4, but at that point, we didn't have any views that we could use to demonstrate it in action. Now's our chance!

As we learned in Chapter 4, any instance variable that's declared in the controller automatically becomes available to the view as an instance variable. Let's take advantage of that fact: edit /app/controllers/story_controller.rb again so that it contains the following code:

File: **11-story_controller.rb**

```
class StoryController < ApplicationController
  def index
    @current_time = Time.now
  end
end
```

Next, replace the contents of app/views/story/index.rhtml with the following:

File: **12-index.rhtml**

```
<%= @current_time %>
```

I'm sure you can guess what's happened here:

1. We've moved the "calculation" of the current time from the view to the controller.

2. The result of the calculation is stored in the instance variable @current_time.

3. The contents of this instance variable are then automatically made available to the view.

The result is that the job of the view has been reduced to simply displaying the contents of this instance variable, rather than executing the calculation itself.

Voila! Our application logic and our presentation logic are kept neatly separated.

Pulling in a Model

All we need to do now is pull some data into our view, and we'll have the entire MVC stack covered!

In case you deleted all of your model records when we experimented with scaffolding earlier, make sure you create at least one story—type the following into a Rails console:

```
>> Story.create(
    :name => 'SitePoint Forums',
    :link => 'http://www.sitepoint.com/forums/')
```

To display this model data within a view, we need to retrieve it from within the controller, like so:

File: **13-story_controller.rb**

```
class StoryController < ApplicationController
  def index
    @story = Story.find_by_name('SitePoint Forums')
  end
end
```

We'll also change our view accordingly:

File: **14-index.rhtml**

```
A random link:
<a href="<%= @story.link %>"><%= @story.name %></a>
```

Reload the page to see the result—it should look like Figure 5.11.

Figure 5.11. MVC in action: a view displaying model data via the controller

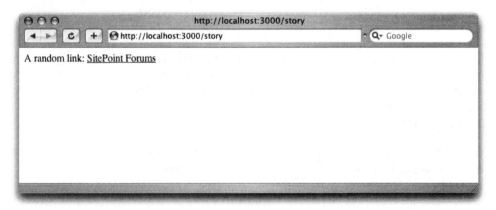

A random link: SitePoint Forums

Of course, Rails wouldn't be doing its job of saving you effort if it required you to manually create links the way we just did. Instead of typing out the HTML for a link, you can use the `link_to` function, which is much easier to remember and achieves the same thing. Try it for yourself:

File: **15-index.rhtml (excerpt)**

```
<%= link_to @story.name, @story.link %>
```

One other point: I'll be the first to admit that the text on the page is a little misleading. Our link is not exactly random—it simply retrieves the same link from the database over and over again.

It's actually quite easy to make our application retrieve random stories, though. Simply modify the part of the controller that fetches the story so that it looks like this:

File: **16-story_controller.rb (excerpt)**

```
@story = Story.find(:first, :order => 'RAND()')
```

This selects a single story, just like before (using the `:first` parameter). However, this time, the database is being instructed to shuffle its records before picking one. Now when you reload your page, random stories should appear (assuming you have more than one story in your database, that is!).

There we have it: the beginnings of our story-sharing application. Admittedly, displaying a random story from our database is only a small achievement, but hey—it's a start!

Summary

This chapter saw us create some real code for each of the components of an MVC application. We generated a model to handle the storage of our stories, and created a corresponding migration; we generated a controller to handle communication between the models and the views; and we created a view that dynamically renders content supplied by our controller.

With the functionality provided by `ActiveRecord`, we've been creating, updating, and deleting data from our SQL database without touching any SQL.

I also introduced you to the `rake` tool, which can be used to run migrations and other tasks. And we learned about the YAML data representation language that's used to store test fixture data for our application.

In Chapter 6, we'll add a layout to our application using HTML and CSS; we'll talk about associations between models; and we'll extend the functionality of our application.

What are you waiting for? Let's get into it!

Helpers, Forms, and Layouts

In Chapter 5, we put in place some basic architecture for our application—a model, a view, and a controller—and were able to display links to stories that are stored in the database. Though the foundation of our application is sound, users can't really interact with it yet.

In this chapter, we'll use some helpers to implement the basic functionality for our application—the capability that allows users to submit stories to the site.

We'll also make a start on building our test suite. In this chapter, we'll create some functional tests to confirm that the form is working as intended. We'll expand on this suite of tests in the coming chapters.

Calling Upon our Trusty Helpers

No, we're not talking about Santa's little helpers. Let me explain.

In Chapter 5, we discussed the importance of keeping application logic in a controller, so that our views contain only presentational code. While it hasn't been apparent in the simple examples that we've looked at so far, extracting code from a view and moving it into a controller often causes clumsy code to be added to an application's controllers.

To address this, another structural component exists—the **helper**. A helper is a chunk of code that can be reused throughout an application, and is stored in a **helper file**. A helper usually contains relatively complicated or reusable presentation logic; because any views that utilize the helper are spared this complexity, the code in the view is kept simple and easy to read, reflecting our adherence to DRY principles. Dozens of helpers are built into Rails, but you can, of course, create your own to use throughout your application.

An example of a good candidate for a helper is code that renders a screen element on a page. Repeating this type of code from one view to another violates the DRY principle, yet sticking it all into a controller doesn't make sense either.

As we saw in Chapter 5, when we generate a controller (using the `generate` script that we've come to know and love), one of the files that's created is a new helper file called `controllername_helper.rb`. In the case of our `StoryController`, the helper file associated with this controller is `story_helper.rb`, and lives in `app/helpers` (take a peek at it if you like).

Helpers associated with a particular controller are available *only* to the views of that particular controller. However, there is one "special" group of helpers—those defined in the file `app/helpers/application_helper.rb`. These helpers are called **global helpers** and become available to *any* view throughout your application.

We'll be relying on a few of Rails' built-in helpers for much of the story submission interface that we'll build in this chapter.

Story Submission

In our brief foray into the world of scaffolding in Chapter 5, we saw that it's possible in Rails to create a quick (and dirty) front end for our data, though this approach doesn't necessarily constitute best practice.

In this section, we'll build a web interface for submitting stories to our Shovell web site without relying on any scaffolding. First, we'll create a view template that contains the actual submission form, then we'll add a new method to our `StoryController` to handle the task of saving submitted stories to the database. We'll also implement a global layout for our application, and we'll create some feedback to present to our users, both when they're filling out the form and after they've submitted a story.

Creating a Form

The topic of HTML forms is one that even seasoned front-end developers have traditionally found intimidating. While it would be possible to create our form elements manually, it's not necessary—Rails offers a number of helpers and shortcuts that make the creation of forms a breeze. One of those is the `form_for` helper, which we'll look at now.

Introducing the `form_for` Helper

Rails offers a few different helper functions for writing forms. `form_for` is a recent addition to the family, and is recommended for use when generating a form that's bound to one type of object. By "bound," I mean that each field in the form maps to the corresponding attribute of a single object, rather than to corresponding attributes of multiple objects. At its most basic, using the `form_for` helper to bind a simple form to a `Story` object would look something like this:

```
<% form_for :story do |f| %>
  <%= f.text_field :name %>
  <%= f.text_field :link %>
<% end %>
```

This syntax boasts a few points that are worth highlighting:

❑ The first and last lines use the ERb tags for silent output (`<% … %>`), while each line within the form uses the ERb tags that display output to the browser (`<%= … %>`).

❑ The parameter that immediately follows `form_for` is a *symbol* with the same name as the object to which the form will be bound. If you're wondering why a symbol is required, rather than the object itself, you're not the only one. The answer's fairly non-technical, though: that's just the way Rails was designed. Just remember to use a symbol, and `form_for` will work fine. In this case, `@story` is the object to which we want to bind the form, so the symbol `:story` is passed as a parameter.

❑ The fields that make up the form live inside a block. As you'll no doubt remember from Chapter 3, a Ruby block is a statement of Ruby code that appears between the keywords `do` and `end`, or between curly braces. This is the first time we've encountered a block within an ERb file, but the principle is the same.

❑ A new object, which I've named `f` in this case, as shorthand for "form," must be passed as a parameter to the block. This object is of type `FormBuilder`, which is a class that contains instance methods designed to work with forms. Using these methods, we can easily create form `input` elements such as `text_field`, `password_field`, `check_box`, and `text_area`.

We receive a number of benefits in exchange for following this syntax:

❑ The `form` tags that signify the start and end of our HTML form will be generated for us.

❑ We gain access to a number of instance methods, via the `FormBuilder` object, that we can use to create fields in our form. In the example, we've used the `text_field` method to create two text fields; these fields will be mapped to our `@story` object automatically.

❑ Appropriate `name` and `id` attributes will be applied to each of these fields—these attributes can then be used as hooks for CSS and JavaScript, as we'll see later in this chapter.

As you can see, using `form_for` and the `FormBuilder` object that comes with it is a powerful way to create comprehensive forms with minimal effort.

Creating the Template

Now that we have a handle on `form_for`, let's use it to create the form that site visitors will use to submit stories to Shovell.

A form is a presentational concept, which means that it should be stored as a view. Our form will allow users to submit *new* stories to Shovell, so we'll give this view the name new. Let's make a template for it: create a new file called `new.rhtml` in the `app/views/story` folder. It should contain the following:

File: **01-new.rhtml**

```
<% form_for :story do |f| %>
<p>
  name:<br />
  <%= f.text_field :name %>
</p>
<p>
  link:<br />
  <%= f.text_field :link %>
</p>
```

```
<p>
  <%= submit_tag %>
</p>
<% end %>
```

Let's break down the ERb code here:

```
<% form_for :story do |f| %>
```

As we just discussed, the form_for helper creates a form that's bound to a specific object—in this case, it's bound to the @story instance variable, as indicated by the inclusion of the :story symbol at the beginning of the block.

```
<%= f.text_field :name %>
```

This line creates a text field called name, which is mapped to our @story object. It will display a text field in which the user can enter the name of the story he or she is submitting.

```
<%= f.text_field :link %>
```

This line creates another text field, this time named link, which is also mapped to our @story object. It will display a text field in which the user can enter the URL of the story he or she is submitting.

```
<%= submit_tag %>
```

This helper generates the HTML code for a Submit button to be displayed in our form. This is a **stand-alone helper**—it's not part of the form_for helper.

Next, make sure that your WEBrick server is running (refer to Chapter 2 if you need a refresher on starting the server). Open your web browser and type the following URL into the address bar: http://localhost:3000/story/new. You should see a page that looks something like Figure 6.1.

Figure 6.1. Our unstyled story submission form

If you see an error message when you try to open this URL, I'd recommend you monitor the terminal window from which you launched your WEBrick server. This process is the heart of our application, so if it's not beating, you won't be able to access any of the functionality that we're going to add in this chapter. Any errors that appear in the terminal window should give you an idea of what went wrong.

You might have assumed that we'd need to include a `new` method in our `StoryController` before this page could display successfully. Not so! The existence of the `new.rhtml` template that we created in the `story` folder was all the impetus Rails needed to go ahead and render the page located at the path `/story/new`.

Of course our form doesn't actually *do* anything yet, but at least we can see it in our browser, ready to go. Rather than allowing our view to gather the information that our user enters (the principles of MVC dictate that this is not its job, after all), let's create a "real" controller action for this form.

Modifying the Controller

To create an action that will process the form, edit the file `app/controllers/story_controller.rb` so that it looks as follows (I've indicated the method to be added in bold):

File: **02-story_controller.rb**

```ruby
class StoryController < ApplicationController
  def index
    @story = Story.find(:first, :order => 'RAND()')
  end
  def new
    @story = Story.new
  end
end
```

It doesn't matter whether you place this new method above or below the existing `index` method. Some people prefer to sort their methods alphabetically, while others group their methods by purpose; the decision is entirely up to you and has no impact on the functionality of your application.

The code that we've added to our `new` method simply instantiates a new `Story` object and stores it in the `@story` instance variable. As it's an instance variable, `@story` will now be available to our view. That's a good start!

Analyzing the HTML

The time has come to find out what kind of HTML the Rails helpers have generated. If you check the HTML for this page (using your browser's View Source option) you should see something that looks like this:

```html
<form action="/story/new" method="post">
<p>
  name:<br />
  <input id="story_name" name="story[name]" size="30"
      type="text" />
</p>
<p>
  link:<br />
  <input id="story_link" name="story[link]" size="30"
      type="text" />
</p>
<p>
  <input name="commit" type="submit" value="Save changes" />
</p>
</form>
```

This markup is basically what we would expect: two text fields and a Submit button have been created for us, and everything has been wrapped up in a `form` element. What *is* interesting is that the target URL (the `action` attribute of the form element) points to the address of the form itself: /story/new. This technique is known as **postback**.

Using postback, we can ensure that if we find an error in user data submitted through the form, that form will simply redisplay for the user, its values intact. It does so without us having to duplicate any code.

Okay, so our markup looks fine. But if you were to submit the form in its current state, you wouldn't be too thrilled with the results: the form is redisplayed, but nothing has been saved—the values you entered have simply disappeared! (Go on, try it!) Let's add some code to save the user's data to the database.

Saving Data to the Database

We're using a single controller action to manage both the display of the form *and* the storage of submissions in the database, so we need to find a way to distinguish between the two.

In order to do this, we'll use the HTTP request method to request the page.[1] Form display is handled by HTTP GET, and form submission is handled by HTTP POST. As the form we're building is being used to submit information, we'll use POST in this case.

In order to check whether a user's browser is in the process of GETting or POSTing information, we might be tempted to look at the raw HTTP headers. However, the built-in Rails request object provides a much easier way to determine whether we're in POST mode or not.

The request object can be used in any controller action. It contains every bit of information about a request issued by a user's browser, including the type of HTTP request method used. To determine whether a browser request is a POST or not, we check the request.post? method. If it is indeed a POST request, we'll need to assign the values submitted via the form to our @story object.

Modify the new method in our StoryController class definition so that it looks like this:

---

[1] The HTTP protocol defines a number of methods for communicating between a web browser and a web server, the most common being GET and POST. GET is used to request information *from* a web site (for example, a page that requires only a minimal amount of information to be supplied by the browser). POST, on the other hand, is used to submit information *to* the web site (for example, the contents of a form).

File: **03-story_controller.rb** (excerpt)

```ruby
def new
  @story = Story.new(params[:story])
  if request.post?
    @story.save
  end
end
```

The `params` object in the first line of our method is a hash that contains all of the content that the user submitted (read up on hashes in Chapter 3 if you need a refresher).

If you look once more at the HTML source of the submission form, you'll notice that the `input` elements all have a `story[]` prefix. As each field has this prefix, the form data passed to Rails will be added to the `params` hash.

We can access this data by passing the hash a symbol that has the same name as our base object, such as `params[:story]`. We can then reference individual elements within the hash by passing the name of the attribute (also a symbol) to the hash. For example, the value of the `name` attribute could be accessed as `params[:story][:name]`. You get the idea.

The result of all this is that user data submitted via the form can be assigned to an object very easily. All we need to do is pass the `params[:story]` hash to the `Story.new` method, and we have ourselves a populated `@story` object.

Not coincidentally, this is exactly what we've done in the first line of our method:

```ruby
@story = Story.new(params[:story])
```

Now, if you enter some data into your form and click Save changes, you should see a different result: the form is displayed again, and the values you entered are still there. There's a good chance that the data has also been saved to the database, but because the page is rather uninformative, we don't really know.

To remedy this situation, let's tell the form to redirect the user to the `index` action immediately after the object is saved:

File: **04-story_controller.rb** (excerpt)

```ruby
if request.post?
  @story.save
  redirect_to :action => 'index'
end
```

Test the form again. This time you should be redirected to the random story selector that we created in Chapter 5, located within the `index` action. That's a little better! However, our application does look a little sparse. Let's make it pretty.

Creating a Layout

In Rails, a **layout** is a specialized form of a view template. Layouts allow page elements that are repeated globally across a site to be applied to every view. Examples of such elements include HTML headers and footers, CSS files, and JavaScript includes.

Layouts can also be applied at the controller level. This can be useful if, for example, you want to apply different layouts to a page depending on whether it's being viewed by an administrator or a regular user.

We'll begin our foray into layouts by creating a global layout for the entire application.

Establishing Structure

Layouts should be stored in the `app/views/layouts` folder. A layout template can basically be given any name, as long as the file ends in `.rhtml`. If the filename is `application.rhtml`, Rails will adopt this as the default layout.

Let's take advantage of that convention: create a file named `application.rhtml` in the `app/views/layouts` folder, and populate it with this code:

File: **05-application.rhtml**

```
<!DOCTYPE html PUBLIC "-//W3C//DTD XHTML 1.0 Strict//EN"
    "http://www.w3.org/TR/xhtml1/DTD/xhtml1-strict.dtd">
<html xmlns="http://www.w3.org/1999/xhtml"
    xml:lang="en" lang="en">
<head>
  <meta http-equiv="Content-type"
      content="text/html; charset=utf-8" />
  <title>Shovell</title>
  <%= stylesheet_link_tag 'style' %>
</head>
<body>
  <div id="content">
  <h1>Shovell</h1>
  <%= yield %>
```

```
  </div>
</body>
</html>
```

There's nothing too radical going on here—we've created a regular XHTML document, and it includes a proper DOCTYPE declaration. However, a couple of ERb calls here warrant some explanation.

`<%= stylesheet_link_tag 'style' %>`

This code generates the HTML that includes an external style sheet in the page.[2] By passing the string style, we ensure that the <link> element that's generated will point to the URL /stylesheets/style.css. We'll create this style sheet in a minute.

`<%= yield %>`

This line is the point at which the content for our specific view is displayed. Now, telling our layout to "yield" might not seem the most intuitive thing to do here, but it does actually make sense. Let me explain.

Remember that our layout will be used by many different view templates, each of which is responsible for displaying the output of a specific action. When the layout receives the command yield, control is handed to the *actual* view template being rendered—that is, the layout *yields* to the view template. Once that template has been rendered, control returns to the layout, and rendering is resumed for the rest of the page.

Seeing as we've linked a style sheet, we'd better make use of it.

Adding some Style

We'll use CSS to make our page look good.[3] To apply a style sheet to your application, create a file called style.css in the public/stylesheets folder, and drop in the following code:

---

[2] Rails ships with a number of helpers that are similar to stylesheet_link_tag, in that they make generating HTML pages easy. They mostly save tedious typing (and thus potential errors). Similar helpers include image_tag and javascript_include_tag.
[3] Don't worry if CSS is not your forte—all you need to do for this project is type out the CSS rules exactly as you see them (or, even better, simply copy and paste them from the code archive). If you're interested in improving your CSS skills, Rachel Andrew and Dan Shafer's book *HTML Utopia: Designing Without Tables Using CSS* [http://www.sitepoint.com/books/css2/] is a good place to start.

File: **06-style.css**

```css
body {
  background-color: #666;
  margin: 15px 25px;
  font-family: Helvetica, Arial, sans-serif;
}
#content {
  background-color: #fff;
  border: 10px solid #ccc;
  padding: 10px 10px 20px 10px;
}
```

Reload the page in your browser. You should see a slightly prettier version of the form, as shown in Figure 6.2s.

Figure 6.2. The new story form with a layout

Excellent! We now have a form that functions correctly, is well structured under the hood, *and* looks good on the outside.

However, our app doesn't deliver any feedback to the user to let them know whether a story submission was successful or not. Enter: the flash!

User Feedback and the Flash

Yes, you read that correctly: flash.

No, we're not going to be switching to Adobe's Flash technology to provide submission feedback. "Flash" also happens to be the name for the internal storage container (actually a kind of hash) that Rails uses for temporary data. In this section, we'll use the flash to pass temporary objects between actions. We'll then apply some validation to the data that is entered.

Adding to the Flash

When I say that the flash is used to store *temporary* items, I'm not talking about items that exist in memory and aren't saved to the database. Items stored in the flash exist for the duration of exactly one action, and then they're gone.

What good is this? Well, using the flash allows us to conveniently communicate information between successive actions without having to save information in the user's browser or the database. The flash is well positioned to store short status messages, such as notifications that inform the user whether or not a form submission or login attempt was successful.

Flash content is usually populated from within a controller action. Using the flash is very easy: to place a message in the flash, simply pass it an identifying symbol (the **flash area**) and a corresponding message. Here's an example:

```
flash[:error] = 'Login unsuccessful.'
```

In our story-sharing application, we want to put a message into the flash immediately after the story is saved, to let the user know that his or her submission was successful. Add the following line to the new action of your `StoryController`:

File: **07-story_controller.rb (excerpt)**

```
def new
  @story = Story.new(params[:story])
  if request.post?
    @story.save
    flash[:notice] = 'Story submission succeeded'
    redirect_to :action => 'index'
  end
end
```

Conventions for Flash Areas

In general, Rails applications use flash areas named after common UNIX logging levels to indicate the level of severity of a message. The common area names are :notice, :warning, and :error.

In this case, the message is not critical, so we've chosen to use :notice. However, the name of the flash area is entirely up to you.

Retrieving Data from the Flash

To retrieve contents from the flash (usually done in the successive action), just access the flash from a view in the same way that you would access any other hash in Rails. You don't need to explicitly populate it in the controller, nor do you have to purge the Flash once the view has been rendered—Rails takes care of this for you.

Since flash content is universally applicable, we'll change our layout file (which is located at app/views/layouts/application.rhtml) so that it *always* renders a notification box, unless there is no content available to render. Modify your layout file as follows:

File: **08-application.rhtml (excerpt)**

```
<div id="content">
  <h1>Shovell</h1>
  <% unless flash[:notice].blank? %>
  <div id="notification"><%= flash[:notice] %></div>
  <% end %>
  <%= yield %>
</div>
```

The condition that we've added here checks whether the flash[:notice] variable is blank; if not, the code renders a simple HTML div element to which an id is attached. Rails considers an object to be "blank" if it's either nil or an empty string.

Before we switch to the browser to test this addition, let's add a few rules to our style sheet to display our notification:

File: **09-style.css (excerpt)**

```
#notification {
  border: 5px solid #9c9;
  background-color: #cfc;
  padding: 5px;
```

```
  margin: 10px 0;
}
```

If you submit another story now, you should see a nice green box on the subsequent page informing you that the submission succeeded, as shown in Figure 6.3. If you're curious, reload the landing page to make sure the contents of the flash disappear.

Figure 6.3. Providing feedback after story submission

However, our form submission process is still flawed—it's possible for a user to submit stories without entering a name. Or a link. Or both!

Applying Validations

To be sure that all the stories submitted to Shovell contain both a name and a link before they're saved, we'll make use of the `ActiveRecord` functionality called **validations**.

Validations come in a variety of flavors: the simplest flavor says, "Check that this attribute (or form input) is not empty." A more complex validation, for example, might be, "Make sure this attribute (or form input) matches the following regular expression."[4] There are varying degrees of complexity in between. A more complex validation might be used, for example, to validate an email address.

Validations are defined in the model. This ensures that the validation is always applied, and, therefore, that an object is always valid, before its data is saved to the database.

Let's look at a simple validation. To add validations to our Story model, edit the model class in app/models/story.rb so that it looks like this:

File: **10-story.rb (excerpt)**

```
class Story < ActiveRecord::Base
  validates_presence_of :name, :link
end
```

You'll notice that the line we've added here is fairly verbose, so it's quite readable by humans. This line makes sure that the name and link attributes have a value before the model is saved.

Tweaking the Redirection Logic

We want to ensure that the user can only be redirected to the index action if the model passes its validation checks. To do so, we need to modify the new action in our controller as follows:

File: **11-story_controller.rb (excerpt)**

```
def new
  @story = Story.new(params[:story])
  if request.post? and @story.save
    flash[:notice] = "Story submission succeeded"
    redirect_to :action => 'index'
  end
end
```

As you can see, we've modified the if clause so that it checks two conditions: first, we check to see if our page request is a POST request. If it is, we then check to see whether @story.save returns true.

---

[4] A regular expression is a string of characters that can be used to match another string of characters. The syntax of regular expressions can be confusing, with particularly long expressions looking much like random characters to a newcomer to the syntax. One of the most common uses of regular expressions is validating whether or not an email address is in the correct format.

These validations will be called before the `save` method writes the object to the database. If the validations fail, this method will return `false`—the object will not be saved, and the user will not be redirected.

It's quite common to use Ruby statements directly within conditions, as we've done with the `save` method here. In general, many of the methods provided by Rails core classes return `true` or `false`, which makes them an excellent choice for use in conditions.

Fantastic—our logic for processing the form is sound. If you were to try to submit a blank name or link now, our app would not allow the object to be saved, and the redirect would not occur. However, we still need to give the user some guidance for correcting any errors that result from a failed validation.

Improving the User Experience

Looking at the generated HTML of the submitted form gives us a hint as to how we might implement some additional feedback for the user when a validation error occurs:

```
<div class="fieldWithErrors">
  <input id="story_name" name="story[name]" size="30" type="text"
      value="" />
</div>
```

As you can see, using the Rails `form_for` helper has paid off—it has wrapped our text field in a `div` element, and assigned it a class called `fieldWithErrors`. We could style this `div` with a red border, for example, to indicate that this field threw an error. In fact, let's do just that. Add the following rule to the `style.css` file:

File: **12-style.css (excerpt)**

```
.fieldWithErrors {
  border: 5px solid #f66;
}
```

The other neat thing that the helper does is populate each field with values that the user entered, as Figure 6.4 shows.

It's also good practice to tell our users what *exactly* is wrong with a particular field—further down the track, we might want to add a validation to our model to ensure that each URL is submitted only once.

Add the following line to the top of the new.rhtml template:

File: **13-new.rhtml (excerpt)**

```
<%= error_messages_for 'story' %>
```

Now, if a user submits the form without entering content into every field, the browser will display:

❑ a useful error message that indicates how many fields are blank

❑ some textual hints as to the nature of the error for each field

❑ a red border that clearly highlights which fields need attention

See Figure 6.4 for an example.

Figure 6.4. Story submission form with validation output

That seems like a pretty functional form submission process to me. And it doesn't look too shabby, either.

However, before we begin loading our application with additional features, we should add some unit and functional test coverage, to make sure that future modifications don't break any of our existing functionality.

Testing the Form

Getting into the habit of writing tests for newly added code is more than just a good idea—it may save your hide in the future!

As I've mentioned before, by writing tests for *all* of your code, you can evolve a suite of automated testing facilities as your application evolves. This suite can then be run periodically or on demand to reveal errors in your application.

You can take a couple of approaches to creating a test suite for your application. One of them—the more radical, in fact—is referred to as **test-driven development** (TDD). When adhering to TDD principles, you *first* write a test, make sure it fails, then fill in the code that causes the test to pass. This approach works best when you've had some experience with the programming language you want to test.

The opposite approach is to write the code first, and make sure it passes *you* (the human testing engine). Once this preliminary test has been passed, you write some automated testing code, then run your application against the automated test. We'll be using this second approach for the rest of the development of our story-sharing application.

A Rails test suite can be split into three fundamental parts:

unit tests	Unit tests cover model-level functionality, which generally encompasses an application's core business logic. Unit tests can test validations, associations (which we'll be covering in Chapter 7), and generic methods that are attached to models.
functional tests	Functional tests in Rails cover controller-level functionality and the accompanying views. A functional test can be quite specific—for example, making sure that a certain HTML element is present in a view, that a variable is populated properly, or that the proper redirection takes place after a form has been submitted.

integration tests   Integration testing goes beyond the relatively isolated approaches of functional and unit testing. An integration test allows you to test complete stages of user interaction with your application. The registration of a new user, and the story submission process as a whole, are good candidates for integration testing.

In this chapter, we'll look at functional and unit testing; we'll cover integration testing in Chapter 11.

Generally speaking, test cases in Rails exist as classes that descend from `Test::Unit::TestCase`. However, when we generated our models and controllers in Chapter 5, the `generate` script created some skeleton files for us. These are located in the `test` folder, which is where all of the files that make up our testing suite reside.

Testing the Model

While our `Story` model doesn't have a great deal of functionality yet, it does have some validations, and we should definitely make sure that they operate as expected. We'll add them to the skeleton test file, then run the test to confirm that our validations are behaving themselves!

Analyzing the Skeleton File

The skeleton test file for our `Story` model is located at `test/unit/story_test.rb`. When you open it, you should see the following code:

File: **14-story_test.rb (excerpt)**

```
require File.dirname(__FILE__) + '/../test_helper'

class StoryTest < Test::Unit::TestCase
  fixtures :stories

  # Replace this with your real tests.
  def test_truth
    assert true
  end
end
```

That first line aside, what we have here is a basic class definition by the name of `StoryTest`. The name of this class, which was created when the file was generated, suggests that its purpose is for testing our `Story` model—and so it is. The fixtures :stories line makes sure that the dummy data for our test is loaded into the database before the test begins. (We looked at dummy data that we can use for testing in Chapter 5.)

That require command at the top of the file is a simple example of one file gaining access to the functionality of another file; the external file in such arrangements is known as an **include file**. By including this file, we gain access to a large amount of testing-related functionality.

Of course, Rails includes other files all the time, but we don't see dozens of require commands littered throughout our code. Why not? The Rails conventions allow it to deduce what is needed, when it is needed, and where it can be found. And this is one reason why following Rails conventions is so important.

Using Assertions

Code is tested in Rails using **assertions**. Assertions are tiny functions that confirm that something is in a certain state. A simple assertion may just compare two values to make sure that they're identical. A more complex assertion may match a value against a regular expression, or scan an HTML template for the presence of a certain HTML element. We'll look at various types of assertions in this section.

Once they have been written, assertions are grouped into **tests**. A test is an instance method that is prefixed with test_. An example of a test is the test_truth method in the previous code listing. These tests are executed one by one using the rake command that we looked at in Chapter 5. If one of the assertions in a test fails, the test is immediately aborted and the test suite moves on to the next one.

Now that we know what assertions are, and how they work, let's write one!

Writing a Unit Test

The test_truth method in our unit test is just a stub that was created by the generate script. Let's replace it with a real test:

File: **15-story_test.rb** (excerpt)

```
def test_should_require_name
  s = Story.create(:name => nil)
  assert s.errors.on(:name)
end
```

We've named our method `test_should_require_name`. As you might've guessed, this method will test the validation of the name. Let's examine each line within the method:

```
s = Story.create(:name => nil)
```

This line creates a new `Story` object—something that we might do in a regular controller action. Note, however, that this time we've purposely left the required `name` attribute blank (`nil`). As the `create` method will attempt to save the new object immediately, the validations that we defined in the model will be checked at the same time.

At this point, we can check the result of the validation by reading the `errors` attribute of our newly created object.

```
assert s.errors.on(:name)
```

Every model object in Rails has an `errors` attribute. This attribute contains the results of any validations that have been applied to it—if the validation failed, errors will exist "on" that attribute. In this case, we deliberately left the `name` attribute empty; passing a symbol to `errors.on` should therefore return `true`, and our `assert` statement confirms exactly that.

The `name` attribute is not the only required attribute for our `Story` model, though—the `link` attribute must be assigned a value before a story can be saved. We've already added one test, so adding a second should be fairly straightforward. Let's add a test that covers the validation of the `link` attribute:

File: **16-story_test.rb (excerpt)**

```
def test_should_require_link
  s = Story.create(:link => nil)
  assert s.errors.on(:link)
end
```

Easy, huh?

Lastly, to complete our first batch of tests, we'll add a test that checks whether or not a new `Story` object can be successfully created and saved, thereby passing all of our validations:

File: **17-story_test.rb (excerpt)**

```
def test_should_create_user
  s = Story.create(
    :name => 'My test submission',
```

```
    :link => 'http://www.testsubmission.com/')
  assert s.valid?
end
```

In this test, a new `Story` object is created, and all mandatory attributes are assigned a value. The assertion then confirms that the created object has indeed passed all validations by calling its `valid?` method—this method returns `true` if no validation errors are present.

Running a Unit Test

With this testing code in place, let's run our small unit test suite. From the applications root folder, execute the following command:

```
$ rake test:units
```

This command will execute all of the test cases located in the `test/unit` folder one by one, and alert us to any assertions that fail. The output of a successful test execution should look something like Figure 6.5.

Figure 6.5. Running a successful suite of unit tests

As you can see, `rake` gives us a nice summary of our test execution. The results suggest that a total of three test cases and three assertions were executed, which is exactly what our test suite contains at the moment.

You'll notice some dots between the Started and the Finished lines of the test suite output—one dot for each test passed. Whenever an assertion fails, an uppercase F will be displayed, and if one of your tests contains an error, an uppercase E will be displayed, followed by details of the error that occurred.

Instead of just boldly assuming that our tests work correctly, let's change a test so that we *know* it's going to fail. In our `test_should_create_user` method, modify the last line so that its output is reversed:

```
assert ! s.valid?
```

Save the file and run the unit testing suite again:

```
$ rake test:units
```

Your output should display an F, indicating test failure, as shown in Figure 6.6. A description of the assertions that may have caused the test to fail is also displayed.

Figure 6.6. Unit testing with a failed test

Armed with this information, locating and fixing an error is easy. We're provided with the name of the test that failed (`test_should_create_user`), the test case to which it belongs (`StoryTest`), and the line on which it failed (line 18). Thus, the (admittedly forged) culprit is easily located and fixed.

For now, undo the change you made to the last line of `test_should_create_user`, so that the test will again pass:

```
assert s.valid?
```

That's it—we've tested the model. We'll add more tests in later chapters as we add more functionality to the model.

Testing the Controller

The functional testing of controllers is, at first glance, not very different from testing models—it's just a different part of the MVC stack. However, there is some extra housekeeping involved in getting the environment properly set up.

Analyzing the Skeleton File

Once again, a skeleton functional test was created as a result of our generating the `StoryController`. This skeleton file resides in `test/functional/story_controller_test.rb`:

File: **18-story_controller_test.rb** (excerpt)

```
require File.dirname(__FILE__) + '/../test_helper'
require 'story_controller'

# Re-raise errors caught by the controller.
class StoryController; def rescue_action(e) raise e end; end

class StoryControllerTest < Test::Unit::TestCase
  def setup
    @controller = StoryController.new
    @request = ActionController::TestRequest.new
    @response = ActionController::TestResponse.new
  end
  # Replace this with your real tests.
  def test_truth
    assert true
  end
end
```

On first inspection, this *looks* similar to the `StoryTest` class that we saw in the previous section, with a couple of exceptions—the most notable being the existence of a `setup` method.

The `setup` method is called automatically before *every* functional test case. It's responsible for setting up a "clean" environment, which is what the creation of new `@controller`, `@request`, and `@response` objects achieves.

We also have a `test_truth` dummy test, which we'll overwrite once again.

Writing a Functional Test

To add the first test for our `StoryController`, replace the `test_truth` method in the skeleton functional test file with the following code:

File: **19-story_controller_test.rb (excerpt)**

```
def test_should_show_index
  get :index
  assert_response :success
  assert_template 'index'
  assert_not_nil assigns(:story)
end
```

Let's look at each line in this method.

```
def test_should_show_index
```

As you might have deduced from the name of the method, what we're checking here is that the `index` action is correctly displayed in the user's browser when the `/index` path is requested.

```
  get :index
```

This line simulates a user requesting the `index` action of the `StoryController` class that we instantiated in the `setup` method. It uses the HTTP request method GET; the `post` function call is the one to use for testing POST requests.

```
  assert_response :success
```

The `assert_response` assertion checks that the HTTP response code we receive is the code that we expect.[5]

```
  assert_template 'index'
```

By invoking `assert_template`, we ensure that the request we made is actually rendered with the template that we expect—not a template with a different name.

---

[5] A complete list of HTTP response codes can be found at
http://en.wikipedia.org/wiki/List_of_HTTP_status_codes.

Shortcuts for Cryptic HTTP Codes

HTTP codes are numeric, so sometimes they're hard to remember. As a result, Rails has implemented a few aliases for the more common codes. In this example we've used the `:success` symbol, which maps internally to the `200 OK` response code that is returned when a page request is successful. Other mappings that can be used with the `assert_response` function include `:redirect` for HTTP redirect headers and `:missing` for the all-too-common "`404 Not Found`" error that occurs when a request is made for a file that doesn't exist.

```
assert_not_nil assigns(:story)
```

This final assertion is not as intuitive as the others, but it's actually quite straightforward. `assert_not_nil` tests whether or not the instance variable `@story` is set to `nil` (that's the easy bit). The `assigns(:story)` construct makes available to the functional test all of the instance variables that have been declared within the controller's actions. The `@story` object is one such variable, so passing the `:story` symbol to the test allows the `@story` variable to be used as part of the test.

We also need some fixtures for this test. As we learned in Chapter 5, fixtures are dummy model objects that provide a consistent data set against which our tests can run. Fixtures are model based, so there's a fixture file for every model class in our application. This means that we need to specify explicitly which fixtures we want to load for each test.

We can do so by adding the line that's highlighted here to the top of the functional test class definition:

File: **20-story_controller_test.rb (excerpt)**

```
class StoryControllerTest < Test::Unit::TestCase
  fixtures :stories
  def setup
    ...

end
```

Running a Functional Test

Now that we've created our test case, we can invoke the functional test suite. Once again, we turn to the trusty `rake` tool:

```
$ rake test:functionals
```

The output that results from the successful execution of our test suite is shown in Figure 6.7.

Figure 6.7. Running a successful functional test suite

More Functional Tests

There's one action for which we haven't yet written a test—the new action. We'll want to create a few different tests for this page. Let's do that now.

To test the inner workings of our new action in GET mode, we'll use a test case that we'll name `test_should_show_new`. Add the following method below the `test_should_show_index` test that we created previously:

File: **21-story_controller_test.rb** (excerpt)

```
def test_should_show_new
  get :new
  assert_response :success
  assert_template 'new'
  assert_not_nil assigns(:story)
end
```

This is quite straightforward—apart from a few textual differences, this test is almost identical to that for `test_should_show_index`. However, our work isn't done yet!

There's a `form` element in the `new` template, and we should certainly test that it appears correctly. Here's another test to do just that:

File: **22-story_controller_test.rb (excerpt)**

```
def test_should_show_new_form
  get :new
  assert_select 'form p', :count => 3
end
```

The `assert_select` helper function that we've used here is a very flexible and powerful tool for verifying that a certain HTML element is present in the document that's returned from a request.[6] `assert_select` can even verify the hierarchy of the HTML element, regardless of how deeply it is nested; it can also test the element's attributes (for example, the value of its `class` or `id`). In fact, it's so flexible that we could potentially devote an entire chapter to its features alone.[7]

But now we're getting sidetracked. Back to this line! `assert_select` checks for the existence of one `form` element in which five `p` elements are nested (the count is supplied using the `:count` argument). These five paragraphs contain the fields that comprise our story submission form.

How do we specify an element in this hierarchy? Easy—by following the simple rules of CSS selectors.

In this example, we want to reference a paragraph element that resides within a `form` element. Now, if we were writing a CSS rule to style these paragraph elements to be bold, it would look like this:

```
form p {
  font-weight: bold;
}
```

In the same way that we reference paragraphs in CSS, the parameter that we use with `assert_select` is simply `'form p'`. We'll look at a few more of the CSS selector features of `assert_select` in the tests we write in later chapters.

Lastly, to test the posting of a new story, we'll write a few more short tests:

---

[6] `assert_select`, originally available as a plugin only, is the successor to `assert_tag`, and was introduced in Rails 1.2.

[7] An `assert_select` cheat sheet is available at the web site of the tool's author: http://labnotes.org/svn/public/ruby/rails_plugins/assert_select/cheat/assert_select.html

File: **23-story_controller_test.rb (excerpt)**

```
def test_should_add_story
  post :new, :story => {
    :name => 'test story',
    :link => 'http://www.test.com/'
  }
  assert ! assigns(:story).new_record?
  assert_redirected_to :action => 'index'
  assert_not_nil flash[:notice]
end
```

Let's break this test down line by line.

```
post :new, :story => {
  :name => 'test story',
  :link => 'http://www.test.com/'
}
```

As I mentioned earlier in this chapter, post is another way to invoke an HTTP request programmatically from a test. post takes a few parameters: in this case, we're simulating the submission of a story. To do this, we need to pass a hash that contains values for the required attributes of a story—symbols representing the name and link attributes.

Immediately after our post call has been issued, the following line checks the results:

```
assert ! assigns(:story).new_record?
```

Here, we're using the new_record? method of the @story instance variable to confirm that the record has actually been saved to the database. Since we want the assertion to tell us if it *hasn't* been saved at this point, we use the exclamation mark (!) to reverse the return value of the new_record? call.

When a story submission has been successful, our application issues a redirection. We can test that this redirection occurs using assert_redirected_to:

```
assert_redirected_to :action => 'index'
```

Lastly, we assert that the contents of the notice flash area is not nil:

```
assert_not_nil flash[:notice]
```

Whew! Our rapidly-expanding test suite is evolving to the point where we can be very confident that the story submission process is functioning correctly.

The final test case we'll add covers the situation in which posting a new story fails. We'll cause the submission to fail by omitting one of the required fields:

File: **24-story_controller_test.rb (excerpt)**

```
def test_should_reject_missing_story_attribute
  post :new, :story => { :name => 'story without a link' }
  assert assigns(:story).errors.on(:link)
end
```

In the first line of this code, we attempt to post a story without a `link`:

```
post :new, :story => { :name => 'story without a link' }
```

After this submission attempt, we use the `errors` attribute to verify that there's an error condition on the `link` attribute, just as we did in the unit test earlier in the chapter:

```
assert assigns(:story).errors.on(:link)
```

That's it! We've written all the tests we need for the time being. Now, let's run the suite.

Running the Complete Test Suite

Now that we have these additional tests in place, we'll need to run all of our tests again. However, this time, we'll use a slightly different approach: instead of invoking our unit and functional tests separately, we'll use a `rake` task to run these test suites successively:

```
$ rake test
```

The output of a successful test run should look like Figure 6.8.

Figure 6.8. Running the complete test suite

Congratulations! Not only have you created a full test suite, but, on running it, you've found that your application is error-free—a discovery that should make even the most seasoned developer a little proud. To finish up, let's turn our thoughts to the application's performance as we inspect the log files generated by ActionPack.

Revisiting the Logs

We took a brief look at the extensive logging functionality that ActiveRecord provides in Chapter 5—this gave us a glimpse into the kind of automation, in terms of SQL generation, that happens behind the scenes in Rails.

If you liked what you saw back then, you'll be glad to learn that ActionPack is also a prolific logger. An example of some of the entries that ActionPack wrote to the development log file are shown in Figure 6.9.

Figure 6.9. Contents of the development log file showing `ActionPack` entries

```
Terminal — bash — 82x25

Processing StoryController#new (for 127.0.0.1 at 2006-11-02 15:50:44) [POST]
  Session ID: 11232bbc0fcabd7a7382e435058f413e
  Parameters: {"commit"=>"Save changes", "story"=>{"name"=>"Coolest Site of the Ye
ar", "link"=>"http://coolestsite.com/"}, "action"=>"new", "controller"=>"story"}
  Story Columns (0.007434)   SHOW FIELDS FROM stories
  SQL (0.000719)   BEGIN
  SQL (0.001804)   INSERT INTO stories (`name`, `link`) VALUES('Coolest Site of th
e Year', 'http://coolestsite.com/')
  SQL (0.001614)   COMMIT
Redirected to http://localhost:3000/story
Completed in 0.02377 (42 reqs/sec) | DB: 0.01085 (45%) | 302 Found [http://localho
st/story/new]


Processing StoryController#index (for 127.0.0.1 at 2006-11-02 15:50:44) [GET]
  Session ID: 11232bbc0fcabd7a7382e435058f413e
  Parameters: {"action"=>"index", "controller"=>"story"}
  Story Load (0.002244)   SELECT * FROM stories ORDER BY RAND() LIMIT 1
Rendering  within layouts/application
Rendering story/index
  Story Columns (0.005072)   SHOW FIELDS FROM stories
Completed in 0.01735 (57 reqs/sec) | Rendering: 0.00473 (27%) | DB: 0.00732 (42%)
| 200 OK [http://localhost/story]
Core:~/shovell/log scoop$ 
```

As you look at these entries, you'll notice a full record of your activities within the application has been logged, complete with SQL statements, page redirections, page requests, templates rendered, and more.

The level of detail in Rails' log files is of real benefit when you're hunting down a problem with your code—the logs provide real insight into what's actually happening as a page is requested. The same level of detail is captured for unit and functional tests in the test log file, which is located in `log/test.log`.

The timing values that are written to the log file are particularly interesting. Consider the following snippet:

```
Completed in 0.03430 (29 reqs/sec) | Rendering: 0.00515 (15%) |
DB: 0.02469 (71%) | 200 OK [http://localhost/story]
```

From this log entry, we can conclude that:

❑ 71% of the time it took Rails to pump out this page was spent talking to the database

❑ only 15% of the total time was spent in actually assembling the page

While 71% might sound like a large portion of the total time—which it is—by looking at the actual number of seconds involved in the process, we see that communications with the database took just 0.02 seconds.

Rails also provides us with a rough estimate of how many instances of this particular page could potentially be served per second (in this case, it estimates 29 page requests per second). Note, though, that this is a very rough estimate—we're running our app in the development environment, which is certainly not optimized for speed. The application is also unlikely to be located on the same server as the one that will be running the application in production. As such, the real numbers for this statistic may vary greatly.

We won't dig any deeper into the logs, but be aware that it's worth keeping an eye on your log files. Incidentally, this is the same information that has been flying past in the terminal window from which you launched your WEBrick server, too. This is another way that you can check your application's log entries in real time, although you'll probably find using a text editor more practical.

We'll revisit the log files once more in Chapter 11.

Summary

We certainly increased the functionality of our application in this chapter—we even made it look a little prettier. We used the Rails form helpers to create a fully functional web interface for submitting stories, and we added a global layout to our application, complete with style sheets.

Along the way, we looked briefly at the flash—Rails's short-term memory container that can be used to pass messages between successive actions. We also added some validations to our Story model, to make sure that our story submissions adhere to our own high standards (or that, at the very least, that each story has a title and a URL!).

Finally, we wrote our first unit and functional test cases, which we used to automate the testing of our models, controllers, and views. We also took a scroll through the Rails log files to see what kind of logging the ActionPack module performs, and how those log entries are useful when we debug our application.

In the next chapter, we'll add the much-anticipated voting feature to our story-sharing application—and we'll do it using cutting-edge Ajax technology, spiced up with some Web 2.0 visual effects. Yes—it's going to be one good-looking chapter! On with the show!

7

Ajax and Web 2.0

The success of a social bookmarking or content-sharing application doesn't rest solely on the submission of stories by users; there must also be some way for site visitors to get an idea of the *value* of each content item. Now, in the world of social bookmarking, popular opinion rules. So on our Shovell site, the value of each story will be gauged by its popularity as indicated by the number of votes the story receives from Shovell users.

In this chapter, we're going to expand the feature set of our story-sharing applic-ation to include this crucial voting functionality. And what better way to do so than with the technology behind some of Web 2.0's biggest buzzwords: Ajax, Prototype, and script.aculo.us? We'll cover them all in the coming pages. Let's dive in!

Generating a Vote Model

At the core of our app's voting functionality lies a data model—a `Vote`—which we'll need to create. Once that's in place, we'll create and apply the necessary changes to our database schema. We learned how to do this using migrations in Chapter 6, so there's no reason to go back to the old ways now!

Creating the Model

Using the `generate` script (you should be feeling pretty confident with this by now), let's add a new model to our application:

```
$ ruby script/generate model Vote
```

The result of running this script is shown in Figure 7.1.

Figure 7.1. Generating a `Vote` model

As you might expect, this command generates a new migration file (among others). This file lives in `db/migrate/002_create_votes.rb`; let's tweak it to suit our needs.

Creating the Migration

The skeleton migration file that was generated for us contains the basic code to create a `votes` table in our database. This is the second migration for our project, so it has been assigned the number `002`.

The `votes` table really only needs two columns for now—replace the `self.up` method of the skeleton migration file with the following code:

File: **01-002_create_votes.rb**

```
def self.up
  create_table :votes do |t|
```

```
    t.column :story_id, :integer
    t.column :created_at, :datetime
  end
end
```

As you can see, to create the schema, we're following the format we used in Chapter 5, but this time, the column types are different. Let's look at them briefly:

```
    t.column :story_id, :integer
```

This line creates a `story_id` column of type `integer`. It's going to be used to store the numerical ID of a story that has received a vote from a user. This column will be populated using associations, which we'll talk about in the next section.

Rails has a handful of "magical" column names, one of which is `created_at` of type `datetime`. The next line in our migration shows an example:

```
    t.column :created_at, :datetime
```

Whenever a new model is saved to the database using the `save` method, Rails will automatically populate the column called `:created_at` with the current date and time.

Its companion, `updated_at`, operates in a similar manner—it automatically populates the column with the current date and time of any successive call to the `save` method—although we won't be making use of this column in our application.

As with the last migration we created, the `self.down` method is fine as is—reversing this migration simply gets rid of the whole table.

Applying the Migration

Our migration is in place, so let's apply it using the `rake` tool once more:

```
$ rake db:migrate
```

The result of applying the migration is shown in Figure 7.2.

Figure 7.2. Applying the second migration

```
Terminal — bash — 80x10 — ⌘5
Core:~/shovell scoop$ rake db:migrate
(in /Users/scoop/Desktop/railsbook/code)
== CreateVotes: migrating =====================================
-- create_table(:votes)
   -> 0.0060s
== CreateVotes: migrated (0.0062s) ============================

Core:~/shovell scoop$ ▌
```

Excellent! Now, I suggest you sit down before we begin the next topic, because things could get a little heavy. It's time for you and me to have an in-depth talk about relationships.

An Introduction to Relationships

Contrary to popular belief, relationships don't have to be hard work.

No, I'm not talking about human relationships—I'm talking about the relationships between objects in our model (also commonly referred to as **associations**). We touched on some of this stuff back in Chapter 4, when we talked about the features of `ActiveRecord`. Now we finally have a practical use for all that theory.

The `Vote` model that we just created needs to be associated with our `Story` model. After all, what good is a vote if you don't know which story it's for?

As we saw back in Chapter 4, Rails can cater for a variety of associations between models. One of the more popular associations is the **one-to-many relationship**, which we'll add to our model now.

Introducing the `has_many` Clause

A one-to-many relationship exists when a single record of type A is associated with many records of type B.

In our application, a single story is likely to be associated with many votes. This relationship is shown in Figure 7.3.

Figure 7.3. The one-to-many relationship between stories and votes

Relationships are usually declared bidirectionally, so that the relationship can be utilized from both sides. Let's begin by examining the Story model's relationship to a Vote; we'll look at the reverse relationship later in the chapter.

To define the first aspect of the relationship, edit the Story class, located in app/models/story.rb, adding the line in bold below:

File: **02-story.rb (excerpt)**

```
class Story < ActiveRecord::Base
  validates_presence_of :name, :link
  has_many :votes
end
```

The addition of this one line has ignited a flurry of activity behind the scenes—fire up a Rails console, and I'll show you what I mean. First, retrieve an existing Story record from our database:

```
$ ruby script/console
>> s = Story.find :first
=> #<Story:0x27482a0..>
```

Next, invoke this object's newly acquired votes method:

```
>> s.votes
=> []
```

The name of this method is derived directly from the has_many :votes relationship that we defined in our class definition (we'll talk more about declaring associations in Chapter 9). Invoking the method grabs all votes for the `Story` and returns them in an `Array` (which, obviously, is empty right now).

So, how would we go about adding some votes to this story?

The easiest way is to call the `create` method of the object returned by `story.votes`, like so:

```
>> s.votes.create
=> #<Vote:0x273d954..>
```

This approach instantiates a new `Vote` object, and saves the object to the database immediately. It works because we haven't specified any validations for the `Vote` model yet, so there's nothing to prevent empty fields from being saved. However, if you assume that the record we just saved to the database is completely empty, you couldn't be more wrong.

Let's take a look at the number of votes that have been created. Call the `size` method for our `Story`'s associated votes, like so:

```
>> s.votes.size
=> 1
```

This is another method to which we gained access by defining the `has_many` relationship. An alternative syntax that achieves the same result combines the name of an associated table (in this case, `votes`) with `_count`, like so:[1]

```
>> s.votes_count
=> 1
```

This Ruby code also instructs Rails to calculate the number of records associated with the current model object. A result of 1 indicates that the `Vote` object that we just created does indeed contain some information, since a `Vote` is associated with the `Story` we retrieved.

To find out more, let's retrieve the same `Vote` object independently from the `Story` with which it's been associated, and inspect its attributes:

```
>> v = Vote.find(:first)
=> #<Vote:0x2732360..>
```

---

[1] This technique for counting records is in fact **deprecated**, meaning that it should no longer be used as it will cease to be available in future versions of Rails. However, I've included it here for a reason—we'll be overriding this method with a database table column of the same name in Chapter 9, so we need to create it now.

```
>> v.attributes
=> {"story_id"=>2, "id"=>1,
#"created_at"=>Thu Jul 20 11:20:24 CEST 2006}
```

As you can see, not only has our `Vote` object automatically been populated with a creation date, but a value has been assigned in its `story_id` field. This value was obtained from the `id` attribute of the `Story` object that was used to create the vote. (In this case, the value is equal to `2`, as that's the `id` of the first `Story` in my database.) Figure 7.4 shows this relationship.

Figure 7.4. A `Story` has many `Votes`

To complete our relationship definition, let's add its counterpart—the `belongs_to` clause—to the `Vote` model.

Introducing the `belongs_to` Clause

As we learned in the previous section, when it comes to relationships, there are usually two sides to the, ahem, story.

In this section, we'll add the second part of our one-to-many relationship. First, edit the `Vote` model class (in `app/models/vote.rb`) so that it looks as follows:

File: **03-vote.rb**

```
class Vote < ActiveRecord::Base
  belongs_to :story
end
```

Now that we've defined the relationship within both models that are affected by it, not only can we access the `votes` of a `Story`, we can also access the `story` of a `Vote`. And I'm sure you can guess how we'd do the latter—back to the Rails console!

```
>> v = Vote.find(:first)
=> #<Vote:0x272a7a0..>
>> v.story
=> #<Story:0x2725570..>
```

With the addition of just one line to our `Vote` class definition, we've gained access to the associated `Story` object. As the code listing above shows, access to this object is possible via a new instance method (`story`) on the model—this method is available as a direct result of the relationship clause that we put in place, and attains its name from the first parameter of the association call (`belongs_to :story`).

Figure 7.5 shows how this relationship works.

Figure 7.5. A Vote belongs to a Story

How's our Schema Looking?

Now that we've established both sides of our one-to-many relationship, let's look at how the information representing this relationship is stored in the database.

If you recall each of the migrations that we've created and applied so far, you'll notice that, although the `Vote` model contains a `story_id` column, the `Story` model doesn't contain a corresponding `vote_id` column.

In fact, this column isn't necessary—there's no need to store association information in both models when defining a one-to-many relationship. The information is always stored on the "many" side of the relationship. With this information in place, Rails is intelligent enough to query the correct table when we instruct it to find objects between which there is an association.

Also note how the terminology used to define the relationship is an accurate reflection of what's going on—the `Votes` *belong to* the `Story` (hence the `belongs_to` call). And the `Vote` model represents the "many" side of the relationship, so each `Vote` stores its own reference to its associated `Story`.

Now that we understand the data structures that underlie it, let's jump to the user interaction part of our voting functionality.

Clean URLs and Permalinks

In terms of viewing stories that have been submitted to Shovell, our users currently only have access to a page that displays a random story. To address this issue, we'll add a new action that displays a single story, along with all of its details, before we implement the voting actions themselves. The story page will serve as a reference point for any given story on the Shovell site, as it will contain a range of information—voting actions, voting history, and so on—about the story.

Before we dive into the creation of our story page, let's take a quick—but important—detour. The development of a story page such as this provides the perfect opportunity for a discussion about clean URLs.

Implementing Clean URLs

If you cast your mind back to Chapter 4, you'll recall that Rails translates URLs of a certain format into actions that are invoked on a controller class. The translation, known as **routing**, is performed by the Rails `Routing` module.

Consider a URL that has the following format:

```
http://domain.com/story/show/1
```

Since most web applications operate on a single domain, we can ignore the domain part of the URL for now. That leaves us with a path that contains several components, separated by forward slashes:

```
/story/show/1
```

By default, the `Routing` module operates as follows:

❑ The first part of the URL is mapped to the corresponding controller. In this example, /`story` would route to our `StoryController` controller.

❑ The second part of the URL routes to the action name. In this case, the `show` action would be invoked.

❑ The third part is used to populate the `id` entry in the `params` hash. In our example, the value of `params[:id]` would be set to 1.

The end result of this routing is that the `show` action of the `StoryController` class would be called, and `params[:id]` would receive a value of 1.

This is all well and good, and such a URL structure is certainly neater than many of the more complicated URLs out there on the Web. But an `id` of 1 isn't exactly meaningful to our users—they're more likely to remember the title of a story. Even if the title was slightly modified (with special characters removed, escaped, or replaced), it would still make for a more usable URL.

So, in referring to a story titled "My Shiny Weblog," the following URL would be ideal:

```
/story/show/my-shiny-weblog
```

As I mentioned, converting a title to a URL like this will require a little work on our behalf (setting all characters to lowercase, and replacing spaces with dashes, in this case). But from a usability perspective, it's quite obvious that the URL relates to the story, so this idea is definitely worth implementing.

To do so, we'll modify the configuration of the Rails `Routing` module to support clean URLs like the one above. The routing configuration is stored in the file `config/routes.rb`, and (once all of the comments are stripped out) looks like this:

File: **04-routes.rb**

```
ActionController::Routing::Routes.draw do |map|
  map.connect ':controller/service.wsdl', :action => 'wsdl'
  map.connect ':controller/:action/:id'
end
```

The two calls to `map.connect` are Rails **routes**—rules that specify how a URL should be mapped. Routes are read from top to bottom; the route with the lowest priority is the one at the very bottom of the list. In almost all cases, this will be the default route, which, as we learned above, is responsible for mapping a controller name, an action name, and an `id`:

```
map.connect ':controller/:action/:id'
```

To implement clean URLs for stories, we'll insert the following line between the two existing routes:

File: **05-routes.rb** (excerpt)

```
map.story 'story/show/:permalink',
  :controller => 'story',
  :action => 'show'
```

This newly added route will match any URLs of the following form:

```
/story/show/my-shiny-weblog
```

In this route, we've explicitly named the controller and the specific action that should handle a URL in this format. As a result, a URL of this form will always be handled by the `show` action of our `StoryController`. The permalink (an abbreviation of **permanent link**) that appears at the end of the route is the part of the URL that will be placed in the `params[:permalink]` hash area.

The syntax for matching the URL is absolutely identical to that used in the default route: any string prefixed with a colon (with the exception of the `:controller` and `:action` reserved words) ends up as a value in the `params` hash, thus becoming available to both the controller and its views.

But why are we using `map.story` instead of the default, `map.connect`? Well, because we can—what we're defining here is a **named route**. A named route is a custom alias for matching an incoming request's URL. Requests with a URL that matches the defined pattern are directed to a specific page within our application (in this instance, the `show` action for our `StoryController`). Assigning the name `story` to this route makes sense, because we're directing requests that relate to `Story` objects. Named routes are available from both controllers and views, and provide an easy way to direct requests to common pages within our application. We'll look at how to take advantage of this later in this chapter.

Now, all we need is a `permalink` value.

Adding Permalinks to Stories

As we discussed in the previous section, our aim is for stories submitted to Shovell to have a permalink that's derived from a story title, with characters such as spaces being removed or replaced with dashes. For now, we'll let the user create the permalink manually, and we'll leave the automatic generation of permalinks for Chapter 9.

A permalink is an attribute of a `Story`, so we'll need to modify our schema so that one can be stored for each story. We've already seen migrations in action—each of our existing migrations was generated when we created a new model. Now we need to expand an existing model, so that we can add a `permalink` attribute to the `Story` model.

To add a migration without adding a new model, we use the `generate` script, passing `migration` as the first parameter:

```
$ ruby script/generate migration AddPermalinkToStories
```

This code generates a single migration file by the name of `db/migrate/003_add_permalink_to_stories.rb`. Edit this file so that its contents reflect the following:

File: **06-003_add_permalink_to_stories.rb**

```
class AddPermalinkToStories < ActiveRecord::Migration
  def self.up
    add_column :stories, :permalink, :string
  end
  def self.down
    remove_column :stories, :permalink
  end
end
```

Unlike our previous migrations, here we're modifying the structure of an existing table, rather than creating a brand new one. The `add_column` function fills this role nicely:

```
add_column :story, :permalink, :string
```

The syntax of the `add_column` function is almost identical to that of the `create_table` function we've used before—we just need to pass it the name of the table we want to modify, and the name and type of the column we want to add.

In this case, we're adding a column with the name `permalink`, of type `string`, to the `stories` table.

In previous migrations, we haven't needed to modify the `self.down` method, but this time we've added a line to it:

```
remove_column :stories, :permalink
```

When this migration is reversed, we want to remove a single column, rather than drop the entire table (which would be extremely bad news). As with `add_column`, `remove_column` takes symbols as its parameters. These symbols represent the table that's being modified, and the name of the column that we're removing. We don't need to specify the column type when we're removing a column, so this isn't included as a parameter.

Go ahead and apply this migration using the `rake` tool:

```
$ rake db:migrate
```

This will add the new column to the stories table, the output of which is shown in Figure 7.6.

Figure 7.6. Adding and executing our third migration

To finish off this little exercise in altering our app's infrastructure, we need to populate our newly added `permalink` column with a value for each of the stories that have already been added to our database. I'll show you how to do this for a single story, and leave it to you to update the rest of your stories. As I mentioned, though, we'll look at how to automate this step in Chapter 9.

From the Rails console, fetch a single `Story`. Update its `permalink` attribute using the `update_attribute` method:

```
>> s = Story.find(:first)
=> #<Story:0x27c7be0..>
>> s.name
=> "My shiny weblog"
>> s.update_attribute :permalink, 'my-shiny-weblog'
=> true
>> s.permalink
=> "my-shiny-weblog"
```

As you can see, the permalink I created for this entry is loosely adapted from the name of the `Story`: spaces have been replaced with dashes, and uppercase letters with lowercase letters.

Right, now we're ready to implement the `show` action of our `StoryController`.

Showing off our Stories

The next step in displaying our stories is to implement the `show` action of our `StoryController`. At the moment, in line with the routing rules that we've put in place, the `Routing` module would try to invoke the `show` method, which doesn't yet exist.

Before we write this method, let's think for a moment about what it's going to do. We told the `Routing` module to extract the `permalink` from the URL and hand it to the controller via the hash entry `params[:permalink]`. Now our controller action needs to go ahead and retrieve a story with this `permalink` from the database, and hand the object it finds to the view, which is in turn responsible for displaying it.

We'll start by adding the following method to our `StoryController` class. Once again, the order of the method definitions within the class definition is not important:

File: **07-story_controller.rb (excerpt)**

```
def show
  @story = Story.find_by_permalink(params[:permalink])
end
```

As we saw in Chapter 5, Rails automatically adds some dynamic `find` methods to the attributes of a model. Now, for our `Story` model, Rails has also defined a find_by_permalink method, even though this attribute was added *after* the table itself was created (using a migration). We didn't need specifically to tell Rails to reprocess everything that it knew about our database structure in order for this new method to become available—Rails just knew. This certainly makes our jobs as developers easier!

The single line of code in our show method executes this dynamic finder by passing the value of params[:permalink] to it. By doing so, we're instructing ActiveRecord to retrieve from the database all columns that have a permalink that's equal to the value in the URL requested by the user (there should only be one in each case!).

Lastly, we need a template with which to display a story. Create a new template file at app/views/story/show.rhtml, and fill it with the following simple HTML and ERb code:

File: **08-show.rhtml**

```
<h2><%= @story.name %></h2>
<p><%= link_to @story.link, @story.link %></p>
```

All this does is display the name of the Story, wrapped in <h2> tags. It also adds a link to the URL that's stored as part of the story.

Let's check that this functionality works as expected. Open the following URL in your browser (if you used a different permalink for your story, substitute it here): http://localhost:3000/story/show/my-shiny-weblog.

As you can see in Figure 7.7, our story has its own page—complete with its own permalink—that displays its name and a link to the story content.

Make Sure your Server is Running!

As with our other examples, connecting to your application requires the WEBrick server to be running. If you need a refresher on how to launch it, flip back to Chapter 2.

Figure 7.7. The finished show action, accessible via a clean URL

While we're at it, let's change our front page so that the random link it displays no longer uses the story's external URL. We'll instead direct users to the story's internal page, to which we'll add some voting functionality very soon.

Let's examine the route that we added to our Routing module configuration earlier in this chapter:

```
map.story 'story/show/:permalink',
    :controller => 'story', :action => 'show'
```

I stated back then that using map.story instead of map.connect creates a shortcut for referencing this particular route. Now we'll see how that works.

Open up the template responsible for the index action of StoryController (located at app/views/story/index.rhtml) and change the link_to call so that it reads as follows:

File: **09-index.rhtml (excerpt)**

```
<%= link_to @story.name,
        story_url(:permalink => @story.permalink) %>
```

The fact that a story_url function exists for our use is a direct result of the map.story call in the route configuration—this is how we take advantage of the named route that we defined earlier. The `story_url` function accepts a hash of values that's used dynamically to generate the URL we're looking for.

In this case, our named route takes only a single parameter—the `permalink`. The value of the `permalink` of the randomly picked `Story` is passed using the `:permalink` symbol.

Reload the `index` page at http://localhost:3000/story—it should now link to the internal story page, as demonstrated in Figure 7.8.

Figure 7.8. The index page linking to the story page

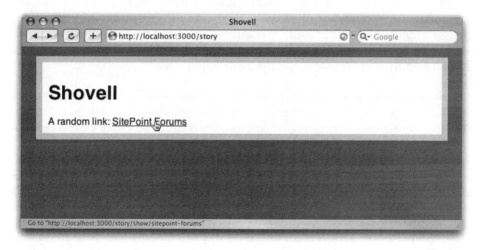

This completes our implementation of a page for each story, and the formation of links to each story page.

At this point, we're ready to start implementing the app's voting functionality. However, as we're going to do this using Ajax techniques, we'll take another slight detour to learn a bit about Ajax and see how it's implemented in Rails.

Ajax and Rails

We mentioned back in Chapter 1 that Rails is a full-stack framework, encompassing code on the client, the server, and everything in between. **Ajax** is a technique for communicating between client and server, so the Rails implementation of Ajax is therefore one of the key parts that makes up this "full-stack."

What is Ajax?

Ajax stands for Asynchronous JavaScript and XML, but represents a technique that encompasses more than just these specific technologies. You've no doubt heard the term, which has become one of the prime buzzwords behind the so-called Web 2.0 movement. Strictly speaking, though, Ajax isn't a new invention—it's actually existed for quite some time.

Basically, Ajax enables a web browser to continue to communicate with a web server without reloading the entirety of the page it's showing—a technique that's also known as **remote scripting**. This communication may include the exchange of form data, or the requesting of additional data to be incorporated into a page that has already been displayed. The end result is that a web application that uses Ajax has the potential to compete with more traditional desktop applications by providing the user with a more dynamic experience.

At the heart of Ajax is the **XmlHttpRequest** object. XmlHttpRequest was originally invented by Microsoft in the late 1990s for Internet Explorer 5, to improve and enhance the user experience of Microsoft's web-based email interface. It has since been implemented in all modern browsers. In 2005, a user-experience designer named Jesse James Garrett invented the term *Ajax* to describe the approach of using the XmlHttpRequest object, along with XHTML, CSS, and the Document Object Model (DOM), to create interactive web sites that *feel* like desktop applications.

While compatibility with certain web browsers was lacking when the first applications that used Ajax hit the Web, this is no longer as much of an issue—all popular web browsers support the XmlHttpRequest object, including Internet Explorer, Firefox, Safari, and Opera.

Ajax has been used in many popular web applications, such as digg, Flickr,[2] del.icio.us,[3] GMail,[4] and the 37signals applications that we talked about in Chapter 1.

As we'll soon see, implementing Ajax in Rails is as easy as implementing a regular link.

---

[2] http://flickr.com/
[3] http://del.icio.us/
[4] http://mail.google.com/

Remote Scripting with Prototype

Being an early adopter of new technologies usually means diving into other people's code—code that usually does not represent best practice—as well as persisting with debugging tools, if such a tool even exists. Not so with Ajax and Rails.

Rails was one of the first—if not *the* first—frameworks to ship with (and even encourage) the use of Ajax in web applications. Rails comes bundled with the **Prototype** JavaScript library,[5] which is responsible for all of the dynamic interaction between browser and application. As it's so easy to use, many Rails-powered web applications were Ajax-enabled from day one.

Visual Effects with script.aculo.us

When web developers first embraced Ajax, it introduced a number of new user-interface problems (interaction designers are still searching to find the best solution for several of these!). These challenges arose from the fact that the way in which users interact with a web application that utilizes Ajax is fundamentally different from the way they use an app that does not. Back in the Web 1.0 days (before Ajax), most users were able to anticipate when communication was occurring between client and server, and when it was not. The interaction was very start-stop in nature, because each back-and-forth transmission resulted in the delivery of a new page to the client.

With Ajax, the web browser might never really stop communicating with the server. We're therefore faced with a problem: how do we let the user know that communication has taken place?

Let me illustrate this point with an example. When users click on an element, such as a link or a button, on a web page that uses Ajax, they expect a new page to load, because this is what's happened with every other link that they've clicked on the Web in the past. Instead, a small amount of content on the page is updated, while everything else stays in place, unchanged. The change that takes place is so minor, though, that the users don't notice it; they begin to wonder whether they might have missed the link when they clicked it, so they try clicking it again. Figure 7.9 shows a hypothetical example of this kind of confusion in action.

---

[5] Although Prototype is bundled with Rails, it can be downloaded as a stand-alone JavaScript library from the Prototype web site [http://prototype.conio.net/], and used independently.

Figure 7.9. An Ajax-powered to-do list without visual feedback

In fact, the only thing that's missing is feedback from the application about what's going on. What would be great in this situation is some kind of visual feedback to let the users know that their click has been processed, so that the results of that action become more obvious. For this very purpose, Rails core team member Thomas Fuchs invented the **script.aculo.us** JavaScript library, which works with the Prototype Library to provide various visual effects. Rails ships with this library by default, and we'll use it to provide feedback to the user.[6]

While they might look like gratuitous eye candy at first, when used sparingly, the visual effects provided by script.aculo.us can provide great user feedback for the Ajax actions handled by Prototype. For example, you can use effects to drop elements off the bottom of the page when a user deletes them, to highlight specific elements that have just been updated, or to "shake" the entire login form if a user supplies an incorrect password.

In addition to these visual effects, script.aculo.us was later expanded to include some other nifty functionality, such as:

drag-and-drop
These helper functions allow for the easy reordering of lists, but could also be applied to a drag-and-drop shopping cart, for example.

edit-in-place
This functionality allows a user to edit text that is displayed on the page (a heading, or a regular paragraph, for example) simply by clicking on it. The text turns into a text field into which the user can type to change the text;

---

[6] While script.aculo.us is bundled with Rails, it can, like Prototype, be downloaded from its own web site [http://script.aculo.us/].

the edits are saved without the page having to be reloaded. You might already have used this functionality on Flickr, for example.[7]

auto-completion of strings
This functionality allows your web application to perform a database lookup as users type text into a form field. This capability could be used to complete path names on a remote server or to suggest search terms—an implementation pioneered by Google Suggest.[8]

An additional benefit of using Rails' built-in helpers to enable Ajax functionality in your application (compared with writing all of the Ajax code from scratch) is that they make it easy to provide a fallback option for browsers that don't support Ajax—a concept known as **graceful degradation**. The browsers that fall into this category include older versions of web browsers, some browsers on newer platforms such as mobile phones or PDAs, and browsers for which the user has deliberately disabled JavaScript. Visitors using these browsers will still be able to use your web application—it won't be as dynamic as it is for other users, but at least they won't be faced with an application that doesn't work at all (a scenario that's almost guaranteed to drive them away from your site).

Armed with this knowledge of Prototype and script.aculo.us, we'll make use of the Rails Ajax helpers to implement functionality that allows users to vote on stories in our Shovell application without waiting for page reloads, and we'll provide those users with a nice visual effect to highlight the altered element after their vote actions are successful.

Making Stories Shove-able

Okay, we've walked through the ins and outs of Ajax. We've discussed the capabilities of the two JavaScript libraries that are bundled with Rails, and explored the role that each of them plays. We're now in a good position to add voting functionality to our application, and to indicate to users that their votes have been recorded. We'll also provide a fallback option for users whose browsers don't support Ajax.

Just to be extra-cheeky, we'll refer to each story's vote as a **shove**, rather than a digg—users can then "shove" stories that they think are worthy of publication on the site's homepage.

---

[7] http://flickr.com/
[8] http://labs.google.com/suggest/

Including the JavaScript Libraries

As both of the helpers that we're going to use—Prototype, for dealing with the `XmlHttpRequest` object, and script.aculo.us, for displaying visual effects—are implemented in JavaScript, we need to include the appropriate JavaScript files into our application's layout. To do so, add the following line to the `app/views/layouts/application.rhtml` file, somewhere in the `head` section:

File: **10-application.rhtml (excerpt)**
```
<%= javascript_include_tag :defaults %>
```

This line calls the `javascript_include_tag` Rails helper, passing it the `:default` parameter. It causes a total of five JavaScript include files to be added to our application:

prototype.js   This file contains the entire Prototype library, which provides our Ajax functionality.

effects.js   This is the visual effects part of the script.aculo.us library.

dragdrop.js   This file contains the JavaScript methods required for adding drag-and-drop functionality, also from the script.aculo.us library.

controls.js   The auto-completion methods are contained within this part of the script.aculo.us library.

application.js   This is an empty file that we can use to store our own custom JavaScript functions. It's located in the `public/javascripts` folder of our application.

To confirm that the helper is indeed doing its job, take a look at the source of any of the pages that exist in our application right now. Remember, since we added these files to the application's layout template, this change will be visible on *every* page. In the header of the page source, you should find `<script>` tags that closely resemble the following:[9]

---

[9] If you're curious about that weird numerical suffix that follows each of the JavaScript files, don't be: this number simply represents the amount of time in seconds between January 1, 1970 (the "Unix epoch"), and the time at which the file was last modified. This information is included in order to force browsers to reload the file in question whenever the file is modified. Normally browsers cache supplementary files such as style sheets and JavaScript files, so this is a good way to force the browser to discard the cached version and apply the new file.

note

It's Not All or Nothing!

If you like, you can be more selective about what you include in your own application, depending on whether you plan to use all of the functionality provided in the JavaScript files that ship with Rails. This might save some download time for your users, since their browsers won't have to load JavaScript files that your app doesn't use anyway.

```html
<script src="/javascripts/prototype.js?1152710301"
    type="text/javascript"></script>
<script src="/javascripts/effects.js?1152710301"
    type="text/javascript"></script>
<script src="/javascripts/dragdrop.js?1152710301"
    type="text/javascript"></script>
<script src="/javascripts/controls.js?1152710301"
    type="text/javascript"></script>
<script src="/javascripts/application.js?1152710301"
    type="text/javascript"></script>
```

Giving Stories a Shove

The next step is to change our existing show view (located at app/views/story/show.rhtml) to display the current number of votes that the story has received; we also need to add a link that allows users to vote on stories. Modify your view so that it looks like this:

File: **11-show.rhtml**

```html
<h2>
  <span id="vote_score">
    Score: <%= @story.votes_count %>
  </span>
  <%= @story.name %>
</h2>
<p>
  <%= link_to @story.link, @story.link %>
</p>
<div id="vote_link">
  <%= link_to_remote 'shove it',
    :url => { :action => 'vote', :id => @story } %>
</div>
```

Let's take a look at what's new here:

```html
<h2>
  <span id="vote_score">
```

```
    Score: <%= @story.votes_count %>
  </span>
  <%= @story.name %>
</h2>
```

The heading that previously displayed just the name of the story now also contains a <span> tag that holds its vote score. To calculate this number, we simply use the votes_count method to add up the number of votes submitted for that story. We've also given the span element a unique id, which we'll use later as a hook to update the score when a user casts a vote. We'll also add some CSS to float this span to the right of the page:

```
<div id="vote_link">
  <%= link_to_remote 'shove it',
    :url => { :action => 'vote', :id => @story } %>
</div>
```

This is where the magic happens! The extra div houses a relative of our much-loved link_to helper: a function called link_to_remote. This function generates the bits of HTML and CSS that are necessary to invoke the specified action (vote) using Ajax, rather than display it as a regular page-loading link.

Using Models in URLs

Readers with an eagle eye might have noticed that the .id part of the @story variable is not included when the variable is passed in as a parameter. Yet the URL that Rails assembles from this function call will contain exactly that—the value of @story.id.

How is this possible? Every ActiveRecord model has an instance method called to_params, which defaults to the value of id. If you'd prefer to use a different identifier in your URLs, you can override this method in your model class (in this case, Story) with another column—for example, permalink:

```
class Story < ActiveRecord::Base
  def to_params; permalink; end
end
```

We'll stick with the default to_params value for our Shovell application.

Styling the Scoreboard

Next let's expand our CSS (it lives in the file located at public/stylesheets/styles.css), to style and position our new elements.

File: **12-styles.css** (excerpt)

```css
#vote_score {
  float: right;
  color: #9c9;
}
#vote_link a {
  padding: 3px 5px;
  border: 3px solid #393;
  background-color: #cfc;
  text-decoration: none;
  color: #393;
}
#vote_link a:hover {
  background-color: #aea;
}
```

There's nothing too mysterious happening here—it's all cosmetic stuff. But who said cosmetics weren't important?

If you access one of your stories through your browser (using the link to a random story on `http://localhost:3000/story`, for example) you should see a page similar to the one in Figure 7.10. However, clicking the shove it link won't do much right now (except that your application may spit out some weird warnings and error messages).

Figure 7.10. Showing a story with voting score and vote link

Storing the Votes

To store the votes that have been submitted, we'll add a `vote` method to our `StoryController`. If you recall the `link_to_remote` helper call from above, you'll notice that it refers to a method called `vote`. Here it is:

File: **13-story_controller.rb (excerpt)**

```
...
def vote
  @story = Story.find(params[:id])
  @story.votes.create
end
end
```

This new method doesn't contain anything we haven't seen before. In the first line of the method, we find the appropriate story record using the unique ID of `Story` for which a vote has been cast. The second line creates and saves a new `Vote`—it only contains auto-generated values, such as the creation date, and the IDs that receive a value because of the `Vote`'s association with a `Story`.

If you were to try clicking the shove it link on your story page now, it would store your vote. But nothing on the page would change yet—even in Rails-land we can only perform so much magic at once.

To update the voting score that's displayed on the page and highlight it with a visual effect, we'll use a new kind of Rails template: an RJS template.

Introducing RJS Templates

While the regular `.rhtml` templates with which we're so familiar deal with a whole page (or partial pages, as we'll see later), templates with an `.rjs` extension (short for *Rails JavaScript*) are used to modify parts of an existing page. When we use RJS templates, the information that's transferred to the user's browser is a series of JavaScript instructions that modify, extend, and apply visual effects to HTML elements. In contrast, `.rhtml` templates transfer HTML elements themselves.

You don't need to add anything special to your controllers or actions in order to have them use `.rjs` templates; simply place a template that has the extension `.rjs` right alongside all your other regular views, and it will be ready for use.

Let's create an RJS template for our `vote` action now. It'll handle the updating of a story's voting score (the number of "shoves"), and it'll highlight the score

after the update, using a visual effect. We'll store this new template in
app/views/story/vote.rjs. Create the template like so:

File: **14-vote.rjs**

```
page.replace_html 'vote_score', "Score: #{@story.votes_count}"
page[:vote_score].visual_effect :highlight
```

That's all: just two lines of code! Let's look at what each line does.

First of all, you'll notice that the window to the world of RJS is the **page** object.
This object provides us with two different approaches for using RJS templates:

❑ The first approach focuses on *what* you do to an element on the page—"replace
the content of an HTML element," for example, or "show this visual effect."
This approach involves calling a specific instance method on the **page** object;
the method usually takes as a parameter the HTML element to be modified
(referenced by its **id** attribute).

❑ The second approach revolves around the question of *which element* you want
to work with first. We can access the HTML element in question—once again
identified by its **id** attribute (well, a Ruby symbol of the same name as its **id**,
anyway)—by treating the **page** object like a hash that contains all the elements
on the page. The actual functionality is then invoked as an instance method
on the element.

The two lines of code I showed above purposely use the two different approaches,
because I wanted to demonstrate each in an example. You could just as easily
(and probably should) choose one approach and use that consistently. We'll leave
our RJS template as is, but as an exercise, you might like to try modifying the
code so that your approach to using RJS templates is consistent.

The first line is responsible for updating the story's score after a new vote has
been cast:

```
page.replace_html 'vote_score', "#Score: {@story.votes_count}"
```

The **replace_html** method of the **page** object takes two arguments: the **id** of
the element whose contents you'd like to replace (**vote_score**, this time as a
string, not a symbol), and the actual text that you want to assign to the element.

One new thing here is the **#{}** syntax that we've used between the quotes of the
last argument. Using this syntax gives us the ability to add dynamic values to
our strings—in this case, we're adding the value of **@story.votes_count**, which,

if you recall, returns the number of votes that the story has received. To use this functionality, you must use double quotes instead of single quotes—the #{} syntax does *not* work with single quotes.[10]

In this example, the code between the parentheses is a simple method call. However, it is possible to put any Ruby code in there. Be mindful, though, not to violate the MVC terms and conditions by placing any complex calculations within your views—that stuff really belongs in your controller code.

```
page[:vote_score].visual_effect :highlight
```

Figure 7.11. The "yellow fade" visual effect

This second line of our RJS Template uses the second syntax that we discussed for the page object. It asks for the element with the id of vote_score, and applies the visual effect highlight to it. By default, this effect will highlight the back-

---

[10] For performance reasons, it's generally a good idea to use single quotes whenever you *don't* need to replace values in a string dynamically.

ground of the element in question with a light yellow, then fade it back to white. The color of the fade can be customized easily, like most of Rails' defaults.

After the user clicks the shove it voting link, the score will update, and the element will be highlighted with the yellow fading background. It's difficult to show the dynamic update and highlighting effect in black-and-white print (I've done my best in Figure 7.11), so you'll just have to go ahead and try it yourself.

Isn't it amazing how much you can do with as little code as this?

Ensuring Graceful Degradation

To implement a fallback action for browsers that don't support Ajax, we first need to modify our Story's template to include a regular HTML link—this will appear when Ajax voting is not an option. Additionally, we need to redirect users back to the story page after we've processed their votes (while users with Ajax-enabled browsers can watch as the total number of votes is updated and highlighted).

Let's start with the story template, which is located in app/views/story/show.rhtml. We can modify the existing link_to_remote call to include a pure HTML link as follows:

File: **15-show.rhtml (excerpt)**

```
<div id="vote_link">
  <%= link_to_remote 'shove it',
    { :url => { :action => 'vote', :id => @story } },
    { :href => url_for(:action => 'vote', :id => @story) } %>
</div>
```

As you can see, we've added another parameter here—a hash that sets the href attribute of the anchor element a, which constitutes a link in HTML. To set this attribute, we're using the url_for Rails helper to turn the :action and :id parameters into a relative URL using Rails routes. The URL that this helper creates will then be used for the HTML link.

For example, if the id of the story we were looking at was 2, the url_for call would return:

```
/vote/2
```

You can confirm that the modified link_to_remote call functions correctly as a fallback option by disabling JavaScript in your browser and clicking on the link.

However, you can perform a quick test by hovering your mouse over the shove it link, as demonstrated in Figure 7.12.

Figure 7.12. Hovering over the voting link reveals the fallback URL

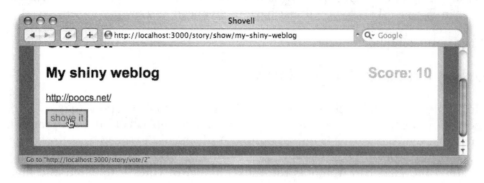

To instruct our story controller to take appropriate action, whether it's dealing with an Ajax request or a regular HTTP GET request, we need to modify the vote action in our StoryController class like so:

File: **16-story_controller.rb (excerpt)**

```
def vote
  @story = Story.find(params[:id])
  @story.votes.create

  respond_to do |wants|
    wants.html { redirect_to :action => 'show',
                             :permalink => @story.permalink }
    wants.js   { render }
  end
end
```

The newly added respond_to block acts as the switchboard for the different requests for which we need to account.[11] By indicating the action that must be taken for each of the different requests, our application will do what's appropriate without duplicating any of the code that stores the vote.

---

[11] Rails uses the HTTP Accept header to determine the request type. This header, among others, is supplied by the user's web browser when it connects to the server.

In the code block that's passed to the respond_to clause, we list the alternatives that we intend to support in our modified show action. Note that the alternatives listed here (wants.html and wants.js) are not filenames—wants is an object that's provided to the code block in order to find out "what the client wants." For each supported request type, a corresponding instance method is defined; each line can be read as "if the client wants this, do that." Let's look at each of them:

```
wants.html  { redirect_to :action => 'show',
                          :permalink => @story.permalink }
```

If we're dealing with a regular HTTP GET request, we want to redirect the user back to the story page. The redirect_to function should be familiar to you from Chapter 6.

Our former Ajax-only show action implicitly called render after the vote had been processed. However, since we've introduced a decision into the mix, we need explicitly to tell Rails to render the RJS template, in case we're dealing with an Ajax request. That's what the second parameter in the block does:

```
wants.js { render }
```

Having made the necessary modifications to both the controller and the view, we're now able to cater to users with—*and* those without—Ajax support in their browsers.

Note, though, that given the app's current state, a search engine crawler would be able to vote on Shovell stories. This is something to keep in mind when you're implementing fallback functionality for your Ajax flourishes. In Chapter 8, we'll remedy this situation by requiring users to log in in order to vote.

Introducing Partials

I've mentioned before that templates ending in .rhtml can be used to display certain pieces of the page independently of the rest of the page. When used in this way, these files are called **partials**. Partials can be helpful for dealing with parts of a page that are constantly being reused (such as a navigation menu), or for retrieving and formatting the items in a collection (such as a list).

In this section, we'll use partials to implement a voting history box for our story page. The history box will show the dates and times at which each vote for a story was submitted.

Adding Voting History

We'll implement the voting history as a list, using the HTML elements for an unordered list (ul). Each vote will be represented as a list item (li) that shows the voting timestamp. The list items themselves will be rendered as partials, so a single template that contains a single list item will be rendered as often as there are votes for a given story.

To begin with, we'll modify the show template located at app/views/story/show.rhtml to render an unordered list of the votes a story has received. To accomplish this, we'll add to the template code right above the paragraph container that houses the story link, like so:

File: **17-show.rhtml (excerpt)**

```
<ul id="vote_history">
  <% if @story.votes.size.zero? %>
    <em>No shoves yet!</em>
  <% else %>
    <%= render :partial => 'vote',
               :collection => @story.votes %>
  <% end %>
</ul>
<p>
  <%= link_to @story.link, @story.link %>
</p>
```

In this code we've started out with a very straightforward ul element that has a unique id, and we've added a condition using an unless ... else ... end construct. This causes the message No shoves yet! to be displayed whenever a story that has not received any votes is rendered.

```
<% if @story.votes.size.zero? %>
  ...
<% else %>
  ...
<% end %>
```

While the if construct is familiar to us from Chapter 3, the votes.size.zero? part is new—it's yet another method to which we have access as a result of specifying the association between our two models. In this case, the zero? method will return empty if a story has associated votes, and true if not.

```
<%= render :partial => 'vote',
           :collection => @story.votes %>
```

It's in this call to render that we add the partial to our page—we instruct Rails to render a template for every Vote that has been added to a story. The render :partial syntax can be used to render a partial once or many times (as in this case)—it's the addition of the :collection argument that indicates we'll be rendering the partial multiple times.

Creating the Partial

Partials, like regular full-page templates, have a .rhtml extension and are stored right alongside their full-page cousins in an application's directory structure. A partial is identified by an underscore (_) prefix in its filename. Let's create a new partial at app/views/story/_vote.rhtml, and populate it with the following line of code:

File: **18-_vote.rhtml**

```
<li><%= vote.created_at.to_formatted_s(:short) %></li>
```

That's all there is to it! This line simply wraps the date on which a vote was made (the value of which is stored in the created_at attribute) in a pair of <li> tags.

Note that we have access to an object named vote. Rails has created this object for us—it does so for every partial—and the object takes the name of the partial (vote, in this case). This object is automatically set to the current element of the collection that's being rendered.

The upshot of all this is that a partial needn't concern itself with determining which Vote it's currently processing, or where that Vote sits within the larger collection of votes. The partial simply operates on a single vote object and lets Rails take care of the rest.

Styling the Voting History

If we printed the date and time exactly as they appear in the database, we'd produce something rather awkward-looking:

```
2006-09-01 11:47:55
```

To address this issue, we've made use of Rails' date-formatting helper. This helper, appropriately named to_formatted_s, is available as an instance method for objects of the classes Date and Time. The helper takes a single argument: one of several pre-defined symbols representing the format that should be applied to the output. Some of the formats include `:short` and `:long`; for a `Time` object, these render as 01 Sep 11:47 and September 01, 2006 11:47 respectively.

Again, to make things a little more pleasing to the eye, we'll add a few CSS rules to our style sheet to define what our voting history box should look like. These rules arrange our voting history nicely, but they also introduce some minor CSS quirks that relate to floated elements. Thankfully, we can rectify these problems easily by adding a few more lines to our style sheet. The additions are marked in bold below:[12]

File: **19-style.css (excerpt)**

```
#content {
  background-color: #fff;
  border: 10px solid #ccc;
  padding: 10px 10px 20px 10px;
  overflow: hidden;
}
* html #content {
  height: 1%;
}
...
#vote_history {
  padding: 5px;
  margin: 0;
  list-style: none;
  border: 3px solid #ccc;
  background-color: #eee;
  float: right;
  color: #999;
  font-size: smaller;
}
```

With all of this code in place, go ahead and reload a story page in your browser—the result should look similar to Figure 7.13 (depending on how much fun you had clicking the shove it link earlier).

---

[12] The explanation of what's happening here—and why these cryptic CSS rules are necessary—is well beyond the scope of this book. However, if you're interested in learning more, this topic (and others) is explained in Rachel Andrew's *The CSS Anthology: 101 Essential Tips, Tricks & Hacks* [http://www.sitepoint.com/books/cssant1/].

Figure 7.13. Showing a story with voting history

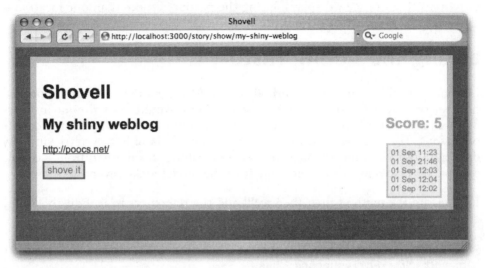

While the page is looking good, there are a few more things that I think we should add: the history should be updated whenever the shove it link is clicked, we should really sort the votes by descending ID (so that the newest is displayed at the top), and we should limit the number of votes that are displayed.

We can achieve the first task easily by adding some code to our RJS template, located at `app/views/story/vote.rjs`. These additions will deal with the voting actions:

File: **20-vote.rjs (excerpt)**

```
page.replace_html 'vote_score', "Score: #{@story.votes_count}"
page[:vote_score].visual_effect :highlight
page[:vote_history].replace_html :partial => 'vote',
                    :collection => @story.votes
```

Can you see where we're heading with this? Once again, we've used the `page` object to gain access to the `vote_history` HTML element. This element is then replaced with a new value. The syntax for replacing the element is the same syntax that we used for the original `render` call in our `show.rhtml` template. The name of the partial is passed using `:partial`, and the collection of votes (available via `@story.votes`) is passed using a symbol called `:collection`.

When we pass `:partial` and `:collection` to the `replace_html` method of an RJS template like this, the method will behave just like the regular call to `render` that we used in show.rhtml. In this case, it will render the exact same collection of partials that our view displays. Using the partial in more than one location is a nice way to avoid writing duplicate code.

Tweaking the Voting History

Lastly, we'll add an instance method to the Story model to return a limited number of votes sorted by descending ID. Why would we write an instance method, and not just retrieve the data from within the view? Well, for a couple of reasons. For one, MVC principles state that we shouldn't be retrieving any data from our view. But the fact that we'll be calling this method from a couple of separate places means that moving it to the model makes even more sense.

Let's create the method first, then we'll add the references to it. Edit the Story class so that it looks like this:

File: **21-story.rb (excerpt)**

```
class Story < ActiveRecord::Base
  validates_presence_of :name, :link
  has_many :votes
  def latest_votes
    votes.find(:all, :order => 'id DESC', :limit => 3)
  end
end
```

This latest_votes method will take advantage of the story's association with the Vote model, and will use a regular find call to retrieve the records we want, up to a total of three records (as specified by the :limit => 3 parameter). The :order => 'id DESC' argument will ensure that they're ordered so that the newest vote is located at the top.[13]

Ordering Records in Rails

In case you're curious, the :order argument is actually a tiny piece of SQL. DESC, quite obviously, stands for descending; there's also ASC for ascending, which is often left off as it's the default.

The rest of the :order argument constitutes a column name by which the records will be ordered (or multiple column names separated by commas—if you want to order by multiple columns—like so: :order => 'id, cre-

---

[13] Even though :all is passed as the first argument, this find call will *not* retrieve all the votes from the database. The :order and :limit arguments will be used in the database query, so a maximum of three votes will be returned to our application.

ated_at'). Rails itself currently offers no way to specify the ordering of records.

Having added this new instance method to the Story class, you can go ahead and replace the two occurrences of @story.votes that are present in our views with @story.latest_votes. The first occurrence is the render call in show.rhtml:

File: **22-show.rhtml (excerpt)**

```
<%= render :partial => 'vote',
           :collection => @story.latest_votes %>
```

The second occurrence is the last line of the RJS template vote.rjs.

File: **23-vote.rjs (excerpt)**

```
page[:vote_history].replace_html :partial => 'vote',
                  :collection => @story.latest_votes
```

Excellent. Reloading the story page should produce the expected results, with the number of votes being limited to three, and the votes ordered by descending ID. Hitting the shove it link will update the voting history and place the new vote at the top of the list. Have a look at Figure 7.14 to see how the updated page looks.

Figure 7.14. The final story page with voting history

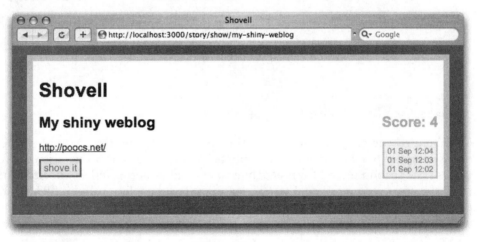

Testing the Voting Functionality

In Chapter 6, we mentioned that our plan is to provide test coverage for all of the functionality in our application. Let's expand our growing test suite now by adding some unit and functional tests.

Testing the Model

While most of the work in this chapter has been on the controller side, we still made some changes to the model—we modified our Story model, we added a Vote model, and we defined an association between the two. We also added an instance method called latest_votes to retrieve the most recent votes of a given Story. All of these features can be tested programmatically, so let's write some unit tests to cover them.

Preparing the Fixtures

Before we write any tests, we'll add some test data to the fixtures for our Vote model, which resides in test/fixtures/votes.yml:

File: **24-votes.yml**
```
first:
  id: 1
  story_id: 1
  created_at: <%= Time.now.to_s(:db) %>
second:
  id: 2
  story_id: 1
  created_at: <%= Time.now.to_s(:db) %>
```

We generated the original contents of this file using the generate script earlier in this chapter, but I've made some enhancements here. First, I've altered the name of the second record from another to second to better reflect the order in which the votes were received. I've also incorporated the relationship information for both votes by adding a story_id field to the fixture file. Both story_ids point to the first Story, illustrating the point that one Story can have multiple Votes.

Additionally, you'll notice some ERb tags in the fixture file. These should be fairly self-explanatory—we're setting the created_at attribute of each vote to the current date and time, using the now method of the Time class. The to_s(:db) method call then transforms the `Time` object into a format that's expected by the database. The value returned by this method will look something like this:

```
Fri Sep 01 20:41:44 CEST 2006
```

We need to set the `created_at` attribute manually because, unfortunately, the automatic population of "magic" columns such as `created_at` and `updated_at` doesn't work within fixtures.

Testing a Story's Relationship to a Vote

At this stage, we're ready to add a test that covers the `Story`'s relationship to the `Vote` model. To do this, open the file `test/unit/vote_test.rb` and change the `VoteTest` class to read as follows:

File: **25-vote_test.rb (excerpt)**

```
class VoteTest < Test::Unit::TestCase
  fixtures :votes, :stories
  def test_story_association
    assert_equal stories(:first), votes(:first).story
  end
end
```

The first line specifies a second fixture file to use in the test:

```
fixtures :votes, :stories
```

We use a comma-separated list of symbols to instruct the test suite to load multiple fixtures into multiple tables. In this case, we're loading the `votes.yml` file that we just modified, as well as our trusty `stories.yml` file from Chapter 5.

The new `test_story_association` test undertakes the testing of the `Story`'s relationship to the `Vote` model. While the underlying Rails association has very good test coverage internally, it's good practice to test all associations that you create as you test your application's behaviour.

```
assert_equal stories(:first), votes(:first).story
```

The `assert_equal` assertion, as the name implies, confirms that two expressions are absolutely equal. In this case, we're simply comparing the return values of two methods.

What's new on this line is the `stories(:first)` and `votes(:first)` syntax, which references our fixture data by name. Making use of a fixture file in a test (using the `fixtures` method) doesn't just load the contents of the file into the database—it also gives us a convenient way to access each record in the fixture file, without having to resort to manual retrieval methods (for example, using `Vote.find(1)` to retrieve the first vote). The records we defined in the `votes.yml` fixture file above are named `first` and `second`. Simply passing these identifiers as symbols to the `votes` method returns the corresponding record.

To give an example, take a look at these two calls—they'd be equal, given the `votes.yml` fixture we created earlier:

```
Vote.find(1)
votes(:first)
```

Incidentally, a method whose name is identical to the name of the fixture file (minus the `.yml` extension) is made available for every fixture we include in a test case. As we've included two fixtures, we have access to both the `votes` and `stories` methods.

In our assertion line, we compare the `Story` named `first` with the `Story` object that's associated with the `Vote` named `first`. We know that this assertion should be `true`, because we associated both votes in the fixture file with the first story.

Testing a Vote's Relationship to a Story

To test the complementary part of the relationship between our models, edit the `test/unit/story_test.rb` file. Once again, we need to expand the `fixtures` call at the top of the class definition to include the `votes` fixture. If we didn't do so, we wouldn't be able to access the fixture data stored in `votes.yml`. And to cover the association with a test, we'll add the following method just below the existing tests:

File: **26-story_test.rb (excerpt)**

```ruby
class StoryTest < Test::Unit::TestCase
  fixtures :stories, :votes

  ...
  def test_votes_association
    assert_equal [ votes(:first), votes(:second) ],
        stories(:first).votes
  end
end
```

This assertion confirms that the votes associated with the `Story` are indeed the votes that we named `first` and `second`. Here, we're manually assembling an array of votes in the order in which we expect them to appear, and comparing that array with the votes that are returned by the `votes` method. If the two arrays match, we know our code works!

Testing the Voting History Order

To test the functionality provided by the `latest_votes` method we added, we'll add two more tests to the `story_test.rb` file, below the others:

File: **27-story_test.rb** (excerpt)

```
def test_should_return_highest_vote_id_first
  assert_equal votes(:second), stories(:first).latest_votes.first
end

def test_should_return_3_latest_votes
  10.times { stories(:first).votes.create }
  assert_equal 3, stories(:first).latest_votes.size
end
```

Let's look at these tests line by line.

The `test_should_return_highest_vote_id_first` test confirms that the `:order` part of the `latest_votes` method is indeed operating correctly.

```
    assert_equal votes(:second), stories(:first).latest_votes.first
```

The assertion compares the first element of the array returned by the `latest_votes` method with the `Vote` object to which we expect it to be equal (the fixture with the highest `id` attribute).

To test whether the `:limit` part of our `latest_votes` method does indeed do its job, we need to add a few more votes to the database, as our fixture file currently contains only two votes. However, because it's unlikely that we'll be using a large number of votes in any other test, we'll create the additional votes right there in the test, using a simple block of Ruby code:

```
    10.times { stories(:first).votes.create }
```

This line programmatically creates ten votes on the fly by calling the `create` method on the `votes` association of the first `Story`.

These dynamically created votes will automatically be wiped from the database before the next test starts, so they won't affect any other tests.

The assertion then goes ahead and compares the size of the array returned by `latest_votes` with the expected number of three, which is the maximum number of votes that `latest_votes` should return.

Running the Unit Tests

At this point, we're ready to run our unit tests with all of the newly added coverage. You remember how to do that, right? With the `rake` tool:

```
$ rake test:units
```

The output should look similar to Figure 7.15.

Figure 7.15. Running unit tests

Testing the Controller

Now that we've created tests that cover all of the extra functionality we added to our model in this chapter, we'll do the same for the new controller actions, `show` and `vote`, and their accompanying views. All these additions will be made to the functional test file located in `test/functional/story_control-ler_test.rb`.

Testing Page Rendering

As with our unit tests, the first thing we need to do here is expand the fixtures that the tests utilize to include the **votes** fixtures. Add the following to the file test/functional/story_test_controller.rb:

File: **28-story_controller_test.rb** (excerpt)

```
fixtures :stories, :votes
```

Next, we'll add two tests for the **show** action; the first will be a test that deals with the basics of displaying a story. Let's add some **permalink** values for the two stories on which we're basing all this testing. Edit the **stories.yml** file as follows:

File: **29-stories.yml** (excerpt)

```
first:
  id: 1
  name: My shiny weblog
  link: http://poocs.net/
  permalink: my-shiny-weblog
another:
  id: 2
  name: SitePoint Forums
  link: http://www.sitepoint.com/forums/
  permalink: sitepoint-forums
```

Now that we have some reliable test data in place, we can write the tests. The code for the first test looks like this:

File: **30-story_controller_test.rb** (excerpt)

```
def test_should_show_story
  get :show, :permalink => 'my-shiny-weblog'
  assert_response :success
  assert_template 'show'
  assert_equal stories(:first), assigns(:story)
end
```

This code doesn't do anything we haven't seen before—we request a page (the "show story" page) using HTTP GET, and make sure that the page returns a code indicating that it displayed successfully. We then check that the template name is correct, and make sure that the story we've requested via the **permalink** is indeed the story we expected.

The next test we'll create will cover the new HTML elements that we added to the story page—specifically those relating to the voting functionality. The test is as follows:

File: **31-story_controller_test.rb (excerpt)**
```ruby
def test_should_show_story_vote_elements
  get :show, :permalink => 'my-shiny-weblog'
  assert_select 'h2 span#vote_score'
  assert_select 'ul#vote_history li', :count => 2
  assert_select 'div#vote_link'
end
```

This is a pretty comprehensive test that checks for the presence of correctly nested HTML tags on the rendered page, as well as proper element attributes. Let's examine it one line at a time:

```ruby
assert_select 'h2 span#vote_score'
```

This assertion introduces more of the CSS selector syntax that can be used with `assert_select`, which we first encountered in Chapter 6. Just as you would regularly style an element on a page by referring to its ID, `assert_select` allows us to test for the presence of an element with a given ID using the exact same syntax we'd apply to style an element on the page.

Here, we're checking for a `span` tag with an `id` of `vote_score` nested within an `h2` element. This test actually confirms that we have a proper story header in place, and that the current voting score appears beneath it.

The next assertion also uses `assert_select`:

```ruby
assert_select 'ul#vote_history li', :count => 2
```

Here, we check for the presence of a `ul` element that has a unique `id` of `vote_history` and a specific number of `li` elements nested within it (these reflect the entries of the voting history for this particular story).

Our final check confirms the presence of a `div` element with a unique `id` of `vote_link`:

```ruby
assert_select 'div#vote_link'
```

We now have a high level of confidence that our pages are displaying everything we expect them to! Now, let's add some tests for our voting functionality.

Testing Vote Storage

To test the basics of the vote-casting functionality, add the following test. It simply confirms that new votes are stored correctly:

```ruby
def test_should_accept_vote
  assert stories(:another).votes.empty?
  post :vote, :id => 2
  assert ! assigns(:story).reload.votes.empty?
end
```

The test uses a before-and-after check to confirm that this action, which is supposed to modify data, is indeed doing its job. Let's look at each line in turn.

The first line confirms that the story initially has no votes:

```ruby
  assert stories(:another).votes.empty?
```

We then submit the vote using HTTP POST:

```ruby
  post :vote, :id => 2
```

Finally, we confirm that the vote we submitted was stored successfully, and is indeed associated with our story:

```ruby
  assert ! assigns(:story).reload.votes.empty?
```

Okay, we now have a basic test in place for the application's basic voting functionality. But our voting pages aren't exactly basic—they use that fancy Ajax stuff, remember? Can we test that, too? You bet we can!

Testing Ajax Voting

Let's test an Ajax voting action. Add the following test to your rapidly expanding collection of functional tests:

```ruby
def test_should_render_rjs_after_vote_with_ajax
  xml_http_request :post, :vote, :id => 2
  assert_response :success
  assert_template 'vote'
end
```

Let's walk through each line of this test.

The first line is our test's way of pretending to perform an actual Ajax request:

```
xml_http_request :post, :vote, :id => 2
```

Obviously this isn't really an Ajax request—it doesn't make use of a browser, and there's no XmlHttpRequest object in sight. But, by prefixing the regular post call with the xml_http_request method, our request receives a header that fools the application into thinking that this is a real Ajax request.

Setup statements like these can be extracted from specific tests into smaller, more succinct helper methods, which can then be used by all tests.

The next block of statements submits the vote itself using HTTP POST, checks for a proper response, and confirms that the correct template was rendered:

```
post :vote, :id => stories(:another).id
assert_response :success
assert_template 'vote'
```

There's nothing here that we haven't seen before, so let's move on to our last test.

Testing Regular HTTP Voting

We still need to test the process of vote submission using regular HTTP GET (that is, without Ajax). To do so, we'll add one more test to the story_controller_test.rb file:

File: **34-story_controller_test.rb (excerpt)**

```
def test_should_redirect_after_vote_with_get
  get :vote, :id => 2
  assert_redirected_to :action => 'show',
      :permalink => 'sitepoint-forums'
end
```

Let's examine each line in this test. The first line casts the vote with a simple HTTP GET:

```
get :vote, :id => 2
```

After the vote has been submitted, we just need to check whether the user is properly redirected to the story page. This is accomplished with an assert_re-directed_to assertion:

```
assert_redirected_to :action => 'show',
    :permalink => 'sitepoint-forums'
```

Excellent! All of our new functionality is covered. Time to run the tests!

Running the Full Test Suite

Invoking the full test suite (using the rake test command) will run through a total of 26 assertions contained in ten tests. The results of a successful test suite execution should look something like Figure 7.16.

Figure 7.16. Running the full test suite

Summary

In this chapter we've equipped Shovell with some fully fledged voting functionality, and we've done it using cutting-edge technologies such as Ajax combined with some good-looking Web 2.0 effects.

Along the way, we covered the principles of the Rails routing module, and we added to our application a page that shows the details of a story that has already been submitted.

We also looked at using RJS templates to modify the contents of pages that have already been rendered, and discussed how we can use visual effects to enhance the usability of our application. We even covered partials—mini page templates that help reduce the amount of template code required to get the job done.

Finally, we established test coverage for all the functionality that we added to our Shovell application in this chapter, so that we'll know immediately if any future change to the application code breaks our existing functionality.

In the next chapter, we'll implement some protective measures in Shovell with user authentication. Our objective will be to let only logged-in users post new story links to the application. The additional benefit that comes with having a user account bound to a story's submission is that we can then implement a per-user history of submissions. Things are looking good!

Protective Measures

Over the last few chapters, we've spent a good deal of time implementing new features for our story-sharing application. However, we've yet to put any effort into preventing those features from being misused.

In this chapter, we'll implement some user authentication techniques that will allow us to protect certain actions from use by individuals who have not registered with, and logged into, the site.

Sessions and Cookies

Before we write any code, let's learn a bit more about the technology behind user logins, including sessions and cookies.

If you already have some experience with sessions and cookies, you might want to skim through this section, or jump forward a few pages to the section called "Modeling the User", where we'll get back into writing the code that will bring these concepts to life.

Identifying Individual Users

Generally speaking, HTTP—the protocol that a web browser uses to talk to an application—is a **stateless protocol**. This means that it doesn't make any assumptions about, or rely upon, previous requests between the client and the server.

This is the crucial difference between stateless protocols and other protocols, including instant messaging systems such as AIM or ICQ: when you start up an instant messenger client, it logs in to the instant messaging server, and remains connected for the time that you use the service. Stateless protocols, such as HTTP, request only a single item—a web page, an image, a style sheet, or a Flash movie, for example—during each connection. Once the item has been requested, the connection is closed. If the requested item is a web page, it is impossible for the application to tell what the users are doing—they may still be reading the page, they may have followed a link to another site, or they may have shut down the machine altogether.

In the world of HTTP, it's also impossible to tell whether two pages requested in succession were actually requested by the same user. We can't rely on the IP address of the user's computer,[1] as that computer might sit behind a proxy server or firewall, in which case it's entirely possible that thousands of other users share the IP address displayed by that machine.

Obviously, we need to use another technique to identify individual visitors. Without it, we'd have to force every user to log in to each and every page of our Shovell application, and that's just not cool. This is where sessions and cookies come into play.

What's a Cookie?

A **cookie** is a tiny snippet of information that a web site places on a user's computer. The cookie is bound to the web site that placed it there—no other site is able to access the cookie. You've probably encountered cookies when using the Web in the past, possibly without even knowing it.

A cookie consists of a name/value pair. For example, a cookie with the name `color` might have the value `green`. Additionally, the cookie's name must be unique—if a cookie is set with the same name as one that already exists, the older cookie will be overwritten.

---

[1] An IP address is a number that uniquely identifies a computer connected to the Internet. You've no doubt encountered them before; here's an example: 123.45.67.123.

All web browsers give users control over the cookies that web sites set on their machines (although some make cookie management easier than others). Firefox, for example, provides a handy tool for inspecting—and removing—the cookies that have been set on a machine. To display the Firefox cookie manager shown in Figure 8.1, select Tools > Options (Firefox > Preferences on a Mac), click Privacy, select the Cookies tab, and click View Cookies. Go take a look—chances are that many of the sites you have visited have left a cookie, without even telling you about it!

Figure 8.1. The Firefox cookie manager

Cookies usually have an expiration date; a browser will delete a cookie automatically once its expiration date has passed. It makes sense for sites to set expiration dates on cookies, because they occupy space on the user's computer. Also, once a cookie is set, it can't be modified by the application that set it, so a cookie that had no expiration date could wind up sitting on the user's hard drive forever!

A site can set the expiration date of a cookie in two ways:

❑ by setting an explicit date (for example, December 31, 2006)

❑ by setting the cookie to expire when the user closes the browser

The latter is the default behavior for Rails' session cookies … which brings us to the next topic: **sessions**.

What's a Session?

Sessions are just what we need to identify returning visitors. A session is like a small container that's stored on the server for each user; it can be used as a temporary storage location for everything that needs to be remembered between successive page views made by the user. Though a session is a less permanent storage solution, the data stored in the session shouldn't be treated any differently from data stored in the application's database.

As an added bonus, the processes of creating sessions and retrieving information from them occurs without us having to write any code, or provide specific instructions.

For our Shovell application, we'll use a session to store information about where a user has come from; we'll use that information when the user attempts to access pages or functionality, to determine whether we should allow the user access, or redirect him or her to the login form. Sessions can also be used to store shopping cart content, custom user preferences, and other information that allows us to enhance and customize users' experiences of a site.

Rails uses a **session cookie** to identify the session of a returning visitor. A session cookie does *not* contain the actual session content—it's just an identifier that our application uses to retrieve the session content from its storage location on the server. By default, session content is stored in the file system on the server.

In fact, if you've been following the code in this book, you may notice that a session cookie has been set by our application already—check your browser's cookie manager for a cookie set by `localhost` or `localhost.local`, with the name `_session_id`. This is a cookie that Rails sets for us automatically, to provide us with a session that we can use within our application.

Sessions in Rails

In Rails, a session is automatically created for each of your application's users, and can be used to store and retrieve data without requiring any special code.

The session container for a user is accessed just like any other hash—to add a new value to the session, simply assign the value that you wish to store to a hash key that doesn't yet exist in the session:

```
session[:page] = 'Index page'
```

The result of this assignment is that a cookie will be written to the user's machine as shown in Figure 8.2 (in this case, the session name is _session_id). This cookie is what ties a user to the session container. With the cookie in place, any data stored in the session becomes available for all successive pages that this user visits.

Figure 8.2. A cookie set by our Rails application

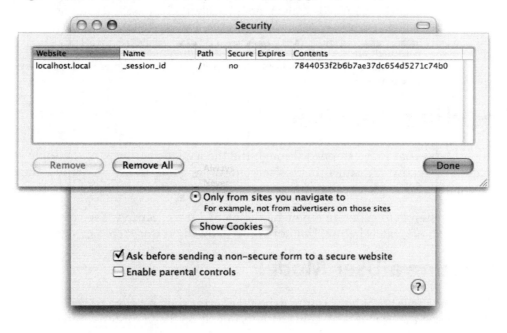

The retrieval of session values is equally simple. To access the value we stored in the previous code snippet, and display it in a view, we'd use the following syntax:

```
<%= session[:page] %>
```

It's actually possible to store data other than strings in a session container—you can use a session to store any type of data you like. The only prerequisite for the storage of such objects is that your application has access to the class definition of the object that's stored. However, in practice, sessions should only be used to store simple objects, such as `String` and `Fixnum` objects.

Tip

The Physical Location of a Session

I mentioned that there are multiple locations in which we can store the contents of a session on the server, the default being the server's file system. The actual directory in which session contents are stored is the `tmp` (short for temporary) folder within your application's directory structure. One file is created per session, and is populated with a textual representation of the session data, which is readable by Rails.

While this solution is fine for local development, it might not work quite so well in a production environment in which many visitors are using the application. The number of files that an operating system can manage within a single directory is limited. Additionally, this approach might not be well suited to a production environment that involves multiple servers.

Although an in-depth discussion on the different session storage options is beyond the scope of this book, we'll briefly explore some of the alternatives in Chapter 12.

Modeling the User

Right! Now that we've stepped through the theory, let's get back to the topic at hand—protective measures. In this section, we're going to lay an architectural foundation for implementing user authentication in Shovell.

The first step is to generate a new model named `User`. Since we've covered the generation of models before, I'm not going to dwell on this step. Let's go!

Generating a User Model

From the `shovell` folder, run the `generate` script shown below to generate the base class of the `User` model, along with its migration files, unit tests, and fixtures. The output of this script is shown in Figure 8.3:

```
$ ruby script/generate model User
```

Figure 8.3. Generating the User model

```
Core:~/shovell scoop$ script/generate model User
      exists  app/models/
      exists  test/unit/
      exists  test/fixtures/
      create  app/models/user.rb
      create  test/unit/user_test.rb
      create  test/fixtures/users.yml
      exists  db/migrate
      create  db/migrate/004_create_users.rb
Core:~/shovell scoop$ █
```

To create the database table for this model, modify the migration file located at db/migrate/004_create_user.rb to look like this:

File: **01-004_create_user.rb**

```ruby
class CreateUsers < ActiveRecord::Migration
  def self.up
    create_table :users do |t|
      t.column :login, :string
      t.column :password, :string
      t.column :name, :string
      t.column :email, :string
    end
    add_column :stories, :user_id, :integer
    add_column :votes, :user_id, :integer
  end
  def self.down
    drop_table :users
    remove_column :stories, :user_id
    remove_column :votes, :user_id
  end
end
```

We'll use this migration to create a brand new users table. Its four columns will hold users' personal information: usernames, passwords, names, and email addresses. Well, the table actually has five columns if you include the automatically created id column.

In addition to creating this new table, we'll insert into each of the existing `stories` and `votes` tables a new column, which will store the `id` of the user who created a particular story or vote, respectively.

While we would normally split migrations into the components that handle small, isolated changes, in this case, it makes sense to group the creation of the `users` table with the modification of the two other tables. We'll keep our schema changes together as one migration, as they're so closely related.

We use the good old `rake` tool to apply the migration we've just written:

```
$ rake db:migrate
```

Figure 8.4 shows the result of a successful migration. We now have in place the database structure necessary to begin writing some code for our `User` model.

Figure 8.4. Applying the migration

Adding Relationships for the User Class

As you've probably gathered from our past endeavors with `ActiveRecord`, a model doesn't require a whole lot of code in order to be functional.

The `User` class is no exception; the only changes we'll make to it now are to specify the relationship between it and our two other models. This will help us keep track of which user submitted a particular story or vote.

Open the `User` class definition, located at `app/models/user.rb`, and modify it as follows:

File: **02-user.rb**

```
class User < ActiveRecord::Base
  has_many :stories
  has_many :votes
end
```

This code sets up a one-to-many relationship between the User class and each of the Story and Vote classes.

As you already know, relationships can (and should) be defined for both of the participating models. So our next step is to add complementary relationship definitions to the Story and Vote classes (located at app/models/story.rb and app/models/vote.rb respectively):

File: **03-story.rb (excerpt)**

```
class Story < ActiveRecord::Base
  belongs_to :user
  ...
end
```

File: **04-vote.rb (excerpt)**

```
class Vote < ActiveRecord::Base
  belongs_to :user
  ...
end
```

These bidirectional relationship definitions allow us to retrieve not only the Vote and Story objects associated with a particular User, but also the User object associated with a particular Story or Vote.

Alright, enough of the architectural building blocks—let's create a user. Then we can start to protect some of our actions from users who haven't logged in.

Creating a User

Creating a User object is no different from creating any other ActiveRecord object. It's easily accomplished from the Rails console (feel free to create an account for yourself, rather than using my name!):

```
>> u = User.new
=> #<User:...>
>> u.name = 'Patrick Lenz'
=> "Patrick Lenz"
>> u.login = 'patrick'
```

```
=> "patrick"
>> u.password = 'sekrit'
=> "sekrit"
>> u.email = 'patrick@lenz.sh'
=> "patrick@lenz.sh"
>> u.save
=> true
```

Implementing Hashed Password Storage

Yes, we *are* using plaintext passwords here. Be sure to implement hashed password storage for yourself before you launch your application to the world though; the `Digest` module[2] that comes bundled with Ruby has the tools for the job.

Developing Login Functionality

In order to handle login and logout actions (and cater for new user registrations down the track), we'll need a second controller to complement our `StoryController`. Once that's in place, we can create some functionality to let users log in and out. It's exciting stuff!

Creating the Controller

We'll name this new controller `AccountController`, and generate it using the generate script, as usual:

```
$ ruby script/generate controller Account login logout
```

Passing the additional `login` and `logout` parameters as arguments to the `generate` script will automatically create blank `login` and `logout` actions in our new `AccountController`. It will also create empty `ActionView` templates in the `app/views/account/` folder, with the names `login.rhtml` and `logout.rhtml`, which saves us a few lines of typing. Figure 8.5 shows the output of the above code.

---

[2] http://www.ruby-doc.org/stdlib/libdoc/digest/rdoc/

Figure 8.5. Generating an `AccountController` class

```
Core:~/shovell scoop$ ruby script/generate controller Account login logout
      exists  app/controllers/
      exists  app/helpers/
      create  app/views/account
      exists  test/functional/
      create  app/controllers/account_controller.rb
      create  test/functional/account_controller_test.rb
      create  app/helpers/account_helper.rb
      create  app/views/account/login.rhtml
      create  app/views/account/logout.rhtml
Core:~/shovell scoop$
```

Creating the View

To better understand what happens when we use extra parameters to generate `ActionView` templates, type http://localhost:3000/account/login into your web browser.

Figure 8.6. The generated login template

The result you see should be similar to Figure 8.6—it's basically a friendly message that lets us know where we can find the template that's being displayed in the browser.

Remember to Start your Server!

As always, to use our Shovell application, you must have the WEBrick web server running. Flip back to Chapter 2 if you need a refresher on this.

Let's modify this template and turn it into an actual login form. As Rails indicates in the browser, the template's located at `app/views/account/login.rhtml`:

File: **05-login.rhtml**

```
<% form_tag do %>
  <p>Please log in.</p>
  <p>
    <label>Username:</label>
    <%= text_field_tag 'login' %>
  </p>
  <p>
    <label>Password:</label>
    <%= password_field_tag 'password' %>
  </p>
  <p><%= submit_tag 'login' %></p>
<% end_form %>
```

Once again, we've created a form using simple HTML markup and a few of the Rails form helpers. This time, our form doesn't deal with a specific model object, so we can't use the `form_for` helper that we used back in Chapter 6. Instead, we use the standard `form_tag` helper that defines the surrounding form with a `do` and `end` block:

```
<% form_tag do %>
  ...
<% end %>
```

This generates the all-important `<form>` and `</form>` HTML tags. To check that they're being created correctly, reload the modified page in your browser and view the source of the page.

The `text_field_tag` and `password_field_tag` helpers generate HTML input elements with `type="text"` and `type="password"` attributes, respectively. These elements will render the text fields into which our visitors will enter their usernames and passwords. The `login` and `password` parameters that we're passing to each of these helpers assigns a name to the HTML tag that's generated; it also causes this value to show up in the `params` hash, which, as we'll see later on, will prove to be very useful.

```
<%= text_field_tag 'login' %>
...
<%= password_field_tag 'password' %>
```

Now that we've put our form in place, we can establish some functionality behind it.

Adding Functionality to the Controller

We're ready to implement the actual login functionality within the login controller action. You'll find the controller class in the file app/controllers/account_controller.rb. Add the following method to this class:

File: **06-account_controller.rb**

```
class AccountController < ApplicationController
  def login
    if request.post?
      @current_user = User.find_by_login_and_password(
        params[:login], params[:password])
      unless @current_user.nil?
        session[:user_id] = @current_user.id
        redirect_to :controller => 'story'
      end
    end
  end
end
```

As Figure 8.7 overleaf shows, we've expanded the previously empty login action to handle circumstances where the user posts information using HTTP POST—which is how a user goes about logging in:

```
if request.post?
  ...
end
```

When handling an HTTP POST request, we attempt to fetch a user using the login and password values that the visitor provided. Notice that we use one of the ActiveRecord dynamic finder methods to do this:

```
@current_user = User.find_by_login_and_password(
    params[:login], params[:password])
```

245

Figure 8.7. The completed login form

![Screenshot of the completed login form in the Shovell application showing a browser at http://localhost:3000/account/login with a Username field containing "patrick" and a masked Password field, and a login button.]

Once we're able to locate a user whose record matches the visitor-entered user-name and password combination, we store within the current visitor's session the `id` of the `User` object that was retrieved. The user is then redirected to the `index` page of the `StoryController`:

```
unless @current_user.nil?
  session[:user_id] = @current_user.id
  redirect_to :controller => 'story'
end
```

ActiveRecord Objects and the Session Container

Be careful when you're storing `ActiveRecord` objects in the session container. `ActiveRecord` objects may change at any time, but the session container won't necessarily be updated to reflect the changes. For example, in our Shovell application, a story object might be viewed by one user, and modified by a second user immediately afterwards. If the entire story was stored in the session container, the first user's session would contain a version of the story that was out of date (and out of sync with the database).

To ensure that this scenario doesn't eventuate, it's best to store only the primary key of the record in question—the value of the `id` column—in the session container. Here's an example:

```
session[:user_id] = myCurrentUser.id
```

On successive page loads, we retrieve the `ActiveRecord` object using the regular `Model.find` method, and pass in the key that was stored in the session container:

```
current_user = User.find session[:user_id]
```

This is all well and good, and if you were to try logging in at http://localhost:3000/account/login using the initial user that we created a few pages back, you would indeed be redirected to the story page. Go on, try it out—it works! Well … sort of.

Since we've stored only the user's `id` in the session container, we need to make sure that we fetch the `User` object for that user before we hand execution control to another controller action. If we failed to fetch the rest of the user's details, we wouldn't be able to display the username of the currently logged-in user—something that we aim to do on every page in our application.

So, before we proceed too much further, let's look at some of the theory behind one of the features of Rails that allows us to execute code globally: filters.

Filters

A **filter** is a function that defines code to be run either before or after a controller's action is executed. Using a filter, we can ensure that a specific chunk of code is rendered no matter which page the user's looking at.

Once we've discussed how filters work, I'll show you how to use one to fetch a `User` object from the database when a user logs in. We'll use another filter to redirect to the login page any anonymous visitors who attempt to access a protected page.

Before Filters

The first type of filter we'll look at is the **before filter**. As you might expect, a before filter executes *before* the code in the controller action is executed.

Like all filters, a before filter is defined in the head of the controller class that calls it. Calling a before filter is as simple as invoking the `before_filter` method and passing it a symbol that represents the method to be executed. The filter can also accept as a parameter a snippet of Ruby code; this code is used as the filter code. However, this practice is discouraged, as it makes for code that is difficult to maintain.

Here's a hypothetical example in which a controller method is called using a symbol:

```
class FooController < ApplicationController
  before_filter :fetch_password
  def fetch_password
    ...
  end
end
```

After Filters

Like a before filter, an **after filter** is defined in the controller class from which it is called. The method to use is appropriately named `after_filter` and, not surprisingly, these filters are executed *after* the controller's action code has been executed. Here's an example:

```
class FooController < ApplicationController
  after_filter :gzip_compression
  def gzip_compression
    ...
  end
end
```

Around Filters

A combination of before and after filters, the **around filter** executes both before *and* after the controller's action code.

In a nutshell, around filters are separate objects that have `before` and `after` methods. These methods are automatically called by the filter framework. Despite being a combination of its simpler siblings, the around filter is significantly more advanced, hence we won't cover it in this book.

A Word on Filter Methods

As we've learned, filters take as a parameter a symbol that represents the controller method to be executed. Consider the hypothetical example of our `FooController` once more:

```
class FooController < ApplicationController
  before_filter :fetch_password
  def fetch_password
    ...
  end
end
```

This all seems fine, until you realize that every method that you implement in a controller can actually be executed directly by a user, using a web browser. For example, in the code listing above, a user would be able to execute the `fetch_password` method of `FooController` simply by visiting http://localhost:3000/foo/fetch_password.

Wait a minute—that's not what we want! The security implications of such an implementation are potentially disastrous, so we definitely want to hide these kinds of methods from the general public.

When we discussed object oriented programming back in Chapter 3, we talked about the interface that an object provides to the outside world—the interface with which other objects can interact. All of the class and instance methods that an object shares this way are called **public methods**, and this is, in fact, the only type of method we've used up to this point.

However, Ruby has two types of methods that are not public: private methods and protected methods.

❏ **Private methods** are available only from within the classes in which they're stored, period. These methods cannot be accessed in any way from another object. In the following example, the keyword `private` signals that all methods that follow it are implemented as private methods.

```
class Formula1Car
  private
  def secret_tuning_option
    ...
  end
end
```

❏ **Protected methods**, like private methods, are unavailable to the outside world. However, a protected method remains available to classes that inherit from the class in which the protected method is defined. For example, in the following code listing, objects of class `FerrariF1` would have access to the

protected method `launch_control`, which is defined in the parent class
`Formula1Car`.

```
class Formula1Car
  protected
  def launch_control
    ...
  end
end
class FerrariF1 < Formula1Car
end
```

The point of all this is that you should *always* implement filter methods as non-
public methods, in order to protect them from being executed independently
from the filtering role for which they were intended. This is exactly what we'll
do now.

Managing User Logins

Okay, we've covered filter theory, so let's modify our application to fetch the
currently logged-in `User` from our database. Once we've done that, we'll display
the user's name on the page, and provide the ability for the user to log out again.

Retrieving the Current User

We're going to use filters to fetch the current user for each and every page of the
Shovell site. That phrase—"each and every page"—should give you a hint as to
where we'll apply the filter. Filters can be inherited from parent classes and, as
we don't want to write numerous filter declarations, we'll stick our filter in the
parent class for all of our controllers: `ApplicationController`.

Methods and filters that are defined in this class are available to all classes that
inherit from `ApplicationController` (located at `app/controllers/applica-
tion.rb`)—which is just what we want:

File: **07-application.rb**

```
class ApplicationController < ActionController::Base
  before_filter :fetch_logged_in_user
  protected
  def fetch_logged_in_user
    return if session[:user_id].blank?
    @current_user = User.find_by_id(session[:user_id])
```

```
    end
end
```

Let's take a look at each of the lines that make up the `fetch_logged_in_user` method:

```
    return if session[:user_id].blank?
```

This line is fairly straightforward. There's no point retrieving a `User` object if the user hasn't logged in yet—we can simply exit the filter method without executing the rest of the code.

The next line tries to fetch from the database a `User` object with an `id` that's equal to the `id` stored in the visitor's session container:

```
    @current_user = User.find_by_id session[:user_id]
```

The fetched object will be assigned to the instance variable `@current_user`, which will then become available to actions in our controller as well as our views.

We've purposely used the `find_by_id` method here, rather than `find`, even though on the surface it appears that the two would produce the same results. In fact, `find` displays an error if it can't retrieve a record that matches the `id` that's passed to it, while `find_by_id` exits more gracefully. It's conceivable that a user may revisit our site after his or her account has been deleted (perhaps because the user submitted the same boring stories over and over again), so we need to make sure the application will handle these cases in a user-friendly manner. Spitting out a bunch of technical-looking errors is not the solution we're looking for—hence our use of `find_by_id`.

Session Security Revisited

As we saw earlier, the value of `session[:user_id]` is not stored in the user's web browser. This means that a user can't, for example, impersonate another user by simply changing the contents of his or her session.

The only way that a user could circumvent the security measures that we've put in place so far would be either to guess the session ID, or to identify it using a brute force attack[3] ... that is, apart from grabbing another user's laptop while he's in the bathroom!

---

[3] A brute force attack involves looping through a list of every possible combination of alphanumeric characters (or sometimes a list of dictionary-based passwords) until a matching phrase is found.

As we're using a randomized string of 32 hexadecimal characters for our session ID, it's not impossible that a malicious user could gain another user's `id` using either of these approaches, but it's certainly highly unlikely.

Our next task will be to display the name of the current user in the global application layout.

Displaying the Name of the Current User

Since we're requiring that our users log in just once to access the entire application, let's add to our global application layout (the file located at `app/views/layouts/application.rhtml`) some code that will display the name of the currently logged-in user. Make the following changes to this file:

File: **08-application.rhtml (excerpt)**

```
<div id="content">
  <div id="login_logout">
    <% unless @current_user.blank? %>
      Logged in as:
      <%= @current_user.login %>
      <em><%= link_to "(Logout)",
              :controller => 'account',
              :action => 'logout' %></em>
    <% else %>
      <em>Not logged in.</em>
      <%= link_to 'Login',
          :controller => 'account',
          :action => 'login' %>
    <% end %>
  </div>
  <h1>Shovell</h1>
  ...
```

Let's step through these changes. Using a simple `unless` condition, we display a link to the action that's most appropriate, based on the user's login status:

```
<% unless @current_user.blank? %>
```

The condition checks whether the instance variable `@current_user` is `blank`—remember that a blank value means the variable contains either an empty string (`""`) or `nil`.

Once we've made sure that the user is actually logged in, we display the user's name along with a link to an action named `logout`, which we'll add to the

`AccountController` in a moment. We wrap the link in an `<em>` tag to make it stand out a little:

```
Logged in as:
<%= @current_user.login %>
<em><%= link_to "(Logout)",
    :controller => 'account',
    :action => 'logout' %></em>
```

If a visitor is *not* logged in, we display a link that the user can follow to the login form:

```
<%= link_to 'Login',
    :controller => 'account',
    :action => 'login' %>
```

To make the page look a little nicer, let's add a snippet of CSS to the global style sheet that's located at `public/stylesheets/styles.css`:

File: **09-styles.css (excerpt)**

```
#login_logout {
  float: right;
  color: #999;
  font-size: smaller;
}
```

This code dims the text colors a little, floats the container to the right, and makes the font size a little smaller. If you reload the page after logging in, you should see the results shown in Figure 8.8. That's much better!

Figure 8.8. Displaying the current user

Next, we'll implement the logout functionality.

Allowing Users to Log Out

Providing our users with a manual logout function is much more user-friendly than forcing them to close their browsers to log out. We'll add this method to our `AccountController` class, located in `app/controllers/account_controller.rb`:

File: **10-account_controller.rb (excerpt)**

```
class AccountController < ApplicationController
  ...
  def logout
    session[:user_id] = @current_user = nil
  end
end
```

Logging a user out of the application is a matter of setting two variables to `nil`:

❑ the `user_id` that's stored in the user's session

❑ the instance variable that holds the current user

```
    session[:user_id] = @current_user = nil
```

This line of code prevents our before filter (the `fetch_logged_in_user` method) from retrieving anything from the database. As we're setting both the current user *and* the user `id` stored in the session to `nil`, no more `User` objects for this user remain in memory. The user has therefore been logged out of the system.

I've taken this opportunity to introduce another piece of shorthand syntax that's used often in Ruby code: what we've done here is assign `nil` to two variables at once. Strictly speaking, we're assigning the result of the statement `@current_user = nil` (which happens to be `nil`) to `session[:user_id]`.

With that code in place, adding a simple message to `app/views/account/logout.rhtml` will confirm for the user that the logout was successful:

File: **11-logout.rhtml**

```
<h2>Logout successful</h2>
<%= link_to 'Back to the story index', :controller => 'story' %>
```

Let's check that this all works as we expect. Click that (Logout) link in the top right-hand corner of the page—if everything goes to plan you should be logged out of the application and presented with a page like the one shown in Figure 8.9.

Additionally, the username that was previously displayed in the upper right-hand corner should not be present on any successive page that you visit—you should see a Login link instead.

Figure 8.9. Successfully logging out of the application

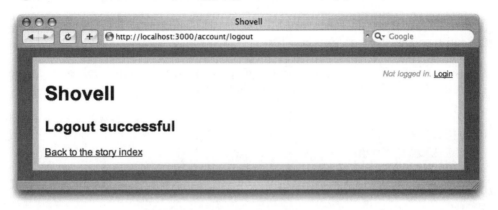

Now that users are able to log in and out of the application, we're in a position to make certain actions available only to logged in users. However, before we begin to make these additions, let's add to our site an element that has been sorely lacking so far: navigation.

Adding a Navigation Menu

You're probably getting a little tired of typing http://localhost:3000/story/new over and over again. Let's create a little navigation menu at the bottom of every page, so that we can move easily between the different pages we've created.

To do so, modify the file `app/views/layouts/application.rhtml`. Right above the closing `</body>` tag at the bottom of the file, place the following unordered list, which contains our navigation menu:

File: **12-application.rhtml (excerpt)**

```
...
<ul id="navigation">
  <li><%= link_to 'Front page stories',
          :controller => 'story' %></li>
  <li><%= link_to 'Submit a new story!',
          :controller => 'story', :action => 'new' %></li>
</ul>
```

```
</body>
</html>
```

We've got two links in our menu at this point:

❏ a link to the story index (which currently displays a random story from the pool)

❏ a link to the story submission form

As usual, we'll also expand our style sheet to make the menu look pretty. The results of these additions are shown in Figure 8.10:

File: **13-styles.css (excerpt)**

```css
#navigation {
  list-style: none;
  padding: 5px 0;
  margin: 0;
  text-align: center;
}
#navigation li {
  display: inline;
  padding: 0 5px;
}
#navigation li a {
  color: #fff;
}
```

Figure 8.10. Story index with navigation

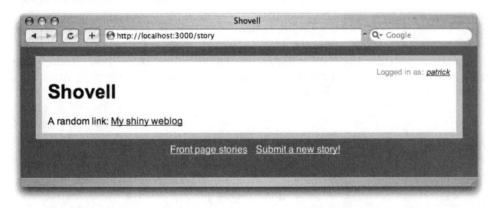

That's much better. With the navigation in place, moving around within our application becomes a lot easier.

Restricting the Application

All this login functionality would be wasted if a guest to our site had access to the same feature set enjoyed by our registered users—what would be the point in logging in?

Now that our login functionality is working, we can restrict certain parts of the application from use by anonymous guests and users who have not logged in.

Protecting the Form

The first action that will benefit from protection is the submission of stories. While we're adding this protection, we'll also check that when a new story is submitted, the application correctly saves the reference to the User who submitted it (as we defined in the relationship between a User and a Story).

The first step we need to take is to figure out how to intercept a request that comes from a user who's not currently logged in to our application. Once we've achieved this, we can direct the visitor to a login form instead of the story submission form. This sounds like a perfect job for a before filter, doesn't it?

Ultimately, our application is likely to consist of more controllers than the two we've created so far, so we'll add our new filter code to the global `ApplicationController` class. This will mean that the filter is available for use by any of the controllers in our application.

The filter will be called `login_required`, which is suitably descriptive. As we're going to check from a few different places in our application whether or not a user is logged in, we'll extract this code into a separate controller method before we create our new filter. (Writing `@current_user.blank?` is becoming a bit tedious, anyway.)

Abstracting Code Using `helper_method`

The reason we're placing this functionality into a controller method (rather than creating a regular helper for it) is that the functionality it provides is useful to both controllers and views. However, regular helpers are available only to views, and controller methods are available only to controllers. We need some sort of magic bridge to make this controller method available to our views.

This magic bridge happens to be the `helper_method` statement, which makes regular controller methods available to views as if they were regular helper methods. We'll add this snippet to the `protected` area of our `ApplicationController` (in `app/controllers/application.rb`):

File: **14-application.rb (excerpt)**

```
...
protected
def fetch_logged_in_user
  ...
end
def logged_in?
  ! @current_user.blank?
end
helper_method :logged_in?
end
```

Here, we've pulled our check of the current user's login status into a new method called `logged_in?`. With the additional call to `helper_method`, we can now use `logged_in?` throughout our application to replace any usage of `@current_user.blank?`.

Requiring Users to Log In

While we're looking at our `ApplicationController`, let's add the `login_required` filter to it—this marks the first use of our new `logged_in?` helper method:

File: **15-application.rb (excerpt)**

```
def login_required
  return true if logged_in?
  session[:return_to] = request.request_uri
  redirect_to :controller => "/account", :action => "login" and
    return false
end
```

Let's break this code down. The first line of the filter exits the method with the value `true` if the user is already logged in:

```
return true if logged_in?
```

However, if the `logged_in?` helper method returns `false`, we need to:

1. Prepare to redirect the user to a location at which he or she can log in.

2. Remember where the user came from, so we can send the person back to that page once the login is complete.

To store the current URL, we grab it from the `request` object and add it to the user's session, so that we can retrieve it later:

```
session[:return_to] = request.request_uri
```

Next, we redirect the user to the `login` action of `AccountController`, and return `false`:[4]

```
redirect_to :controller => "/account", :action => "login" and
    return false
```

A return value of `false` is crucial here, because a filter that returns `false` halts the processing of any subsequent filters and exits the current controller method.

Right! Now that the form's protected, it's time to restrict access to the application's story submission capabilities to users who are logged in.

Restricting Access to Story Submission

While we don't want to let anonymous visitors submit new stories to our site, we want them to be able to view stories. This situation—restricting user access to certain specific actions—is the perfect opportunity to use a filter condition.

Introducing Filter Conditions

A **filter condition** is simply a parameter that's passed to a filter, and specifies how the filter is applied. The parameter can control whether the filter is applied to either:

❏ every method *except* those listed

❏ *only* the actions listed

---

[4] The **and** keyword that's used here is in fact optional: the logic of this method would be identical if the **return** was placed on its own line. However, using **and** in this case adds to the readability of our code—and code that is more readable is more maintainable.

In this case, the `:only` parameter is the best way for us to restrict a single action.

Let's apply the `login_required` filter to the top of our `StoryController` class, which is located at `app/controllers/story_controller.rb`. The `:only` parameter accepts a symbol (or list of symbols) that represents the methods to which it should be applied.

File: **16-story_controller.rb (excerpt)**

```
class StoryController < ApplicationController
  before_filter :login_required, :only => :new
  def index
  ...
```

There, that was easy! However, we've yet to make use of that `:return_to` URL that we stored in the user's session on the previous page. Let's put it to work next.

Redirecting the User

The part of our application that redirects users after they've successfully logged in is the `login` method of the `AccountController` class, which is located in `app/controllers/account_controller.rb`.

Let's modify the redirection code to specify the location to which a user is redirected based on whether or not the user's session actually contains a `:return_to` URL. The changes that you'll need to make are listed in bold:

File: **17-account_controller.rb (excerpt)**

```
def login
  ...
  unless @current_user.nil?
    session[:user_id] = @current_user.nil?
    unless session[:return_to].blank?
      redirect_to session[:return_to]
      session[:return_to] = nil
    else
      redirect_to :controller => 'story'
    end
  end
  ...
```

The aspect of this code that's really worth a mention is the fact that we're resetting the `:return_to` URL to `nil` after a successful redirect—there's no point in carrying around old baggage.

Now, fire up your web browser and execute the following steps to test out this new feature:

1. Log out of the application if you're currently logged in.

2. Click the Submit a new story! link, and confirm in your browser's address bar that you are redirected to /account/login.

3. Log in using the login form, and verify that you're redirected back to the story submission form.

All good? Great!

Associating Stories with Users

The last enhancement that we'll add in this chapter is to associate a story with the ID of the user who submitted it. This will give us a record of who submitted what to Shovell.

Storing the Submitter

As we established the association between stories and user ids at the beginning of this chapter, we simply need to tell Rails *what* we want to store. Add the following line to the new action of the StoryController, located at app/controllers/story_controller.rb:

File: **18-story_controller.rb (excerpt)**

```
def new
  @story = Story.new(params[:story])
  @story.user = @current_user
  ...
end
```

It's as simple as that! We know that the currently logged-in user is stored in @current_user, because we set it using the fetch_logged_in_user before filter. And I hope you'll remember from Chapter 7 that referencing an associated object is as simple as treating the referenced object like an attribute, just as we've done here:

```
@story.user = @current_user
```

But what good is storing information if we're not going to display it somewhere? You guessed it—displaying the submitter's details is our next task.

Displaying the Submitter

Lastly, we'll modify each story's display page to show the name of the user who submitted it. This page corresponds to the `show` action of our `StoryController` class, the template for which is located at `app/views/story/show.rhtml`:

File: **19-show.rhtml (excerpt)**

```
<ul id="vote_history">
  ...
</ul>
<p class="submitted_by">
  Submitted by:
  <span><%= @story.user.login %></span>
</p>
```

Here we're using `@story.user` to fetch the user object that's associated with the currently displayed story. We then display the value of the user's `login` attribute to produce the result shown in Figure 8.11:

```
<span><%= @story.user.login %></span>
```

Data Integrity in Development

One of the down-sides of using an iterative approach to development is that our data is not necessarily complete at each stage of the development process. For example, unless you've specifically added values of `user_id` and `permalink` to every `Story` object in your database, you're probably seeing the odd page error. You could use any of three approaches to rectify this issue:

1. Manually add the missing values to your objects from the Rails console, remembering to use the `save` method so that the value is stored permanently.

2. If you're comfortable writing basic SQL commands, update the values using the MySQL Query Browser.

3. Delete all data in your database (either via the Rails console or the MySQL Query Browser), and begin to add your data from scratch via the application.

We need only two or three objects at this stage of development, so none of these options should be too onerous for you.

Figure 8.11. The name of a story's submitter displays with the story

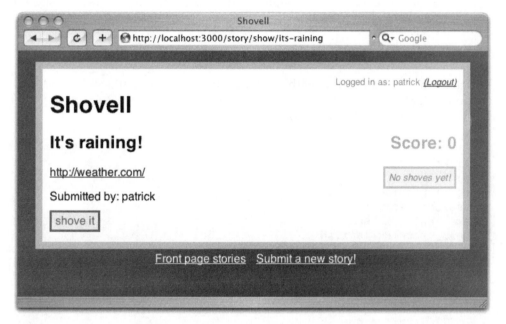

We've accomplished quite a lot in this chapter, both in theory and in code. Being professional Rails coders, our next step is to add tests for all of these cool features.

Testing User Authentication

To develop our testing suite, we'll create unit tests to cover changes to the application's model, followed by functional tests for each of our controllers.

Testing the Model

We haven't extended our models much in this chapter, so our unit tests will be fairly straightforward. Basically, all we've done is:

❑ Create a new model (User).

❑ Add a relationship between the User and Story model.

❏ Add a relationship between the `User` and `Vote` model.

Before we can write any tests, though, we need to make sure that our test data is up to date.

Preparing the Fixtures

The `User` model didn't come with very meaningful fixture data, so let's address that now. Replace the contents of the model's fixture file (located at `test/fix-tures/users.yml`) with the following data:

File: **20-users.yml**

```
patrick:
  id: 1
  login: patrick
  password: sekrit
  name: Patrick Lenz
  email: patrick@lenz.sh
john:
  id: 2
  login: john
  password: gh752px
  name: John Doe
  email: john@doe.com
```

To test the associations between the three models properly, we'll also need to modify the fixtures for both our `Story` and `Vote` models. Only a small change is required—the addition of some data for the `user_id` attribute that we inserted at the start of this chapter.

Make the following changes in `test/fixtures/stories.yml`:

File: **21-stories.yml (excerpt)**

```
first:
  …
  user_id: 1
second:
  …
  user_id: 1
```

And make these alterations in `test/fixtures/votes.yml`:

File: **22-votes.yml** (excerpt)

```
first:
  ...
  user_id: 1
second:
  ...
  user_id: 2
```

Now that our fixtures contain appropriate data, we can start writing some unit tests.

Testing a User's Relationship to a Story

The unit tests for our User belong in test/unit/user_test.rb. First we'll test the relationship between a User and a Story. Make the following changes to this file:

File: **23-user_test.rb** (excerpt)

```
class UserTest < Test::Unit::TestCase
  fixtures :users, :stories, :votes
  def test_stories_association
    assert_equal 2, users(:patrick).stories.size
    assert_equal stories(:first), users(:patrick).stories.first
  end
end
```

The first thing that we're doing here is incorporating all of the fixtures that are required for our tests, including the users and stories fixtures, as well as the votes fixture data that we just created.

```
  fixtures :users, :stories, :votes
```

We use two assertions to test the association between the Story and User models. The first assertion confirms that the total number of Story objects associated with the user patrick is indeed 2:

```
    assert_equal 2, users(:patrick).stories.size
```

The second assertion identifies whether or not the first Story associated with patrick is the first Story object in our fixture file.

```
    assert_equal stories(:first), users(:patrick).stories.first
```

With this test in place, let's add a test for the inverse of this relationship.

Testing a Story's Relationship to a User

By now, you're no doubt very familiar with the directory and file naming conventions we're using. The complementary unit test for the relationship between a User and a Story tests the Story's relationship to a User, and belongs in `test/unit/story_test.rb`. Make the following changes to this file:

File: **24-story_test.rb (excerpt)**

```
class StoryTest < Test::Unit::TestCase
  fixtures :stories, :votes, :users

  ...

  def test_user_association
    assert_equal users(:patrick), stories(:first).user
  end
end
```

The assertion we've written here simply confirms that the user associated with the first story is the user we expect, based on our fixture data (that is, `patrick`):

```
assert_equal users(:patrick), stories(:first).user
```

Let's add some similar tests for the other relationship that our User model has—its relationship with a Vote.

Testing a User's Relationship to a Vote

While we haven't yet added anything to our application's user interface to store or display the details of users associated with votes, we've put the infrastructure in place to do so. For this reason, we can test the relationship between a User and a Vote using a very similar approach to that which we took with the unit tests we created for the relationship between a Story and a User.

To test a User's relationship to a Vote, add the following test to `test/unit/user_test.rb`:

File: **25-user_test.rb (excerpt)**

```
  ...
  def test_votes_association
    assert_equal 1, users(:patrick).votes.size
    assert_equal votes(:second), users(:john).votes.first
  end
end
```

The first assertion compares the number of `Vote` objects associated with a test user with the number of votes that the same user was assigned in our fixture data:

```
assert_equal 1, users(:patrick).votes.size
```

The second assertion makes sure that the first `Vote` object associated with the user `john` matches our fixture data:

```
assert_equal votes(:second), users(:john).votes.first
```

Excellent! Only one more unit test to write: a test for the inverse of this relationship.

Testing a Vote's Relationship to a User

The test that confirms a `Vote`'s relationship to a `User` belongs in `test/unit/vote_test.rb`. Add the following test to this file:

File: **26-vote_test.rb (excerpt)**

```
class VoteTest < Test::Unit::TestCase
  fixtures :votes, :stories, :users

  ...
  def test_user_association
    assert_equal users(:john), votes(:second).user
  end
end
```

This last test confirms that the user associated with the second vote of a story is indeed the second user who voted for the story, as defined by our fixture data.

Keeping the Test Schema up to Date

You might be wondering how migrations are applied to the test database on which we're running our tests (as you'll recall, this database is quite separate from the development database to which our migrations are applied).

Rails is smart enough to figure out that testing should occur on a database with a structure that's identical to the one used for development. So Rails clones the structure of your development database, and applies it to the test database every time you execute your unit or functional tests.

Should you ever need to complete this cloning process manually, use this `rake` task:

```
$ rake db:test:clone_structure
```

Running the Unit Tests

We can now run our updated suite of unit tests using the following code, the results of which are shown in Figure 8.12:

```
$ rake test:units
```

Figure 8.12. Results expected from execution of the unit tests

```
Core:~/shovell scoop$ rake test:units
(in /Users/mattymcg/shovell)
/opt/local/bin/ruby -Ilib:test "/opt/local/lib/ruby/gems/1.8/gems/rake-0.7.1/lib
/rake/rake_test_loader.rb" "test/unit/story_test.rb" "test/unit/user_test.rb" "t
est/unit/vote_test.rb"
Loaded suite /opt/local/lib/ruby/gems/1.8/gems/rake-0.7.1/lib/rake/rake_test_loa
der
Started
...........
Finished in 0.284403 seconds.

11 tests, 13 assertions, 0 failures, 0 errors
Core:~/shovell scoop$
```

Testing the Controllers

The majority of the functional code that we wrote in this chapter was in the `AccountController`, although we also made a few changes to the `StoryController`. Consequently, we have quite a few tests to write to ensure that all of this new functionality is covered.

Testing the Display of the Login Form

The first test we'll add to our functional test file (`test/functional/account_controller_test.rb`) is a simple HTTP GET operation that looks for the display of our login form:

File: **account_controller_test.rb** (excerpt)
```
class AccountControllerTest < Test::Unit::TestCase
  fixtures :users
  ...
  def test_should_show_login_form
```

```
    get :login
    assert_response :success
    assert_template 'login'
    assert_select 'form p', 4
  end
end
```

There's not too much here that we haven't encountered before: the addition of the users fixture ensures that we have proper sample data located in the test database when the tests are run. The test itself asserts that:

❑ The page request was successful.

❑ The page is rendered with the template we expect.

❑ A form tag is contained in the result, with four <p> tags nested below it.

Testing a Successful Login

The following test, to be added to the same file, will attempt an actual login:

File: **27-account_controller_test.rb (excerpt)**

```
...
def test_should_perform_user_login
  post :login, :login => 'patrick', :password => 'sekrit'
  assert_redirected_to :controller => 'story'
  assert_equal users(:patrick).id, session[:user_id]
  assert_equal users(:patrick), assigns(:current_user)
end
end
```

Let's look at each line of this test in more detail.

As was the case when we tested the submission of stories, in this test, we need to pass additional arguments to the login action—values for the login and password parameters.

```
    post :login, :login => 'patrick', :password => 'sekrit'
```

The values we've used here match the values in our users.yml fixture file—if you added your own user to that file, you'll need to change this test accordingly.

If you think about how our login method works, you'll recall that we redirect users after they've logged in successfully. However, the URL to which a user is redirected varies depending on whether or not the user's session contains a URL. In this test, the user's session is empty, so we expect the user to be sent to the story page. The `assert_redirected_to` method comes in handy here:

```
assert_redirected_to :controller => 'story'
```

Lastly, a successful login means that:

☐ The `id` of the user will be stored in the user's session.

☐ The instance variable `@current_user` will be set.

Within the test, we have access to the session of the hypothetical user who just logged in, so we can compare both the session value and the instance variable with the corresponding details that we set for the user in our fixture data:

```
assert_equal users(:patrick).id, session[:user_id]
assert_equal users(:patrick), assigns(:current_user)
```

In a perfect world, this would be the last of the tests that we need to write. However, in the real world, not every login attempt is successful.

Testing a Failed Login

Login attempts fail for various reasons—users may type their passwords incorrectly, or try to guess someone else's login details. When a login attempt fails, the application should not reveal any content that's intended for users who have logged in. As such, login failures need to be tested too!

Here's the test:

File: **28-account_controller_test.rb (excerpt)**

```
def test_should_fail_user_login
  post :login, :login => 'no such', :password => 'user'
  assert_response :success
  assert_template 'login'
  assert_nil session[:user_id]
end
```

If a user tries to log in to our application using a non-existent user name, the login form should redisplay. Our first assertion confirms that the page loads correctly, while the second assertion verifies that the page uses the `login` template:

```
assert_response :success
assert_template 'login'
```

The last assertion checks the `user_id` value that's stored in the user's session, to make sure it's `nil`:

```
assert_nil session[:user_id]
```

Okay, we've tested all our code that relates to our login procedures. But what happens *after* a user logs in?

Testing Redirection After Login

To trial the redirection of a user who logs in to his or her original destination, we'll add a test that populates the `return_to` value within the user's session before he or she logs in.

File: **29-account_controller_test.rb (excerpt)**

```
def test_should_redirect_after_login_with_return_url
  post :login, { :login => 'patrick', :password => 'sekrit' },
      :return_to => '/story/new'
  assert_redirected_to '/story/new'
end
```

Aside from the fact that we explicitly test for redirection to the story submission URL, this test is identical to the regular login test that we wrote earlier.

Testing a Logout

The last part of the `AccountController` that we need to test is the `logout` action. To emulate a user logging out, we actually need to create something that resembles an integration test. Why? Because before we can log out, we need to log in:

File: **30-account_controller_test.rb (excerpt)**

```
def test_should_logout_and_clear_session
  post :login, :login => 'patrick', :password => 'sekrit'
  assert_not_nil assigns(:current_user)
  assert_not_nil session[:user_id]

  get :logout
  assert_response :success
  assert_template 'logout'
  assert_select 'h2', 'Logout successful'
```

```
    assert_nil assigns(:current_user)
    assert_nil session[:user_id]
  end
```

This test is longer than most of our previous tests, but with the number of tests that you have under your belt at this stage, you should be able to comprehend each line without much trouble.

The first thing we do is make sure that variables such as the `@current_user` instance variable and the `user_id` stored in the session are populated before the user logs out:

```
    assert_not_nil assigns(:current_user)
    assert_not_nil session[:user_id]
```

If we don't take this step, we can't guarantee that the `logout` action is really doing its job.

The crux of this test lies in its last two lines:

```
    assert_nil session[:user_id]
    assert_nil assigns(:current_user)
```

Here we're confirming that the all-important variables that we populated when the user logged in are set to `nil` once the user has logged out.

Whew, that was quite a number of tests! We're not done with functional testing just yet, though. Grab a cup of coffee before tackling the rest of the functional tests, in which we'll be testing the changes we've made to our `StoryController` and `ApplicationController` classes.

Testing the Display of the Story Submitter

To test that the name of the user who submitted a story is displayed correctly on a story's page, we first require a user to be logged in. The following test should do the trick—add it to `test/functional/story_controller_test.rb` (and don't forget to add a call to our new fixture file at the top of the class definition while you're at it):

File: **31-story_controller_test.rb (excerpt)**

```
class StoryControllerTest < Test::Unit::TestCase
  fixtures :stories, :votes, :users
  …
  def test_should_show_story_submitter
```

```
      get :show, :permalink => 'my-shiny-weblog'
      assert_select 'p.submitted_by span', 'patrick'
  end
end
```

We've seen all this before—confirming that an element that contains our submitter's name is present is simply a matter of scanning the HTML code for a p element of class submitted_by, which contains the name of the submitter inside a span.

Testing the Display of Global Elements

To test the global elements that we added to the application.rhtml layout file, we'll add two tests. For the sake of convenience, both tests will utilize the index action of our StoryController:

File: **32-story_controller_test.rb (excerpt)**

```
def test_should_indicate_not_logged_in
  get :index
  assert_select 'div#login_logout em', 'Not logged in.'
end

def test_should_show_navigation_menu
  get :index
  assert_select 'ul#navigation li', 2
end
```

We've covered these assert_select statements several times already, so I won't bore you by going through them again. Instead, let's move on to test that our Shovell application displays the name of the logged-in user at the top of every page.

Testing Display of the Username

The div element in the top right of the browser window displays the name of the user who's currently logged in. We've checked the contents of this element when a user *hasn't* logged in; we still need to add a test to check whether the login has been successful.

Before we do so, though, let's add to our test case two methods that will make the authoring of this test (and others related to it) a whole lot easier:

File: **33-story_controller_test.rb** (excerpt)

```ruby
class StoryControllerTest < Test::Unit::TestCase
  ...
  protected
  def get_with_user(action, parameters = nil, session = nil,
                    flash = nil)
    get action, parameters, :user_id => users(:patrick).id
  end
  def post_with_user(action, parameters = nil, session = nil,
                     flash = nil)
    post action, parameters, :user_id => users(:patrick).id
  end
end
```

As you can see above, the utility methods wrap `get` or `post` calls with a session container that contains the `id` of a logged-in user. Using this approach, we can test an action that was previously only available to users who were logged in, just by calling `get_with_user` or `post_with_user`. Using these methods will eliminate the need to worry about parameters each time we call `get` or `post`.

These utility methods take the same arguments as the original `get` and `post` methods provided by Rails, so they replace our original methods seamlessly. It is, of course, possible to make these utilities much more sophisticated than we've done here, but they'll serve us well for now.

Let's see them in action! Before that little detour, we were on the way to writing a test that confirms the contents of the `login_logout` div. These contents should include a (Logout) link as well as the user's name, which is set by our before filter, `fetch_logged_in_user`:

File: **34-story_controller_test.rb** (excerpt)

```ruby
def test_should_indicate_logged_in_user
  get_with_user :index
  assert_equal users(:patrick), assigns(:current_user)
  assert_select 'div#login_logout em a', '(Logout)'
end
```

Using our new utility method, `get_with_user`, to simulate a logged in user, requesting the `index` action of our `StoryController` class is a no-brainer:

```ruby
get_with_user :index
```

Once we've gained access to the index page, it's easy to use some assertions (of which we're now absolute masters!) to confirm that the contents of the `div` are as we expected.

Testing Redirection After Logout

Our next few tests will cover the changes that we made to the `new` action of our `StoryController`.

First, we'll check that a user who isn't logged in is correctly redirected to the login page if he or she tries to access our story submission form:

File: **35-story_controller_test.rb (excerpt)**

```
def test_should_redirect_if_not_logged_in
  get :new
  assert_response :redirect
  assert_redirected_to '/account/login'
end
```

This is a pretty straightforward test—the `get` statement tries to request the story submission form without logging in first:

```
get :new
```

The remainder of the test confirms that the request results in the user being redirected to the `login` action of our `AccountController`:

```
assert_response :redirect
assert_redirected_to '/account/login'
```

Our test suite is certainly expanding. We have just two more tests to write in this chapter!

Testing Story Submission

If you've been particularly eager, and tried executing your functional test suite prematurely, you'll have noticed that a few tests that worked previously now fail. These failures occur because we modified our story submission form—it requires that a `user_id` is present in the session before a page request can be successful. Our old tests didn't account for this change, so they now fail.

We need to modify the four tests that are affected, so that each of them includes a user id in the session. At this point, it should become obvious that it was well worth the effort for us to create the `get_with_user` and `post_with_user` utility methods:

File: **36-story_controller_test.rb (excerpt)**

```ruby
class StoryControllerTest < Test::Unit::TestCase
  ...
  def test_should_show_new
    get_with_user :new
    ...
  end

  def test_should_show_new_form
    get_with_user :new
    ...
  end

  def test_should_add_story
    post_with_user :new, :story => {
      ...
    }
    ...
  end
  def test_should_reject_missing_story_attribute
    post_with_user :new, :story => {
      ...
    }
    ...
  end
end
```

As you can see, the changes are very small—the method that performs the request in each of the tests is modified from `get` and `post` to `get_with_user` and `post_with_user`, respectively.

Testing Storage of the Submitter

The last test we'll add checks that the user who's currently logged in is correctly associated with any stories that he or she submits:

File: **37-story_controller_test.rb (excerpt)**

```ruby
def test_should_store_user_with_story
  post_with_user :new, :story => {
    :name => 'story with user',
    :link => 'http://www.story-with-user.com/'
  }
```

```
    assert_equal users(:patrick), assigns(:story).user
  end
```

Excellent. If you've made it this far, you're probably itching to see the results of executing our rapidly expanding test suite.

Running the Full Test Suite

Run the full test suite with our trusty `rake` tool. If everything has gone well, you should see results similar to Figure 8.13:

```
$ rake test
```

Figure 8.13. Running the test suite

```
Core:~/shovell scoop$ rake test
(in /Users/scoop/Desktop/railsbook/code)
/opt/local/bin/ruby -Ilib:test "/opt/local/lib/ruby/gems/1.8/gems/rake-0.7.1/lib
/rake/rake_test_loader.rb" "test/unit/story_test.rb" "test/unit/user_test.rb" "t
est/unit/vote_test.rb"
Loaded suite /opt/local/lib/ruby/gems/1.8/gems/rake-0.7.1/lib/rake/rake_test_loa
der
Started
...........
Finished in 0.224811 seconds.

13 tests, 15 assertions, 0 failures, 0 errors
/opt/local/bin/ruby -Ilib:test "/opt/local/lib/ruby/gems/1.8/gems/rake-0.7.1/lib
/rake/rake_test_loader.rb" "test/functional/account_controller_test.rb" "test/fu
nctional/story_controller_test.rb"
Loaded suite /opt/local/lib/ruby/gems/1.8/gems/rake-0.7.1/lib/rake/rake_test_loa
der
Started
.....................
Finished in 0.501743 seconds.

21 tests, 55 assertions, 0 failures, 0 errors
/opt/local/bin/ruby -Ilib:test "/opt/local/lib/ruby/gems/1.8/gems/rake-0.7.1/lib
/rake/rake_test_loader.rb"
Core:~/shovell scoop$
```

If any of your tests failed, the error message that's displayed should help you to determine where things went wrong. The error will direct you to the location of the erroneous class and method, and the exact line number within that method. And before you pull your hair out, remember that you can double-check your code against the code archive for this book—it went through considerable testing before release, so you can count on the code in it to work!

Even more rewarding than seeing the number of tests and assertions that our test suite now covers is to take a look at the output of the **stats** task. This command displays a number of statistics relating to the architecture of our application, including the ratio of lines of application code to lines of test code. We've been extremely busy writing tests in this chapter, so let's see the results:

$ rake stats

My application reports a ratio of 1:2.4, as Figure 8.14 indicates.

Figure 8.14. The current test-to-code ratio

```
● ● ●                Terminal — bash — 80x20
Core:~/shovell scoop$ rake stats
(in /Users/mattymcg/shovell)
+----------------------+-------+-------+---------+---------+-----+-------+
| Name                 | Lines |  LOC  | Classes | Methods | M/C | LOC/M |
+----------------------+-------+-------+---------+---------+-----+-------+
| Helpers              |     7 |     6 |       0 |       0 |   0 |     0 |
| Controllers          |    75 |    63 |       3 |       9 |   3 |     5 |
| Components           |     0 |     0 |       0 |       0 |   0 |     0 |
|     Functional tests |   180 |   148 |       4 |      27 |   6 |     3 |
| Models               |    16 |    16 |       3 |       1 |   0 |    14 |
|     Unit tests       |    69 |    54 |       3 |      11 |   3 |     2 |
| Libraries            |     0 |     0 |       0 |       0 |   0 |     0 |
|     Integration tests|     0 |     0 |       0 |       0 |   0 |     0 |
+----------------------+-------+-------+---------+---------+-----+-------+
| Total                |   347 |   287 |      13 |      48 |   3 |     3 |
+----------------------+-------+-------+---------+---------+-----+-------+
  Code LOC: 85    Test LOC: 202    Code to Test Ratio: 1:2.4

Core:~/shovell scoop$ ▌
```

Wow! That means we've written more than twice the amount of code to test our application than we've written for Shovell itself. This is a good thing! It means that we can be confident that our application is high quality.

Summary

In this chapter, we explored an approach for sectioning off the parts of a Rails application, so that some features are available to everyone and others are available only to users who have logged in.

First, we discussed some theory about sessions and cookies. We then created a new model—the User—and built a login form that allows users to log in to Shovell. We stored the login functionality in a new AccountController class, which made extensive use of the session container. The end result was that we were able to restrict access to the story submission form to users who were logged in, and direct other visitors to the login form. And to top things off, we verified that the changes to our code are free of bugs by writing a number of tests.

The next chapter, in which we'll add the last of the features to our Shovell application, will cover more complex ActiveRecord associations. Though things are getting more advanced, we'll keep moving through each task step by step, so don't be nervous. Let's add the finishing touches to Shovell!

Advanced Topics

As we enter the final section of this book, we'll implement the last of the features that we listed back in Chapter 1, in preparation for Shovell's much-anticipated first release.

Along the way, we'll cover some of the more advanced topics that are involved in developing web applications with Ruby on Rails, such as writing your own helpers, using callbacks, and creating complex associations.

Promoting Popular Stories

To start this chapter, we'll make a change to the way our users view our application. We'll separate the display of our stories into two pages: one for stories with a score *above* a certain threshold, and one for stories with a score *below* the threshold. This will encourage readers to "shove" stories to the front page by voting for them. This functionality will replace the story randomizer that currently appears on the `index` page of our `StoryController`—it's getting a little boring and doesn't really meet the needs of our application.

However, before we can start hacking away at these new pages, we need to refine our existing models a little. In particular, we need an easy way to select stories on the basis of their voting scores.

Using a Counter Cache

We've already seen how we can count the number of votes associated with a given story by calling the `size` method on the associated `Vote` object:

```
>> Story.find(:first).votes.size
=> 3
```

Behind the scenes, this snippet performs two separate SQL queries. The first query fetches the first story from the `stories` table; the second query counts the number of `Votes` whose `story_id` attributes are equal to the `id` of the `Story` object in question.

This approach to counting records isn't usually a problem in small applications that deal with only a handful of records. However, when an application needs to deal with several thousand records or more, these double queries can significantly impede the application's performance.

One option for tackling this issue is to use some more advanced SQL commands, such as `JOIN` and `GROUP BY`. However, like you, I don't really enjoy writing SQL queries. Instead, I'll introduce you to another funky Rails feature: the counter cache.

Introducing the Counter Cache

The **counter cache** is an optional feature of `ActiveRecord` associations that makes counting records fast and easy. The use of the word *counter* here is as in "bean counter," not as in "counter-terrorism." The name "counter cache" is intended to reflect the caching of a value that counts records. You can enable the counter cache by including the parameter `:counter_cache => true` when defining a `belongs_to` association.

From a performance point of view, the counter cache is superior to an SQL-based solution. When we're using SQL, the number of records for an object associated with the current object needs to be computed by the database every time that object is requested. The counter cache, on the other hand, stores the number of records of each associated object in its own column in the database. This value can be retrieved as often as is needed, without requiring potentially expensive computation to take place.

The Counter Cache doesn't Actually Count!

IMPORTANT

The counter cache doesn't actually go through the database to calculate the number of associated records every time an object is added or removed, effective from the point at which it was turned on. Instead, it increases the counter for every object that's added to the association, and decreases it for every object that's removed from the association, from the point at which it's enabled.

As the counter cache needs to be stored somewhere, we'll create room for it in our Story model with the help of a migration.

Making Room for the Cache

We'll generate a new migration template using the generate script. Figure 9.1 shows the results of this task:

```
$ ruby script/generate migration AddCounterCacheToStories
```

Figure 9.1. Generating a migration to add the counter cache

As expected, our new migration template is stored in the file db/migrate/005_add_counter_cache_to_stories.rb. This migration will be used to add a new column to the stories table—the column will store a value that represents the number of Vote objects associated with each Story. The name of the column should match the method that we would normally call to retrieve the object count, so we'll call it votes_count:

File: **01-005_add_counter_cache_to_stories.rb**

```
class AddCounterCacheToStories < ActiveRecord::Migration
  def self.up
```

```
    add_column :stories, :votes_count, :integer, :default => 0
    Story.find(:all).each do |s|
      s.update_attribute :votes_count, s.votes.length
    end
  end
  def self.down
    remove_column :stories, :votes_count
  end
end
```

Let me explain what's going on here. Columns that store the counter cache need a default value of 0 in order to operate properly. This default value can be provided to `add_column` using the `:default` argument, as we've done in the first line of our `self.up` method:

```
    add_column :stories, :votes_count, :integer, :default => 0
```

In the past, we've used migrations to make schema changes, but migrations can also be used to migrate data. As I mentioned earlier in this chapter, the number of objects associated with the model using the counter cache is never actually calculated by Rails—values are just incremented and decremented as records are modified. Consequently, the next line in our migration loops through the `Story` objects in the database, and manually calculates each `Story`'s initial voting score:

```
    Story.find(:all).each do |s|
      s.update_attribute :votes_count, s.votes.length
    end
```

`Story.find(:all)` returns an array of all stories in the database. We then use the `each` method to pass each of the `Story` objects, one after another, to the block of Ruby code that follows. The block calculates the voting score for the current story (which is held in the variable `s`) by calling the `length` method on the `votes` association—this is effectively the same as counting all of the `Vote` objects associated with the current `Story`. The result of the `votes.length` calculation is then stored in the newly added `votes_count` attribute of the current `Story`, using the `update_attribute` method.

As usual, we reverse the changes that we made in `self.up` in the `self.down` method:

```
  def self.down
    remove_column :stories, :votes_count
  end
```

Right, let's make use of this migration.

Applying the Migration

Go ahead and apply this migration using the `rake` tool:

```
$ rake db:migrate
```

Once that's completed, there's just one more small change we need to make to ensure that our association between a `Vote` and a `Story` uses the counter cache that we've just set up. Change the `belongs_to` association in `app/models/vote.rb` to the following:

File: **02-vote.rb** (excerpt)

```
belongs_to :story, :counter_cache => true
```

Excellent. Let's get that new front page happening!

Updating the RJS Template

One side-effect of using a counter cache is that the cached values are not refreshed when the number of votes associated with a story changes via an Ajax call. This is easily rectified by forcing a reload of the object after we cast our vote, like so:

File: **03-vote.rjs** (excerpt)

```
page.replace_html 'vote_score',
    "Score: #{@story.reload.votes_count}"
...
```

Implementing the Front Page

The core concept of social news sites like digg is that they're user-moderated. Stories that have yet to receive a certain number of votes don't appear on the site's front page—instead, they reside in a "voting area," where they can be viewed and voted upon by the site's users.

The story promotion system that digg uses is actually rather complicated. It takes into account a range of factors other than the number of votes a story receives, including the amount of activity the site was experiencing at the time the vote was cast, and the rate at which a story receives votes. However, we'll implement a much simpler algorithm for Shovell: stories with a voting score *above* a certain threshold will appear on the front page, while stories with a score *below* that threshold will be displayed on the voting page, ready to be "shoved."

First, we'll make all the changes required to get our front page running smoothly, utilizing standard templates and partials. We can then make use of these templates to implement our voting bin.

Modifying the Controller

The first change that we'll make is to our `StoryController`. We need to replace the current `index` action (which displays a random story) with one that retrieves the list of stories that have received enough votes to appear on the front page. Modify the `StoryController` class located in `app/controllers/story_controller.rb` so that it looks like this:

File: **04-story_controller.rb** (excerpt)

```
class StoryController < ApplicationController
  ...
  def index
    @stories = Story.find :all,
      :order => 'id DESC',
      :conditions => 'votes_count >= 5'
  end
  ...
end
```

Let's take a look at this code.

`Story.find :all`, as you already know, fetches from the database all stories that match an optional criterion. We're specifying that our records be ordered by descending `id` here, which will ensure that the newest stories appear at the top of the results, and older ones show at the bottom.

To implement the voting threshold, we've specified a condition that the total `votes_count` must be greater than or equal to five, using the counter cache that we created in the previous section. The result of the `find` operation will then be stored in the `@stories` instance variable.

Modifying the View

Now that we've retired the story randomizer, we also have to rip apart the `index.rhtml` template, which was formerly responsible for rendering a single story link. Our new template will render a collection of stories, each displaying its current voting score and the name of the user who submitted it.

Modify the corresponding index template (located at app/views/story/index.rhtml) so that it looks like this:

File: **05-index.rhtml**

```
<h2>
  <%= "Showing #{ pluralize(@stories.size, 'story') }" %>
</h2>
<%= render :partial => 'story', :collection => @stories %>
```

The first line of ERb code outputs the number of stories being displayed.

```
  <%= "Showing #{ pluralize(@stories.size, 'story') }" %>
```

To display this value, we're making use of the pluralize helper provided by Rails. pluralize displays the noun that's passed in as an argument, either in singular or in plural form. If there's only one story to show, the header will read Showing 1 story; in all other cases it will read Showing *x* stories, where *x* is the number of stories available.

Most of the time, Rails is smart enough to correctly pluralize the most common English nouns automatically. If this doesn't work for some reason, you have the option of passing both singular *and* plural forms, like so:[1]

```
  <%= "Showing #{ pluralize(@stories.size, 'story', 'stories') } %>
```

To render each story in the collection we retrieved, we're using a partial—something that we first encountered when displaying voting history back in Chapter 7:

```
<%= render :partial => 'story', :collection => @stories %>
```

The next item on our list is the creation of the partial.

Modifying the Partial

Create the file app/views/story/_story.rhtml, and edit it to appear as follows:

File: **06-_story.rhtml (excerpt)**

```
<div class="story">
  <h3><%= link_to story.name,
             story_url(:permalink => story.permalink) %></h3>
  <p>
```

---

[1] If you need to "train" Rails to correctly pluralize a noun in more than one spot, it might be worth adding your own pluralization rules to the Rails Inflector. See the bottom of config/environment.rb for an example.

```
      Submitted by: <%= story.user.login %> |
      Score: <%= story.votes_count %>
    </p>
  </div>
```

This partial is responsible for displaying the core facts of a story in the listings on the application's front page (and, as you'll see later, in the voting bin). It's a fairly straightforward template that you should have no trouble understanding: the title of the story is displayed in an h3 element, which links directly to the story page, and the original submitter of the story and current voting score are displayed underneath. The whole story is then wrapped in <div> tags, with a class attribute of story, which we'll use to apply some CSS styling.

Styling the Front Page

Now that we have some new elements on the front page, let's add style rules for those elements to our style sheet, which is located at pub-lic/stylesheets/styles.css:

File: **07-styles.css (excerpt)**

```
.story {
  float: left;
  width: 50%;
}
.story h3 { margin-bottom: 0; }
.story p { color: #666; }
```

While we're giving our front page an overhaul, let's also get rid of the default Rails welcome page that's displayed when a user accesses http://localhost:3000/, and make our new front page the default page instead.

Setting the Default Page

To set the default page, we once again need to alter Rails's routing configuration, which is located in the file config/routes.rb. If you look closely, you'll notice a commented line like this (if you deleted it earlier, don't worry—you can just type out the line you need in a moment):

```
# map.connect '', :controller => "welcome"
```

By removing the # character and making a slight change to the route, we can set the destination for requests for the address http://localhost:3000/ to be the index action for our StoryController:

File: **08-routes.rb (excerpt)**

```
map.connect '', :controller => "story"
```

Before you jump into your browser to test this new route, you should be aware of one small caveat: the default Rails welcome page is a simple HTML page (it contains no ERb code at all). It lives at `public/index.html`, and when present, it will be displayed in favor of any other action that you might configure in the Rails routing configuration file. So, in order to display our story index, this file has to be removed—go ahead and delete it now.

Alright, let's take a peek at our new front page; mine's shown in Figure 9.2. Depending on how many votes you've given your stories, you may or may not see any stories listed.

Figure 9.2. The all new (but empty) front page

If, like me, your front page is looking rather empty, you're probably keen to get voting! Let's quickly cover the implementation of the voting bin, so you can use it to start voting on stories in the queue.

Implementing the Voting Bin

To create a voting bin, create a new method called `bin` in the file `/app/controllers/story_controller.rb`, like so:

File: **09-story_controller.rb (excerpt)**

```ruby
class StoryController < ApplicationController
  ...
  def bin
    @stories = Story.find :all,
      :order => 'id DESC',
      :conditions => 'votes_count < 5'
    render :action => 'index'
  end
end
```

Most of that code probably looks straightforward enough—but what about that `render` call that's hiding in there?

Well, before I explain that line of code, let me point something out to you, in case you haven't spotted it already: this code is almost identical to the code we wrote for our `index` action—it just applies a different condition to the collection of stories.

That fact should trigger the realization that this is a good opportunity to reuse some code. Let's extract most of the code that's used in these two controller methods (`index` and `bin`) and place it in a protected controller method called `fetch_stories`, which we'll then use from both locations within our code.

As we discussed earlier, protected methods are only accessible from within a class and its subclasses; they're not accessible from anywhere outside the class. If we were to make `fetch_stories` a publicly accessible method, it would be exposed via the URL http://localhost:3000/story/fetch_stories, which is certainly not what we want.

Here's that extracted method:

```ruby
def fetch_stories(conditions)
  @stories = Story.find :all,
    :order => 'id DESC',
    :conditions => conditions
end
```

As the only part that differs between the `index` and `bin` actions is the condition, we'll allow the condition to be passed to the new protected method as an argument.

Our `StoryController` should now look a bit like this (only the code relevant to this section is shown):

File: **10-story_controller.rb** (excerpt)

```ruby
class StoryController < ApplicationController
  ...
  def index
    fetch_stories 'votes_count >= 5'
  end

  def bin
    fetch_stories 'votes_count < 5'
    render :action => 'index'
  end
  ...
  protected
    def fetch_stories(conditions)
      @stories = Story.find :all,
        :order => 'id',
        :conditions => conditions
    end
end
```

Now, back to that peculiar render call in the bin action:

```ruby
render :action => 'index'
```

I mentioned earlier that the two actions we have for listing stories (index and bin) are almost identical; well, another thing that they have in common is the template that they use. The above line of code makes sure of that. It specifies that the view template for the index action should also be used by the bin action. As such, we're rendering the exact same template for a slightly different set of stories.

For this very reason, we don't have to add much more to our code in order to complete our story voting bin. However, the two pages currently lack sufficient visual distinction—they need headings that read something like Showing 3 upcoming stories or Showing 7 front-page stories. At the moment, our users would have a difficult time determining which page of the application they're looking at.

We'll rectify this problem now by adding these headings with a little assistance from some ActionView helpers.

Abstracting Presentation Logic

In this section, we'll look at a way to abstract any presentation logic that you find yourself adding to your view templates. First, let's look at why we need to bother extracting Ruby code from our views.

Avoiding Presentation Logic Spaghetti

Recall that our intention is to display in the index template a heading that's appropriate, depending on whether the list of stories being displayed contains front-page stories or upcoming stories.

Of course, we could implement this functionality by adding the logic directly to the `app/views/story/index.rhtml` template (don't do this just yet!):

```
<h2>
  <% if controller.action_name == 'index' %>
    <%= "Showing #{pluralize(@stories.size,'front page story')}" %>
  <% else %>
    <%= "Showing #{pluralize(@stories.size,'upcoming story')}" %>
  <% end %>
</h2>
```

However, you'll notice that this solution entails a fair amount of duplication—all we're changing in the `else` block is a single word! Additionally, the fact that in view templates Ruby code is always wrapped in ERb tags (`<% %>` and `<%= %>`) means that these templates can sometimes begin to look like a dish of spaghetti, containing chained method calls, nested levels of parentheses, `if` clauses, and other complexities.

When your own code starts to look like spaghetti, it might be time to consider extracting some of that code into an `ActionView` helper.

Introducing `ActionView` Helpers

As you've heard countless times now, a view should contain presentational code only. To adhere to the MVC paradigm as strictly as possible, you should aim to place all logic outside the views—in a controller (for application logic) or a model (for business logic). There's a third option for any presentation-related logic that doesn't quite belong in a controller or a model: the **`ActionView` helper**.

We talked about making helper methods available to views in Chapter 8, when we implemented the `logged_in?` method. However, back then, we implemented this functionality as a protected controller method, which was then made available to our views using the `helper_method` statement.

Native `ActionView` helpers differ from protected helper methods in that they're *not* available to controllers—hence the name. An `ActionView` helper is a function that helps to reduce the clutter in your view templates.

Writing an `ActionView` Helper

`ActionView` helpers are available in two basic forms.

The first is the global helper, which is stored in the file `app/helpers/application_helper.rb`. You can think of a global `ActionView` helper as being the "view" equivalent to the `ApplicationController` class in the "controller" world. Any helper that you add to this file will be available from every view of every controller.

The second form of `ActionView` helper is one that's specific to the views of a particular controller. We'll use this approach for our `ActionView` helper—we'll create a new helper method for our `StoryController` in the file `app/helpers/story_helper.rb`. That way, it will be available to every view of `StoryController`, but no other views.

Here's the helper method you'll need to add:

File: **11-story_helper.rb**

```
module StoryHelper
  def story_list_heading
    story_type = case controller.action_name
        when 'index': 'front page story'
        when 'bin': 'upcoming story'
      end
    "Showing #{ pluralize(@stories.size, story_type) }"
  end
end
```

Let's step through this code. The first thing it does is populate a variable `story_type` using a Ruby `case` statement:

```
    story_type = case controller.action_name
        when 'index': 'front page story'
        when 'bin': 'upcoming story'
      end
```

This statement compares the value of `controller.action_name` (which contains the text value of the controller action that's being executed, exactly as it appears in the URL) with a couple of pre-defined values (namely, the values `'index'` and `'bin'`).

Next, we display the same Showing ... string with the `pluralize` helper that we used in our previous attempt at writing this view:

```
"Showing #{ pluralize(@stories.size, story_type) }"
```

However, this time, we're passing `story_type` as the part of the string that's being pluralized. This string is either set to `front page story` or `upcoming story`.[2] While this isn't necessarily a shorter solution than the previous one, it certainly removes a lot of clutter from our view, which we can now reduce to a single line!

File: **12-index.rhtml**

```
<h2><%= story_list_heading %></h2>
<%= render :partial => 'story', :collection => @stories %>
```

Now we just need to add our voting bin page to the navigation menu in the footer of each page, and we're done!

Expanding the Navigation Menu

To add a link to our navigation menu, we simply add another list item to the unordered list at the bottom of the application layout. The layout is stored in `app/views/layouts/application.rhtml`:

File: **13-application.rhtml (excerpt)**

```
<ul id="navigation">
  <li><%= link_to 'Front page stories',
          :controller => 'story' %></li>
  <li><%= link_to 'Upcoming stories',
          :controller => 'story', :action => 'bin' %></li>
  <li><%= link_to 'Submit a new story!',
          :controller => 'story', :action => 'new' %></li>
</ul>
```

---

[2] If we wanted to be extra pedantic about reducing code duplication, we could even extract the word "story" from that string, and simply set the `story_type` variable to "front page" or "upcoming." But you have to draw the line somewhere!

Excellent—now we can finally give our changes a whirl. Point your browser to `http://localhost:3000/` and click the Upcoming stories link at the bottom of the page.

The resulting page, an example of which is depicted in Figure 9.3, should contain all the stories in your database that have a voting score below 5.

Figure 9.3. The story voting bin

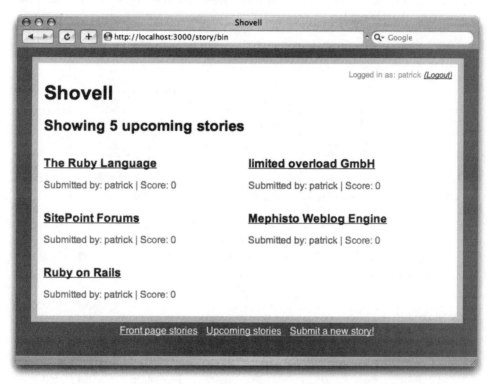

Remember that our application requires each of our stories to have a permalink value—something that must still be created manually at this point—and you might see some strange errors if a story doesn't have such a value. Soon, we'll be generating permalinks for our stories automatically as they're submitted—I promise!

Before you use this unique opportunity to promote the first story to Shovell's front page, we'll go ahead and require users to be logged in before they can vote. This will give us the ability to check a user's voting history later on.

Our application is looking much more like a story-sharing site. On to the next feature!

Requiring that Users Log In to Vote

The next enhancement we'll make will ensure that users log in before they are able to vote. First, we need to modify `StoryController` so that the `vote` method responds only to users who are logged in; we then need to store the `id` of the current user as part of the new vote.

The first step is to modify the existing `before_filter` in `app/control-lers/story_controller.rb`, like so:

File: **14-story_controller.rb** (excerpt)

```
class StoryController < ApplicationController
  before_filter :login_required, :only => [ :new, :vote ]
    ...
end
```

By changing the `:only` option of the `before_filter` call to include an array of two action names, we ensure that the filter is applied to both of them.

Now, it doesn't make much sense to display a feature to visitors if they can't make use of it. Let's add a little login teaser to the story page, to suggest that visitors might like to log in if they want to vote for stories. Make the following changes to `app/views/story/show.rhtml`:

File: **15-show.rhtml** (excerpt)

```
<% if logged_in? %>
  <div id="vote_link">
    <%= link_to_remote 'shove it',
      { :url => { :action => 'vote', :id => @story } },
      { :href => url_for(:action => 'vote', :id => @story) } %>
  </div>
<% else %>
  <p>
    <em>
      You would be able to vote for this story if you were
      <%= link_to 'logged in', :controller => 'account',
          :action => 'login' %>!
    </em>
  </p>
<% end %>
```

This *if* clause decides whether or not to display the shove it link to the visitor, depending on his or her login status. If the user isn't logged in, That person is presented with a teaser and a link to the `login` action, as shown in Figure 9.4.

Figure 9.4. Hiding the voting link from visitors

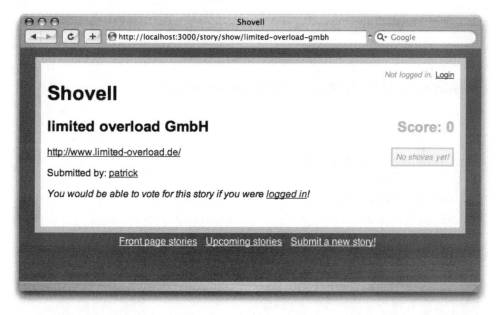

To complete this feature addition, we need to modify the `vote` action of our `StoryController` so that it stores the current user with each vote:

File: **16-story_controller.rb** (excerpt)

```
class StoryController < ApplicationController
  ...
  def vote
    @story = Story.find(params[:id])
    @story.votes.create(:user => @current_user)
    ...
  end
end
```

This new line saves the reference to the current user with each vote.

Excellent! Now it's time to create some additional stories and start submitting some votes, if you haven't done so already.

Visit the voting bin by selecting the Upcoming stories link from the navigation menu, and click on a story's title to visit the story page. From there, you can click the shove it link a few times until the story has five or more votes. Visit the front page, and you should see your story appear! The result of my serial voting is shown in Figure 9.5.

Figure 9.5. Viewing stories on the front page

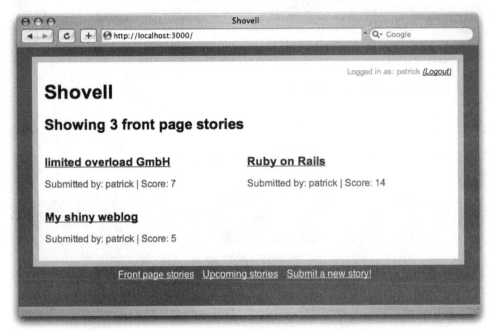

That's another feature crossed off the list. Next!

Adding Story Attributes

In the next enhancement to our application, we'll add a couple of extra attributes to our Story model:

❑ a created_at column that stores the creation date of each story

❑ a description column that allows users to write a few paragraphs about their submissions

Since we're talking about adding attributes, you might expect that there's a new migration ahead—and indeed there is. Let's generate the migration file that will store the code we'll use to add these new attributes:

```
$ ruby script/generate migration
  AddStoryCreationDateAndDescription
```

The contents of this migration (stored in db/migrate/006_add_story_cre-ation_date_and_description.rb) are very straightforward, so they won't need much explanation:

File: **17-006_add_story_creation_date_and_description.rb (excerpt)**

```
class AddStoryCreationDateAndDescription < ActiveRecord::Migration
  def self.up
    add_column :stories, :created_at, :datetime
    add_column :stories, :description, :text
  end
  def self.down
    remove_column :stories, :created_at
    remove_column :stories, :description
  end
end
```

As you can see, we're adding two columns to the stories table. In order for the created_at column to work its magic, we've created it as a column of type dat-etime. We've specified that the description column must be of type text, because a column of type string can only store up to 255 characters, and it's possible that story descriptions may exceed this limit.

The final step is to apply this migration using the rake task. The output of this migration is shown in Figure 9.6:

```
$ rake db:migrate
```

The next thing we'll do is hop into the Story model to remedy a piece of functionality that has no doubt become quite tedious for you by now: the fact that we have to manually generate permalinks for newly submitted stories through the console. As the permalink resembles the story name, let's generate it automatically—this functionality is long overdue!

Figure 9.6. Adding and applying our sixth migration

```
Core:~/shovell scoop$ ruby script/generate migration AddStoryCreationDateAndDesc
ription
      exists  db/migrate
      create  db/migrate/006_add_story_creation_date_and_description.rb
Core:~/shovell scoop$ mate db/migrate/006_add_story_creation_date_and_descriptio
n.rb
Core:~/shovell scoop$ rake db:migrate
(in /Users/scoop/Desktop/railsbook/code)
== AddStoryCreationDateAndDescription: migrating ===========================
-- add_column(:stories, :created_at, :datetime)
   -> 0.0880s
-- add_column(:stories, :description, :text)
   -> 0.0306s
== AddStoryCreationDateAndDescription: migrated (0.1190s) ==================

Core:~/shovell scoop$ ▌
```

Auto-generating Permalinks

To implement this feature, I'll introduce you to a feature of Rails models that we haven't touched on yet: **callbacks**. Callbacks are little snippets of code that are triggered by model events—for example, they're triggered when a model is created, updated, or destroyed.

Introducing Model Callbacks

Callbacks in models can be prefixed or appended to certain actions, such as the creating, updating, or destroying of a model. The concept of a callback might sound similar to the filters we applied to our controllers in Chapter 8—and they certainly are similar.

In fact, we've already encountered a callback in our application—it was used to apply the validation we implemented in Chapter 6. Internally, ActiveRecord prefixes validations to the save method that writes a model to the database. If the callback result allows the request to continue (meaning that the request has passed the defined validations), the save operation is executed.

The names of the available callback methods are fairly intuitive: `before_create`, `before_save`, and `before_delete` are called before the model in question is created, saved, and deleted, respectively. There are also a number of `after_` callbacks that, as expected, are called after the operation.

Like filters in controllers, callbacks in models are usually defined as protected methods. The callback resides in a model class, and is referred to by the class method via a symbol—here's an example:

```
class MyModel < ActiveRecord::Base
  before_create :generate_permalink
  ..
  protected
    def generate_permalink
      ...
    end
end
```

We can use either of two callbacks to hook into our `Story` model and generate the permalink: `before_save` or `before_create`. We'll use `before_create`, because permalinks should be, well, permanent. If we were to use `before_save`, the permalink would change whenever the name of the story changed, for whatever reason.

An Alternative Callback Syntax

note

In your experimentation with Rails you might come across the following syntax for model callbacks. In this syntax, the code that's to be executed when an event occurs is defined as an instance method named after the callback:

```
class MyModel < ActiveRecord::Base
  def before_save
    ...
  end
end
```

While this approach is technically correct, I prefer to define my callbacks using descriptive method names, and to refer to them using the `before_save :my_method` syntax instead.[3] This way, it's much easier to see what's going on, because you can glance at the header of the model class, in which the callbacks are declared, then look at each of the callback methods separately.

---

[3] The `after_find` callback actually *needs* to be defined using this alternative syntax, due to performance implications associated with defining it using the preferred syntax.

The reason why we're using `before_create` instead of `after_create` should be obvious: if we were to set the permalink *after* the model itself had already been saved to the database, we'd either lose the generated permalink, or have to save the model *again*, neither of which options makes much sense.

Adding a Callback

Let's add a callback to our `Story` model. Add the following code to the file `app/models/story.rb`:

File: **18-story.rb (excerpt)**

```ruby
class Story < ActiveRecord::Base
  before_create :generate_permalink
  ...
  protected
    def generate_permalink
      self.permalink = name.downcase.gsub(/\W/, '-')
    end
end
```

Once again, just one line of Ruby code is enough to accomplish the task at hand. Let's dissect what this line actually does, and why things are the way they are.

First, you'll notice that we're using two different approaches to access the attributes of the model: `self.permalink` and `name`.

```ruby
self.permalink = name.downcase.gsub(/\W/, '-')
```

When you're assigning a value to a model attribute, you should use the `self.my_attribute` syntax (`self` refers to the current class) to prevent potential variable scope issues. However, the `self` prefix can be omitted safely from the right-hand side of the expression—it's not necessary for the `name` attribute because Rails automatically defines a shortcut, known as an **attribute reader**, for this attribute. All attributes that map to a database column can be accessed in this way.

The permalink is generated by removing "special" characters from the story name and replacing them with a hyphen. The story name is first converted to lowercase using the `downcase` method of the `String` class (which, unlike the `downcase!` method, doesn't change the story name). The output of that method is then passed through a regular expression replacement pattern.

```ruby
self.permalink = name.downcase.gsub(/\W/, '-')
```

As we discussed briefly in Chapter 6, regular expressions allow us to compare strings against a set of rules that match characters, numbers, word boundaries, and more. Regular expressions (often shortened to regex) are very powerful tools, but they can take a while to fully comprehend.[4]

In Ruby, regular expressions are either wrapped between two forward slashes (as we've done in the above code listing) or applied as an instance of the Regexp class. More complex regular expressions can also be declared using the %r() syntax.

In this case, the regular expression we're applying is very simple—it uses the pattern \W. This pattern matches all "non-word characters," which includes everything except the alphanumeric characters a to z, the numbers 0 to 9, and the underscore character (_).

Lastly, we use the gsub (short for "global substitution") method provided by the String class to replace with a hyphen (-) all the characters that are matched by the regular expression. The result is then stored in the permalink attribute.

Here are a few examples of this code in action, as viewed from the Rails console:

```
>> "My shiny weblog".downcase.gsub(/\W/, '-')
=> "my-shiny-weblog"
>> "Rails: A success story".downcase.gsub(/\W/, '-')
=> "rails--a-success-story"
>> "The good (old) Ruby Idiom".downcase.gsub(/\W/, '-')
=> "the-good--old--ruby-idiom"
```

As you can see, it's not perfect (we end up with a double-hyphen when the story title contains two successive non-alphanumeric characters), but it'll do the trick.

Expanding the Submission Form

One last change we'll make before we test our permalink generation code is to add another field to the story submission form—a field for the description column that we added earlier in the chapter. The form lives in the file app/views/story/new.rhtml:

---

[4] If you're eager to master regular expressions, the book *Mastering Regular Expressions* [http://www.oreilly.com/catalog/regex3/], from O'Reilly Media, is the definitive reference. You may also find Harry Fuecks' four-part tutorial on sitepoint.com useful: http://www.sitepoint.com/blogs/2006/09/26/the-joy-of-regular-expressions-1/.

File: **19-new.rhtml (excerpt)**

```
<% form_for :story do |f| %>
  …
<p>
  description:<br />
  <%= f.text_area :description %>
</p>
<p><%= submit_tag %></p>
<% end %>
```

Figure 9.7 shows the form after we apply this change.

Figure 9.7. Allowing users to add a story description

To accommodate a larger story description (remember that we've given our users plenty of room by making the description column of type text), we're using a textarea instead of a one-line input field:

```
<%= f.text_area :description %>
```

We also need to display the story's description on the story's page, just above the `submitted_by` paragraph in the file `/app/views/story/show.rhtml`:

File: **20-show.rhtml** (excerpt)

```
...
<p>
  <%= @story.description %>
</p>
<p class="submitted_by">
...
```

Right! Let's hop over to our browser and submit a new story to see whether the automated generation of the permalink works as expected. (It sure does—as Figure 9.8 shows!)

Figure 9.8. A story with an auto-generated permalink

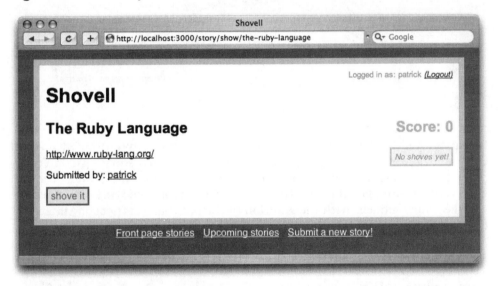

Adding User Pages

In order to track the history of our site's usage on a per-user basis, we'll need to create a place where this information can be displayed.

We'll add a user page, which will list the six stories most recently submitted by the logged-in user and the six stories for which that person most recently voted.

To select the most recently voted-for stories, we'll make use of another type of relationship: the join model.

Introducing the Join Model Relationship

A **join model** relationship is a relationship between two models that relies upon a third—there's no direct relationship between the two models that are being linked. This relationship is illustrated in Figure 9.9.

Figure 9.9. A join model relationship

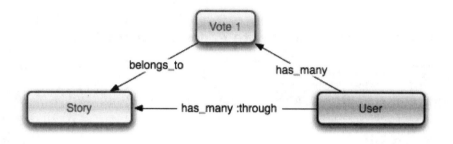

In our Shovell application, an association only exists between our Story and User models when we're talking about who *submitted* each story—we don't currently have the ability to find out who *voted* for each story. This is where the join model comes into play: the Vote model is already associated with both the User and the Story models; with the addition of the has_many :through statement, the Vote can serve as the connecting element in this new relationship.

The Vote model is the join model because it joins the User and the Story models.

Introducing the `has_many :through` Association

The code that implements a join model relationship is the line has_many :through. Let's use it to add a join model relationship to our User model. Open the file app/models/user.rb and make the changes in bold below:

File: 21-user.rb (excerpt)

```
class User < ActiveRecord::Base
  has_many :stories
```

```
  has_many :votes
  has_many :stories_voted_on,
    :through => :votes,
    :source => :story
end
```

Normally, Rails is smart enough to figure out associated class names on its own, so long as the associations are given a name that matches the plural form of the class name (for instance, :stories). However, because our User model already has a has_many relationship (has_many :stories), we need to assign this new association a different name (:stories_voted_on). We also need to specify the model with which we're associating the users, which is what the :source => :story argument does.

The code that defines this relationship as a join model relationship is the :through => :votes argument, which can be read as, "a User *has many* Stories *through* the Vote model."

With this association in place, we find that several new instance methods are available to every User object:

```
>> u = User.find(:first)
=> #<User:...>
>> u.stories_voted_on.size
=> 1
>> u.stories_voted_on.first
=> #<Story:...>
```

As you can see, this association behaves like a regular has_many association, and if you were none the wiser, you'd never actually know that three models were involved in retrieving the associated data.

Modifying the Controller

Our user page will be implemented in the AccountController, in a newly created show action. Add the code below to the file /app/controllers/account_controller.rb:

File: **22-account_controller.rb (excerpt)**

```
class AccountController < ApplicationController
  ...
  def show
    @user = User.find_by_login(params[:id])
    @stories_submitted = @user.stories.find(:all,
```

```
      :limit => 6, :order => 'id DESC')
    @stories_voted_on  = @user.stories_voted_on.find(:all,
      :limit => 6, :order => 'id DESC')
  end
end
```

Let's look at this code. Remember that the `params` hash stores the various parts of the current URL, as defined in the application's routing configuration. We want the URL for the user page to be identified by the user's login name, rather than that person's numeric ID, so we need to use the `find_by_login` method to retrieve the user:

```
@user = User.find_by_login(params[:id])
```

The data we're going to display on the user page is fetched using the associations that are available via the `User` object. We then populate a couple of instance variables using `find` calls—first to sort the items in the desired order, and again to limit the number of items retrieved:

```
@stories_submitted = @user.stories.find(:all,
    :limit => 6, :order => 'id DESC')
@stories_voted_on  = @user.stories_voted_on.find(:all,
    :limit => 6, :order => 'id DESC')
```

The next task on our list is to create the view template for this page!

Creating the View

The view template for our user page is a new file—create it in `app/views/account/show.rhtml`. This template uses the instance variables that we created in our controller to display the recently submitted stories and votes. It does so by rendering a collection of partials:

File: **23-show.rhtml**

```
<h2>Stories submitted by <%= @user.name %></h2>
<div id="stories_submitted">
  <%= render :partial => 'story/story',
       :collection => @stories_submitted %>
</div>
<h2>Stories voted for by <%= @user.name %></h2>
<div id="stories_voted_on">
  <%= render :partial => 'story/story',
       :collection => @stories_voted_on %>
</div>
```

The partial we're rendering with this code already exists. We're re-using the story partial from StoryController, which is why the partial name looks odd at first glance:

```
<%= render :partial => 'story/story',
    :collection => @stories_submitted) %>
```

We specify story/story as the partial name so that Rails will look for the partial in app/views/story/_story.rhtml. If we only specified story as the partial name, Rails would look in app/views/account/_story.rhtml instead.

Next, we'll add a link to the user page by linking the name of the submitter as it's displayed on the story page (/app/views/story/show.rhtml), like so:

File: **24-show.rhtml** (excerpt)

```
...
  <%= @story.description %>
</p>
<p class="submitted_by">
  Submitted by:
  <span><%= link_to @story.user.login,
        :controller => 'account',
        :action => 'show',
        :id => @story.user.login %></span>
</p>
<% end %>
```

Lastly, we'll make a small addition to our style sheet:

File: **25-styles.css** (excerpt)

```
...
.story p {
  color: #666;
  font-size: 0.8em;
}
#stories_submitted, #stories_voted_on {
  clear: both;
}
h2 {
  margin: 0;
  padding: 10px 0;
}
```

There we go! As Figure 9.10 shows, we now have a user page that makes use of our newly added has_many :through association to list both the stories that were submitted by a given user and the stories for which that person recently voted.

Figure 9.10. Example of a user page

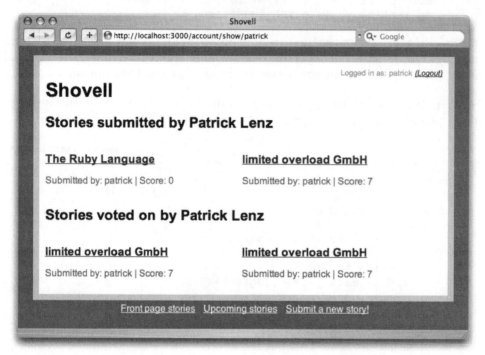

Testing the New Functionality

As usual, we'll add test coverage by writing unit tests, then adding functional tests, for all of the enhancements we've made.

Testing the Model

We made a number of changes to our model in this chapter, including utilizing the counter cache and introducing the join model relationship. Let's write some unit tests for those changes now.

Testing Additions to the Counter Cache

The first change we made in this chapter was to modify the Story model so that it uses the counter cache to track the number of votes associated with any given Story. To test this feature, we have to pull a few tricks out of our sleeves, as there are numerous conditions to take into account.

To begin with, let's add a test to the test case for the scenario in which a vote is cast. The test case is located in test/unit/story_test.rb:

File: **26-story_test.rb (excerpt)**

```
class StoryTest < Test::Unit::TestCase
  ...
  def test_should_increment_votes_counter_cache
    stories(:another).votes.create
    stories(:another).reload
    assert_equal 1, stories(:another).attributes['votes_count']
  end
end
```

We haven't encountered a couple of these methods before, so let's dissect this code.

The purpose of this test is to verify that the cached votes count is properly incremented when a new vote is added. Therefore, the first thing we need to do is to create a new vote:

```
stories(:another).votes.create
```

The second line is where things get interesting—we're forcibly reloading the model from the database.

```
stories(:another).reload
```

We do this because once a new vote has been added, the number of stories that are cached in each model's attributes is suddenly out of sync with the database.

If we were to check the log file when we come to run our tests later on, we'd find lines like the following:

```
UPDATE stories SET votes_count = votes_count + 1 WHERE (id = 2)
```

This is the SQL statement that Rails generates to update the counter cache. You'll notice that the statement doesn't bother to check the current value of votes_count—it just tells the database to increment votes_count by one. And with good reason! You see, in a live application, many users may be using the site at the same time, and some of them might even be casting votes in parallel. The value of votes_count would be totally negated if the SQL for each vote submission relied upon its own copy of votes_count at the time the statement was executed.

As such, you need to reload the model if you ever require access to the current number of votes immediately after a new vote is added. This isn't likely to occur very often—normally you'd redirect your user to a new page anyway. But when we're writing tests that simulate user behavior, it's important to be mindful of this issue.

There's also something special about the assertion in this test: instead of comparing the return value of the votes_count instance method, we're accessing the "raw" attribute as it comes out of the database:

```
assert_equal 1, stories(:another).attributes['votes_count']
```

If we had used the instance method, we wouldn't have had to enable counter caching at all in order for our test to pass—votes_count would simply have issued a second database query to count the votes. By using the attribute itself, we're asserting that the counter cache is doing its job.

Testing Deletions from the Counter Cache

With that first test out the way, this second test, which covers the deletion of votes, should be fairly straightforward. Our application doesn't yet allow users to delete votes, but we'll include this test anyway, for the sake of completeness:

File: **27-story_test.rb** (excerpt)

```
class StoryTest < Test::Unit::TestCase
  …
  def test_should_decrement_votes_counter_cache
    stories(:first).votes.first.destroy
    stories(:first).reload
    assert_equal 1, stories(:first).attributes['votes_count']
  end
end
```

Here, we're basically doing the opposite to the previous test. First, we destroy the first vote from the first story:

```
stories(:first).votes.first.destroy
```

Once again, we need to reload the model to reflect this change:

```
stories(:first).reload
```

Finally, we compare the cached `votes_count` value to the value we expect it to have:

```
assert_equal 1, stories(:first).attributes['votes_count']
```

Preparing the Fixtures

As if those tests didn't contain enough work-arounds, we also need to set the initial `votes_count` value for each story in our fixture file. Like the "magical" auto-populating column names that we first encountered in Chapter 7, the counter cache is not properly populated when fixtures are transferred to the database. Add the following values into the fixture file at `test/fixtures/stories.yml` to reflect the way in which the vote fixtures are associated with the story fixtures; while we're changing this file, we'll add an all-new story to our fixture data. We'll make use of this in the functional tests that we'll write later on:

File: **28-stories.yml (excerpt)**

```
first:
  ...
  votes_count: 2
another:
  ...
  votes_count: 0
promoted:
  id: 3
  permalink: promoted-story
  user_id: 2
  votes_count: 5
```

Testing the Generation of Permalinks

The next test covers the new functionality that we added to our model for generating permalinks:

File: **29-story_test.rb (excerpt)**

```
class StoryTest < Test::Unit::TestCase
  ...
  def test_should_generate_permalink
    s = Story.create(
      :name => 'This#title*is&full/of:special;characters',
```

```
    :link => 'http://example.com/'
  )
  assert_equal 'this-title-is-full-of-special-characters',
      s.permalink
end
```

You should be able to follow this test quite easily. To test the simple regular expression that we used to convert special characters to hyphens, we're creating a story whose name is sprinkled with special characters:

```
s = Story.create(
    :name => 'This#title*is&full/of:special;characters',
    :link => 'http://example.com/'
)
```

The assertion of this test confirms that our regex substitution performs its job properly, by comparing the value that our before_create filter produced with the value that we expect:

```
assert_equal 'this-title-is-full-of-special-characters',
    s.permalink
```

Testing the Join Model Relationship

Lastly, we need to add a test to deal with the new has_many :through association that we added to our User model. Expand the test cases (located in test/unit/user_test.rb) as follows:

File: **30-user_test.rb (excerpt)**

```
class UserTest < Test::Unit::TestCase
  …
  def test_stories_voted_on_association
    assert_equal [ stories(:first) ],
        users(:patrick).stories_voted_on
  end
end
```

This test relies on fixture data. Therefore, we can assert immediately that the list of stories for which our test user voted is equal to the list that we expect:

```
assert_equal [ stories(:first) ],
    users(:patrick).stories_voted_on
```

Next, we've got some functional tests to write.

Testing the `StoryController`

In this chapter, we've added to `StoryController` quite a bit of functionality that needs testing. The functionality that we've added is a little more complicated than in previous chapters, so the corresponding tests will also be more complex.

Testing the Rendering of Templates

We'll start by adding a few basic tests that cover correct template rendering:

File: **31-story_controller_test.rb (excerpt)**

```
class StoryControllerTest < Test::Unit::TestCase
  ...
  def test_should_show_index
    get :index
    assert_response :success
    assert_template 'index'
  end

  def test_should_show_bin
    get :bin
    assert_response :success
    assert_template 'index'
  end

  protected
  ...
end
```

Both tests are very similar in nature and neither exposes any new functionality. Each calls its respective action, checks that the request was responded to successfully, and confirms that the proper template is rendered (remember, we're using exactly the same template for both the `index` and `bin` actions).

Testing the Story Index Pages

As a next step, we're confirming that each of the story-listing actions (`index` and `bin`) picks the proper records from the database. One list shows only "promoted" stories, which have a voting score of at least 5; the other shows the remaining stories:

File: **32-story_controller_test.rb (excerpt)**

```
class StoryControllerTest < Test::Unit::TestCase
  ...
  def test_should_only_list_promoted_on_index
    get :index
    assert_equal [ stories(:promoted) ], assigns(:stories)
  end

  def test_should_only_list_unpromoted_in_bin
    get :bin
    assert_equal [ stories(:another), stories(:first) ],
      assigns(:stories)
  end

  protected
  ...
end
```

In both of these tests, we're comparing the value that is assigned to the @stories instance variable (which is accessible using the assigns(:stories) construct) with our fixture data.

Testing the Routing Configuration

We also altered the routing configuration in this chapter; let's add a test to confirm that our changes are working properly:

File: **33-story_controller_test.rb (excerpt)**

```
class StoryControllerTest < Test::Unit::TestCase
  ...
  def test_should_use_story_index_as_default
    assert_routing '', :controller => 'story', :action => 'index'
  end
  ...
end
```

The assert_routing assertion confirms that a given request is translated into an expected set of parameters, mostly consisting of a controller and an action name:

```
    assert_routing '', :controller => 'story', :action => 'index'
```

Our assertion here confirms that a request for "nothing" (the front page of our domain) is indeed routed to the index action of StoryController.

Testing Page Headings

The next pair of tests deals with the view side of the index and bin actions and confirms that the header tag contains a proper heading, complete with the expected number of stories:

File: **34-story_controller_test.rb (excerpt)**

```
class StoryControllerTest < Test::Unit::TestCase
  ...
  def test_should_show_story_on_index
    get :index
    assert_select 'h2', 'Showing 1 front page story'
    assert_select 'div#content div.story', :count => 1
  end

  def test_should_show_stories_in_bin
    get :bin
    assert_select 'h2', 'Showing 2 upcoming stories'
    assert_select 'div#content div.story', :count => 2
  end
  ...
end
```

The second assert_select assertion tests for an appropriate number of div elements with a class attribute of story. These divs come out of the _story.rhtml partial and, as such, we're looking for one div per story. Each story div is contained in the all-encompassing div that has an id of content.

Testing the Story Submission Form

This chapter also saw us add to the story submission form a new field that allows users to submit story descriptions. To test this functionality, change the existing test_should_show_new_form test to match the following:

File: **35-story_controller_test.rb (excerpt)**

```
class StoryControllerTest < Test::Unit::TestCase
  def test_should_show_new_form
    get_with_user :new
    assert_select 'form p', :count => 4
  end
end
```

In this test, the `assert_tag` call counts the number of p elements below the
`<form>` tag, and checks the total against our expected number of 4—three form
fields plus a Submit button.

Testing Restricted Functionality

As we've made the `vote` action available only to users who have logged in, we
need to revise those tests that request the `vote` action to log in to the application
first. These revisions mostly involve modifying the `get` and `post` calls:

File: **36-story_controller_test.rb (excerpt)**

```
class StoryControllerTest < Test::Unit::TestCase
  …
  def test_should_accept_vote
    …
    post_with_user :vote, :id => 2
    …
  end

  def test_should_render_rjs_after_vote_with_ajax
    xml_http_request :post_with_user, :vote, :id => 2
    …
  end

  def test_should_redirect_after_vote_with_get
    get_with_user :vote, :id => 2
    …
  end
  …
end
```

Testing User Voting History

Additionally, we'll add a test to confirm that the vote action indeed stores the
current user with the submitted vote:

File: **37-story_controller_test.rb (excerpt)**

```
class StoryControllerTest < Test::Unit::TestCase
  …
  def test_should_store_user_with_vote
    post_with_user :vote, :id => 2
    assert_equal users(:patrick), assigns(:story).votes.last.user
  end
```

```
...
end
```

Testing the Story Display Page

Since users who are not logged in no longer see the shove it button, we need to revise an existing test and add a new one:

File: **38-story_controller_test.rb (excerpt)**

```
class StoryControllerTest < Test::Unit::TestCase
  ...
  def test_should_show_story_vote_elements
    get_with_user :show, :permalink => 'my-shiny-weblog'
    ...
  end

  def test_should_not_show_vote_button_if_not_logged_in
    get :show, :permalink => 'my-shiny-weblog'
    assert_select 'div#vote_link', false
  end
end
```

We pass `false` to `assert_select` to confirm that there are *no* elements on the page that match the given CSS selector.

Testing the Navigation Menu

We added an item to our navigation menu, so we need to increase the number of list items that we check for in the following test from two to three:

File: **39-story_controller_test.rb (excerpt)**

```
def test_should_show_navigation_menu
  get :index
  assert_select 'ul#navigation li', 3
end
```

Testing the Story Submitter Link Text

Lastly, let's add a test to confirm that the link to the story submitter's user page is displayed on the story page:

File: **40-story_controller_test.rb** (excerpt)

```ruby
class StoryControllerTest < Test::Unit::TestCase
  ...
  def test_should_show_story_submitter
    get :show, :permalink => 'my-first-story'
    assert_select 'p.submitted_by a', 'patrick'
  end
end
```

Whew! That was quite a litany of tests. Let's now turn our thoughts to one final test of the workings of our controller.

Testing the AccountController

Without further ado, we'll add three tests to cover the functionality encapsulated within the user page we added to AccountController:

File: **41-account_controller_test.rb** (excerpt)

```ruby
class AccountControllerTest < Test::Unit::TestCase
  fixtures :users, :stories, :votes
  ...
  def test_should_show_user
    get :show, :id => 'patrick'
    assert_response :success
    assert_template 'show'
    assert_equal users(:patrick), assigns(:user)
  end

  def test_should_show_submitted_stories
    get :show, :id => 'patrick'
    assert_select 'div#stories_submitted div.story', :count => 2
  end

  def test_should_show_stories_voted_on
    get :show, :id => 'patrick'
    assert_select 'div#stories_voted_on div.story', :count => 1
  end
end
```

All three tests use basic assertions to confirm that the proper user is found by the show action, and that that user's story submissions and story votes are displayed properly on the page.

Running the Complete Test Suite

We've made a massive number of additions to our suite of tests in this chapter, so it should be especially rewarding to run the full suite now, using:

```
$ rake test
```

Figure 9.11 shows the results of all of our tests.

Figure 9.11. Running the test suite

Summary

Wow, what a journey! In this chapter, we've added a stack of features to Shovell, such as the display of popular story listings on the front page and the implementation of a voting bin containing stories that people can vote on.

Along the way, we learned that the counter cache is an easy way to store the number of records associated with any given model, and used ActiveRecord callbacks as a means to hook into certain events that are occurring on our models. We used a `before_create` callback to implement the auto-generation of permalinks, and we also tackled `ActionView` helpers to reduce clutter in our shared view.

Lastly, we covered an additional type of association: the join model relationship. It was used to implement a user page to show the story submissions and voting history of each registered user.

Some 45 tests and 93 assertions later we can attest that, indeed, Shovell is in really good shape. Of course, there are countless enhancements that we could make to our little application; some of the functionality that comes to mind includes:

❑ creating a form that allows new users to register

❑ sending an email to new users to inform them of their passwords

❑ encrypting user passwords in the database

❑ allowing users to comment on stories

❑ restricting users to vote for each story only once

I'm sure your mind is racing with ideas for a number of killer features that you could use to set your application apart from the pack! While the addition of all of these features is more than we could possibly cover in this book, I've given you a solid grounding—both in theory and in practice—that you can build on to further develop Shovell on your own. Don't forget to keep expanding your test suite to include all the cool new features that you add!

In the next chapter, we'll take a quick look at the Rails plugin architecture, and use one of the existing plugins to expand Shovell's feature set—implementing tagging functionality for our story submissions.

10 Rails Plugins

While this book is unable to cover all of the built-in functionality that ships with Rails (there's plenty remaining for you to discover and experiment with once you've finished this book), the plugins architecture of Rails warrants our attention.

What is a Plugin?

A **plugin** is a component that you can add to your application to extend its functionality. While you can certainly write your own plugins, we'll limit our discussion here to using existing plugins. Plugins have been developed for various parts of the Rails framework, and add functionality in a range of areas, including:

❑ extensions to `ActiveRecord` functionality

❑ helper methods

❑ completely new template engines (for coding a view using an alternate templating language)

Compared with the rest of the Rails core framework, plugins are still a fairly new addition. For this reason, at the time of writing, no official, easily browsable plugin repository has been developed, nor has an easy-to-use plugin manager been created to simplify the installation and management of plugins. Various efforts are being made to address these needs, but nothing has been set in stone as yet. The original list of plugins is located in the Rails wiki; each entry simply links to the plugin code that various people have contributed and published.[1]

Plugins are installed using a command line script that's available in the `script` subdirectory of every Rails application. By default, this script will only install the plugins contained in the official Rails repository. To install a plugin from a different location, you must know the exact URL from which the plugin is available—information that's usually provided by the plugin developer.

Let's explore what the `plugin` script can do for us.

Invoke the script from the command line, without arguments, so that we can view its usage instructions:

```
$ ruby script/plugin
```

You should be presented with a set of usage instructions that numbers several pages, and even includes examples. An excerpt of this output can be seen in Figure 10.1.

Using the `plugin` script, plugins can be installed, removed, and even updated should a newer version than the one you originally installed become available. The other commands listed in Figure 10.1 relate to adding, listing, and removing additional plugin repositories; we won't cover them in this book.

Plugins you've installed for your application usually reside in the `vendor/plugins` folder within your application's root folder. Each plugin resides in its own subdirectory, where it will be automatically found and loaded by Rails. The upshot of this is that you don't have to tell Rails "load plugin A from location B."

Every Rails plugin ships with a `README` file that contains instructions for using the plugin. Many plugins also ship with test cases that assert their proper functioning.[2]

Okay, enough theory! Let's go ahead and install our first plugin.

---

[1] http://wiki.rubyonrails.org/rails/pages/HowTosPlugins
[2] Sadly, the plugin we're going to install does not, so we'll be writing our own tests.

Figure 10.1. Usage instructions for `script/plugin`

```
Terminal — bash — 80x23 — ⌘2
Core:~/shovell scoop$ ruby script/plugin
Unknown command:
Usage: plugin [OPTIONS] command
Rails plugin manager.

GENERAL OPTIONS
  -r, --root=DIR                    Set an explicit rails app directory.
                                    Default: /Users/scoop/Desktop/railsbook/code
  -s, --source=URL1,URL2            Use the specified plugin repositories instead
 of the defaults.
  -v, --verbose                     Turn on verbose output.
  -h, --help                        Show this help message.

COMMANDS
  discover   Discover plugin repositories.
  list       List available plugins.
  install    Install plugin(s) from known repositories or URLs.
  update     Update installed plugins.
  remove     Uninstall plugins.
  source     Add a plugin source repository.
  unsource   Remove a plugin repository.
  sources    List currently configured plugin repositories.
```

Adding Tagging to Shovell

The Web 2.0 craze that we mentioned at the start of Chapter 7 not only encourages the (mindful) use of Ajax functionality, it almost dictates that a web application *must* have "tagging" to be classified as a Web 2.0 application. And Shovell is no exception!

Tagging is the process by which content creators attach simple, textual labels to their data—be it a photo, a link, a story, or a restaurant review. These tags vary widely in their nature—they may be location-related, content-related, and so on. The result is that everyone seems to have a unique system for tagging the data he or she deals with.

Tags are definitely more flexible than a simple category tree—they let you assign as many or as few tags as you like to any item of data. The convention that has evolved around this functionality is for the user to enter tags for a content item into a text field. Multiple tags should be separated by a space or a comma.

Introducing the `acts_as_taggable` Plugin

Instead of reinventing the wheel and implementing our own tagging system for Shovell, we'll use one of the available Rails plugins for this job: `acts_as_taggable`.

What `acts_as_taggable` Does

As this isn't the most obvious name for a plugin, allow me to explain a little bit about the history of the `acts_as_*` naming convention.

Rails already ships with a number of **acts**, which are functional extensions to an `ActiveRecord` model. These acts equip models with certain functionality that usually can be enabled using a single line of code.

As this functionality typically enables models to "act as something else," the convention of calling these functional additions "acts" arose, and the code that enables the functionality `acts_as_something` shortly followed.

At the time of writing, Rails ships with three related acts: `acts_as_list`, `acts_as_tree`, and `acts_as_nested_set`. While some are more complex than others, each of these acts applies a hierarchy to a set of model objects. In the case of `acts_as_list`, objects are positioned in a flat list; with `acts_as_nested_set`, the resulting hierarchy is a sophisticated tree system, such as that used in a threaded forum, for example.

But what about `acts_as_taggable`? As the name suggests, this plugin provides a simple yet effective means by which you can make your models taggable. It ships with its own `ActiveRecord` model class called `Tag`, as well as functionality for parsing a list of tags separated by spaces into separate model objects of class `Tag`.

Of course, before we can play with this plugin, we'll need to install it.

Installing the `acts_as_taggable` Plugin

To install the plugin, change directory to the application root folder, and execute the following command:

```
$ ruby script/plugin install acts_as_taggable
```

In the output of the `plugin` script you'll see all the files that were added to your `vendor/plugins/` directory. The six files that make up the `acts_as_taggable` plugin are placed in a folder that has the same name as the plugin, as Figure 10.2 shows.

Figure 10.2. Installing the `acts_as_taggable` plugin

```
Core:~/shovell scoop$ ruby script/plugin install acts_as_taggable
+ ./acts_as_taggable/init.rb
+ ./acts_as_taggable/lib/README
+ ./acts_as_taggable/lib/acts_as_taggable.rb
+ ./acts_as_taggable/lib/tag.rb
+ ./acts_as_taggable/lib/tagging.rb
+ ./acts_as_taggable/test/acts_as_taggable_test.rb
Core:~/shovell scoop$ 
```

IMPORTANT

Removing Deprecated Code from `acts_as_taggable`

Unfortunately, the version of `acts_as_taggable` that resided in the official Rails repository at the time of writing contained deprecated code that threw warnings with Rails 1.2. I've made an updated version available for you in this book's code archive, but the change that's necessary to update this plugin (thus preventing warning messages from occurring when you run your test suite) is actually quite small, so let's go ahead and make it now.

Edit the file `vendor/plugins/acts_as_taggable/lib/acts_as_taggable.rb` and modify the last word on line 17, as shown in bold below:

```
module ClassMethods
  ...
    has_many :taggings, :as => :taggable,
        :dependent => :destroy
  ...
end
```

As I mentioned, you don't have to load this plugin explicitly, so here's where the installation instructions end!

Creating a Migration for the Plugin

Our plan is to allow users of our application to add tags to stories that are submitted to Shovell, so we'll need to make our `Story` model "taggable." As both the tags themselves and the relationships between tags and stories need to be stored somewhere—you guessed it!—we need to use a migration to create new tables. And while this plugin makes use of a new model (the `Tag` model provided by the `acts_as_taggable` plugin), the model wasn't created by the `generate` script, so we don't yet have a migration to go with it—let's create a skeleton migration file now:

```
$ ruby script/generate migration AddTags
```

The `acts_as_taggable` plugin uses two tables:

❑ The `tags` table stores the `Tag` model, which is just a regular `ActiveRecord` model. This table contains one entry for each tag. So, for example, if you tagged two or more `Story` models with the tag `book`, only one `Tag` object (`book`) would be stored in the database. This approach makes it easy for our application's users to find content: if a user was interested in finding stories about books, he or she could browse through all of the stories to which the `book` tag was applied.

❑ The `taggings` table stores the actual mappings between the `Tag` model and those models that make use of the `acts_as_taggable` functionality.

Add the following migration code to the `db/migrate/007_add_tags.rb` file:

File: **01-007_add_tags.rb**

```ruby
class AddTags < ActiveRecord::Migration
  def self.up
    create_table :tags do |t|
      t.column :name, :string
    end

    create_table :taggings do |t|
      t.column :tag_id, :integer
      t.column :taggable_id, :integer
      t.column :taggable_type, :string
    end
  end
  def self.down
    drop_table :tags
    drop_table :taggings
  end
end
```

We're starting out simple here: we create the **tags** table that contains just one column: **name** (in addition to the **id** column that every table has).

While it may appear simple on the surface, the **taggings** table is a little more complex than a mere list of objects and their tags. As I mentioned, it's possible to make more than one model in your application taggable. However, the mappings between the **Tag** model and those models to which tagging functionality has been added use a single table.

acts_as_taggable uses each of the columns created in the **taggable** table as follows:

❑ **tag_id** stores the **id** of the **Tag** model.

❑ **taggable_id** stores the **id** of the object that is *being tagged* (for example, the **id** of a **Story**).

❑ **taggable_type** stores the class of the object that is being tagged (for example **Story**).

Before we can give our **Story** model a little **acts_as_taggable** goodness, we need to apply the migration we just completed:

```
$ rake db:migrate
```

Figure 10.3 shows the outputs that result when this migration is created, and then applied.

Figure 10.3. Adding and applying the `AddTags` migration

```
Terminal — bash — 80x15 — ⌘2
Core:~/shovell scoop$ ruby script/generate migration AddTags
      exists  db/migrate
      create  db/migrate/007_add_tags.rb
Core:~/shovell scoop$ mate db/migrate/007_add_tags.rb
Core:~/shovell scoop$ rake db:migrate
(in /Users/scoop/Desktop/railsbook/code)
== AddTags: migrating ========================================
-- create_table(:tags)
   -> 0.0906s
-- create_table(:taggings)
   -> 0.0232s
== AddTags: migrated (0.1143s) ===============================

Core:~/shovell scoop$
```

Great! Now we can make our `Story` model taggable—but what's really going on here?

Understanding Polymorphic Associations

We've looked at the underlying tables utilized by the `acts_as_taggable` plugin, and we know which columns are used to store what. But what kind of association is this?

It's not a one-to-many relationship, because one tag may be applied to many items *and* one item may have many tags. It's a kind of bi-directional, one-to-many relationship. While traditionally Rails developers have always used the `has_and_belongs_to_many` (sometimes abbreviated to "habtm") relationship to express this kind of functionality, a recent Rails release introduced a new type of relationship that is well suited for this situation. This relationship called a **polymorphic association**.

In a polymorphic association, a model is associated with objects of more than one model class, as Figure 10.4 illustrates. In order to store this relationship in the database accurately, the object's class name *and* its ID need to be stored. Take a peek at the migration that we just created, and you'll see that this is exactly what's achieved by the schema that it creates.

Figure 10.4. Two models are assigned the same tag

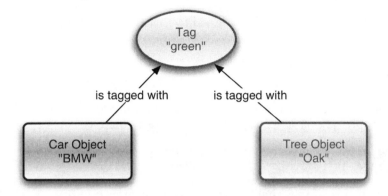

If the schema didn't save both the class name and ID of the object, we could potentially be faced by a situation in which a tag was applied to both a User object with an id of 1 and a Story object *that also* had an id of 1. What chaos that would be!

Fortunately, Rails handles most of the details that implement this relationship automatically and transparently for you.

Making a Model Taggable

To use acts_as_taggable, modify the Story class definition located in app/models/story.rb as follows:

File: **02-story.rb (excerpt)**

```
class Story < ActiveRecord::Base
  acts_as_taggable
  ...
end
```

Yes, that *is* it! With the plugin in place, it takes just 16 characters to make a model taggable.

Next, we'll hop into the Rails console to play with our Story model's new functionality. The acts_as_taggable plugin has added a variety of extra methods to our model—let's take a look at some of them.

First, retrieve a story from the database:

```
>> s = Story.find(:first)
=> #<Story:..>
```

We can look at the tags already assigned to this story by using the `tag_list` instance method:

```
>> s.tag_list
=> ""
```

The plugin provides us with the `tag_with` instance method to tag an object. This method simply takes a space-separated list of tags to apply:

```
>> s.tag_with 'sitepoint forum community'
=> ["sitepoint", "forum", "community"]
```

To refresh the list of tags that we've assigned, be sure to reload the model from the database. Then use the `tag_list` instance method to request the list of tags assigned to the model.

```
>> s.reload
=> #<Story:…>
>> s.tag_list
=> "sitepoint forum community"
```

The `tag_list` method is in fact a shortcut to the association data, which is available through the `tags` instance method. This method provides access to an array of the `Tag` objects with which this particular story is associated:

```
>> s.tags.size
=> 3
```

As I mentioned earlier in the chapter, we can also use methods of the `Tag` class to retrieve a list of stories that are tagged with a particular word. Below, we load up an existing tag (which we've just created through the `tag_with` instance method of the `Story` model) using a standard `ActiveRecord` dynamic finder method:

```
>> t = Tag.find_by_name("sitepoint")
=> #<Tag:…>
```

Each `Tag` instance collects a list of all the objects to which it has been assigned—information that's available through the `tagged` instance method. Let's request the size of the array:

```
>> t.tagged.size
=> 1
```

Based on the value returned by the `size` method, we can hazard a guess that the object available in this array is the `Story` object that we tagged earlier. Let's use the `first` method to be sure:

```
>> t.tagged.first
=> #<Story:...>
```

Yes, we were right!

The objects contained in this `tagged` array are the fully functional model objects to which our tag has been applied. We can therefore invoke the same methods and access the same attributes that we would when dealing with a regular `Story` object. Let's request the name of the story that we've tagged with the `sitepoint` tag:

```
>> t.tagged.first.name
=> "SitePoint Forums"
```

Pretty straightforward stuff, eh?

One last thing—because it's conceivable that a tag may be applied to more than one type of model, each model is equipped with a new dynamic finder that fetches only objects of that object's class that have been assigned a certain tag. That dynamic finder is `find_tagged_with`:

```
>> s = Story.find_tagged_with "sitepoint"
=> [#<Story:..>]
>> s.size
=> 1
>> s.first.name
=> "SitePoint Forums"
```

Okay, enough with the console! Let's give users the ability to tag stories through our application's Web interface.

Enabling Tag Submission

Before we get all fancy about *displaying* tags all over our site, we need to add a way for users to *submit* tags with a new story. Let's add a new form field to the story submission form.

Modifying the View

To add the form field, modify the submission form that's located in the file app/views/story/new.rhtml:

File: **03-new.rhtml (excerpt)**

```
<% form_for :story do |f| %>
  ...
  <p>
    Tags:<br />
    <%= text_field_tag 'tags', params[:tags] %>
  </p>
  <p><%= submit_tag %></p>
<% end %>
```

Users will be separating each tag with a space, so a simple text field for tag entry will do the job nicely:

```
<%= text_field_tag 'tags', params[:tags] %>
```

The only tricky thing about this line is the use of `text_field_tag` (rather than the regular `text_field` method that we normally use in conjunction with the `form_for` helper). This is because `form_for` is restricted to dealing with the actual attributes of a model, and `tags` isn't one of the `Story` model's attributes.

The `text_field_tag` helper takes two arguments: the name of the form field, and the destination of the final submitted value. For our application, we're passing `text_field_tag` the parameter `params[:tags]`, which is the location at which the submitted value will be stored. Therefore, the `input` HTML element that's created looks like this:

```
<input id="tags" name="tags" type="text" />
```

By storing the submitted value in `params[:tags]`, we ensure that any tags that the user entered during the submission process will be retained if an error occurs, and re-presented in the submission form when the user is returned there to correct the error.

Modifying the Controller

To assign the submitted tags to the new story, modify the `new` action of the `StoryController` class. While, in the past, we could add a regular attribute such as `description` without making any changes, tags are stored as an association and, as such, need a little tweaking.

Open `app/controllers/story_controller.rb` and add to it the bold line below:

File: **04-story_controller.rb (excerpt)**

```
class StoryController < ApplicationController
  ⋯
  def new
    ⋯
    if request.post? and @story.save
      @story.tag_with params[:tags] if params[:tags]
      ⋯
    end
  end
end
```

As you can see, we're taking the same approach that we used to test the tagging functionality when we were fooling around with the `console` script. We call the `tag_with` instance method provided by `acts_as_taggable` to add the tags that were submitted with the story:

```
    @story.tag_with params[:tags] if params[:tags]
```

As tags are not mandatory, I've wrapped an `if` clause around this method, so that the logic for assigning tags is skipped completely if `params[:tags]` is empty.

Right, our users can submit tags with their stories! Let's display them then, shall we?

Enabling Tag Display

We want our tags to appear in a few places. First of all, they need to be visible on the story page itself. It would also be nice to see them in the story listings on the front page, and on the page showing stories in the voting bin.

Modifying the View

To display the assigned tags on the story page, modify the `show` template, located at `app/views/story/show.rhtml`. Add the following code between the containers of the story submitter (`submitted_by`) and the voting link (`vote_link`):

File: **05-show.rhtml (excerpt)**

```
...
</p>
<% if @story.tags.size.nonzero? %>
  <p class="tags">
    <strong>Tags:</strong>
    <%= render :partial => 'tag', :collection => @story.tags %>
  </p>
<% end %>
<% if logged_in? %>
  ...
```

Once again, if a story doesn't have tags, we don't bother to list them, so we wrap the logic in an if clause:

```
<% if @story.tags.size.zero? %>
  ...
<% end %>
```

If tags *are* associated with a story, we go ahead and render a partial for every assigned tag:

```
<%= render :partial => 'tag', :collection => @story.tags %>
```

Hang on—we've just instructed our application to render a partial that doesn't exist! We'd better create it now.

Creating a tag Partial

To render a collection of tags assigned to a story, we need a tag partial. Create the file app/views/story/_tag.rhtml, and edit the contents to contain the following single line:

File: **06-_tag.rhtml (excerpt)**

```
<%= link_to tag.name, :action => 'tag', :id => tag.name %>
```

The new partial links each tag name to a new tag page, which we'll create in a moment. That page will list all stories that have been assigned a given tag.

Updating the story Partial

Last of all, we'll display tags for each story that appears in the story listings on the front page and in the voting bin. To add this information to the display, we'll modify the app/views/story/_story.rhtml partial like so:

File: **07-_story.rhtml (excerpt)**

```
<div class="story">
  …
  <p>
    Submitted by: <%= story.user.login %> |
    Score: <%= story.votes_count %><br />
    Tags: <%= story.tag_list %>
  </p>
</div>
```

This code prints a simple, space-separated list of the tags assigned to a story using the `tag_list` instance method.

Updating the Style Sheet

To give our tag links a little room to breathe on the page, let's add the following snippet of CSS to our style sheet, located at `public/stylesheets/style.css`:

File: **08-styles.css (excerpt)**

```
.tags a { padding: 0 3px; }
```

Excellent. Let's see how things look then, shall we?

Assigning our First Tags

With a solid foundation in place for the assignment and display of tags in the application, you can now start experimenting with this exciting new piece of functionality. Submit a new story from your browser using the story submission form, and this time include a few tags, as I've done in Figure 10.5.

Figure 10.5. Submitting a story with tags

When you view the front page, the upcoming page, or the individual story listings, you should see the tags that you submitted display nicely below your story, as in Figure 10.6.

Figure 10.6. Tags displaying for the new story

Everything looks good! However, those tags currently link to a `tag` action that we have yet to write. This page will display yet another list of stories, so it would make sense to reuse a template that we already have: the `index` template. We reused it for the `bin` action, and we'll use it again for the `tag` page.

Viewing Stories by Tag

At this stage, creating a page that allows users to view stories by tag should be quite easy for you. Try implementing it yourself, before reading ahead to see how I've gone about it.

Modifying the Controller

The new `tag` action of our `StoryController` should look like this:

File: **09-story_controller.rb** (excerpt)

```
class StoryController < ApplicationController
  ...
  def tag
    @stories = Story.find_tagged_with(params[:id])
    render :action => 'index'
  end
  ...
end
```

There's nothing too taxing here; first we retrieve all of the stories that are tagged with a particular tag using a method that we played with in the `console` script earlier in this chapter—`find_tagged_with`:

```
  @stories = Story.find_tagged_with(params[:id])
```

Then, as we did in the `bin` action, we render the `index` template, which already contains everything necessary for us to render a list of stories:

```
  render :action => 'index'
```

The last thing this page needs is an appropriate heading to distinguish it from our other story lists.

Displaying Tagged Stories

To show an appropriate heading for our newly added `tag` action, add the following line to the `story_list_heading` helper, located in the file `app/helpers/story_helper.rb`:

File: **10-story_helper.rb** (excerpt)

```
  ...
  def story_list_heading
```

```
    story_type = case controller.action_name
        when 'index': 'frontpage story'
        when 'bin': 'upcoming story'
        when 'tag': 'tagged story'
      end
    "Showing #{ pluralize(@stories.size, story_type) }"
  end
end
```

Clicking one of the tag links from an individual story page now takes the user to a page similar to the one in Figure 10.7. The page lists all of the stories that have been given that particular tag. Lovely!

Figure 10.7. Listing all stories tagged with "rails"

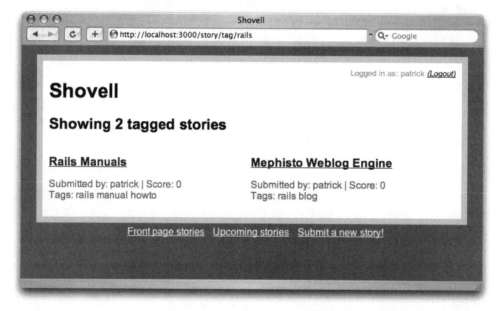

Testing the Tagging Functionality

Some plugins come bundled with complete test coverage; others do not. Unfortunately `acts_as_taggable` does not have any such coverage. However, even if it did, it's good practice to add tests to your test suite to ensure that you're testing *your usage* of the plugin, which definitely isn't covered by the standard test suite for the plugin.

Testing the Model

To test the tagging functionality that our `Story` model has inherited, we're going to add two more unit tests to the `StoryTest` test case.

Testing the Assignment of Tags

The first test we'll add to the `/test/story_test.rb` file follows:

File: **11-story_test.rb (excerpt)**

```
class StoryTest < Test::Unit::TestCase
  ...
  def test_should_act_as_taggable
    stories(:first).tag_with 'book english'
    stories(:first).reload
    assert_equal 2, stories(:first).tags.size
    assert_equal 'book english', stories(:first).tag_list
  end
end
```

This test uses the `tag_with` method to apply two tags to the first story in our fixture data:

```
    stories(:first).tag_with 'book english'
```

To reflect the newly added tags, we need to reload the object in question:

```
    stories(:first).reload
```

The two assertions in this test confirm that the number of tags assigned to the story is as expected, and that the list of tags returned by the `tag_list` method contains the correct tags, each separated from its neighbors by a space:

```
    assert_equal 2, stories(:first).tags.size
    assert_equal 'book english', stories(:first).tag_list
```

Testing the Finding of a Story by Tag

The next unit test we need to add for our `Story` model is as follows:

File: **12-story_test.rb (excerpt)**

```
class StoryTest < Test::Unit::TestCase
  ...
  def test_should_find_tagged_with
```

```
    stories(:first).tag_with 'book english'
    assert_equal [ stories(:first) ],
      Story.find_tagged_with('book')
  end
end
```

This test confirms that the functionality for finding stories by tag works as expected. After tagging a story, the test uses the `find_tagged_with` class method to retrieve a list of stories with the `book` tag, and compares it with the list of stories that we expect to be returned:

```
    stories(:first).tag_with 'book english'
    assert_equal [ stories(:first) ],
      Story.find_tagged_with('book')
```

Great, we're done! Let's go do some functional testing.

Testing the Controller

We need to add a few tests to our `StoryControllerTest` to confirm that our tagging feature works correctly from a controller perspective.

Testing the Submission of a New Story with Tags

The first test confirms that the process of adding a new story with tags works:

File: **13-story_controller_test.rb (excerpt)**

```
class StoryControllerTest < Test::Unit::TestCase
  ...
  def test_should_add_story_with_tags
    post_with_user :new, :tags => 'rails blog', :story => {
      :name => 'story with tags',
      :link => 'http://www.story-with-tags.com/'
    }
    assert_equal 'rails blog', assigns(:story).tag_list
  end
end
```

In this test, we need to be careful not to specify the tags as part of the `:story` hash—remember, tags are submitted separately from the other fields in the story submission form:

```
    post_with_user :new, :tags => 'rails blog', :story => {
      :name => 'story with tags',
```

```
      :link => 'http://www.story-with-tags.com/'
   }
```

The assertion then makes sure that the `tag_list` method of the newly added Story returns the tags that we submitted:

```
   assert_equal 'rails blog', assigns(:story).tag_list
```

Testing the Display of Tags on a Story Page

The next test checks whether a story's individual page displays its tags properly:

File: **14-story_controller_test.rb (excerpt)**

```
class StoryControllerTest < Test::Unit::TestCase
  …
  def test_should_show_story_with_tags
    stories(:promoted).tag_with 'apple music'
    get :show, :permalink => 'promoted-story'
    assert_select 'p.tags a', 2
  end
end
```

In this test, we confirm that the container element on the story page contains an appropriate number of elements. We do this by counting the number of links within the p element that has a **class** of **tags**:

```
   assert_select 'p.tags a', 2
```

Testing the **tag** Action for Listing Tagged Stories

To test our new **tag** action, add the following test to our `StoryController` test case:

File: **15-story_controller_test.rb (excerpt)**

```
class StoryControllerTest < Test::Unit::TestCase
  …
  def test_should_find_tagged_stories
    stories(:first).tag_with 'book english'
    get :tag, :id => 'book'
    assert_equal [ stories(:first) ], assigns(:stories)
  end
end
```

We start this test by assigning some tags to one of our stories, then call the `tag` method to find all stories tagged with `book`:

```
stories(:first).tag_with 'book english'
get :tag, :id => 'book'
```

The assertion then confirms that the `@stories` instance variable actually contains all the stories we expect it to:

```
assert_equal [ stories(:first) ], assigns(:stories)
```

Testing the Display of Stories by Tag

The next test we need to add to our `StoryControllerTest` is the following:

File: **16-story_controller_test.rb (excerpt)**

```
class StoryControllerTest < Test::Unit::TestCase
  ...
  def test_should_render_tagged_stories
    stories(:first).tag_with 'book english'
    get :tag, :id => 'english'
    assert_response :success
    assert_template 'index'
    assert_select 'div#content div.story', :count => 1
  end
end
```

In this test, we put the template code through its paces. The `assert_select` call confirms that the resulting page contains the expected number of `div` elements with a `class` of `story`:

```
assert_select 'div#content div.story', :count => 1
```

Testing the Display of the Story Submission Form

As we added a new field to the story submission form, we have to edit our `StoryControllerTest` class so that the `test_should_show_new_form` test counts an additional paragraph element:

File: **17-story_controller_test.rb (excerpt)**

```
class StoryControllerTest < Test::Unit::TestCase
  ...
  def test_should_show_new_form
    get_with_user :new
```

```
    assert_select 'form p', :count => 5
  end
end
```

And that, dear reader, is the last test that I'll make you write! Well, for this chapter, anyway.

Running the Test Suite ... Again!

To assure ourselves that all of these new tests (and our existing ones) pass, we'll run the whole suite again using rake, as illustrated in Figure 10.8.

Figure 10.8. Running the test suite

```
$ rake test
```

If all of your tests passed, give yourself a congratulatory pat on the back for a job well done! And if there are any errors or failures, double-check your code against the code in the book and the book's code archive to see where you might have gone wrong—the error messages displayed in your console will of course help (and if you get truly stuck, you might want to jump ahead to Chapter 11 to read about debugging your Rails application).

Summary

In this chapter, we briefly looked at using an existing Rails plugin to extend our application's functionality without reinventing the wheel. After installing the plugin and applying the necessary migration, we only had to add a single line of code to make use of the rich functionality provided by the plugin. When we'd ascertained how the plugin worked, we expanded the story submission form to take a space-separated list of tags, and expanded several views to display the tag data.

Our work is not done yet, though—we still have a bit to learn about debugging our application, running integration tests, and configuring our environment for production; these topics will be the focus of the coming chapters.

11

Debugging, Testing, and Benchmarking

Welcome to a chapter full of topics nobody likes to talk about—errors, bugs, flaws and exceptions. These are all things that other hands-on technical books rarely address—they prefer to pretend that development is easy and results in perfect, error-free code.

However, once you begin developing applications on your own, the first thing you'll learn—probably the hard way—is that bugs arise all the time, regardless of how proficient you are as a developer. It's your job to find and fix them, so you'd better be good at it!

Of course, the fun doesn't stop at bugs and errors. It may be that your finished application is not as speedy as you'd like. If this is the case, you'll need tools on hand to profile your application, so you can locate the bottlenecks that are responsible for slowing things down.

In this chapter, we'll explore all three topics.

Debugging your Application

When you're building a web application, there are times when you know exactly and immediately the cause of a problem and how to fix it. For example, if you notice a broken image on your web site, you'll instantly realize that you've forgotten to upload it, or that the path to the image is incorrect. With other bugs, however, you'll have no idea what's happened. It's at times like these that knowing how to debug your code comes in *very* handy.

There are various approaches to debugging. The simplest involves printing out the values of some of the variables that your application uses while it runs, to get a better idea of what's going on at each step in your code. A more complex approach involves complicated but powerful techniques—setting breakpoints, hooking into the running application, and executing code in the context in which you suspect it's misbehaving.

We'll begin our discussion with something simple: we'll look at the `debug` statement that's available for use within `ActionView` templates. Over the course of the next two sections, we'll work to squash a real, live bug in our Shovell application—I've deliberately introduced problems into our existing, perfectly working application code so we can get our hands dirty with a practical application. As you follow along, try to think of the potential causes for the problems we encounter.

Are you ready? Let's try our hands at a little debugging.

Debugging within Templates

I've deliberately broken our application by removing a specific line of code (obviously, I won't tell you which—that's the whole point of this section!). The result of this code removal is that the story page for a newly submitted story throws an exception and no longer displays the story. Figure 11.1 shows how this bug appears in the browser.

To complete this exercise, you'll first need to follow these steps to set up the purposefully buggy version of Shovell:

1. Copy the folder named `shovell-debug-01` from the code archive, and place it alongside your existing `shovell` application folder.

2. Ensure that `shovell-debug-01/config/database.yml` is configured to point to your existing `shovell_development` and `shovell_test` databases.

3. Start up your broken version of the Shovell application using the now familiar `ruby script/server` command.

4. Log in and add a new story to Shovell; I've given my story the name All About Debuggers.

5. Once you've submitted your new story, point your browser to http://localhost:3000/story/show/all-about-debuggers.

When your browser has finished loading the page, you should see something very similar to Figure 11.1. Don't worry if the line number doesn't match exactly; as long as the error is the same, everything's working as expected.

Figure 11.1. A mystery bug causing an error to display when we view a story

Where do we go from here? How should we approach such an error? Let's begin by taking a closer look at the error message:

```
Showing app/views/story/show.rhtml where line #22 raised:
You have a nil object when you didn't expect it!
The error occurred while evaluating nil.login
```

The obvious deduction here is that our application tried to call the `login` method on a `nil` object in our `show.rhtml` template. Understandably, Rails could not perform such an action, as the object `nil` certainly doesn't have a `login` method.

The error message also includes an excerpt of the code that Rails believes was responsible for the exception:

```
Extracted source (around line #22):
20: <p class="submitted_by">
21:    Submitted by:
22:    <%= link_to @story.user.login,
23:         :controller => 'account',
24:         :action => 'show',
25:         :id => @story.user.login %>
```

The error message directs us to line 22 of the template, which is where the link_to helper tries to assemble a link to the user page associated with the user who originally submitted the story. This line also contains the call to the login method that raised the exception. We're calling the login method on the user object associated with the story that's currently being viewed:

```
22:    <%= link_to @story.user.login %>
```

Re-reading the error message, we get the impression that @story.user must actually must be nil. But what good are impressions in web application programming? No good at all. We need cold, hard facts!

Let's put two tasks on our to-do list:

❑ Confirm that @story.user is indeed nil.

❑ Find out *why* it is nil.

To tackle the first item on our list, let's change the parts of the template that raised the exception, in order to inspect the contents of @story.user. To do so, open the app/views/story/story.rhtml template and change the following sections:

File: **01-story.rhtml (excerpt)**

```
...
<p class="submitted_by">
  Submitted by:
  <%= @story.user.class %>
  <%# link_to @story.user.login,
       :controller => 'account',
       :action => 'show',
       :id => @story.user.login %>
</p>
...
```

I made two changes to the template. First, I added a statement to print the class of the @story.user variable to our browser. Then, I used the <%# %> syntax to comment out the link_to statement. If we don't do this, the application will continue to raise an exception when we reload the page, and we won't receive the output of the line we added. This line is now considered a comment, rather than a part of the working code, and as such it won't be executed.

When we reload the page, we see that @story.user is indeed nil, which explains the exception we're seeing. Figure 11.2 shows the results of our work. The first item on our to-do list is done!

Figure 11.2. @story.user visible in the rendered template

To find out *why* @story.user is nil, we'll need to skip to the point where @story.user is actually assigned a value: the new action of StoryController. Before we do so, though, we should revert the changes that we just made to the `show.rhtml` template. Remove the statement that prints the class name, and make the `link_to` statement active again:

File: **02-story.rhtml** (excerpt)

```
...
<p class="submitted_by">
  Submitted by:
  <%= link_to @story.user.login, … %>
</p>
...
```

When we implemented user authentication in Chapter 8, we started to populate this variable with the currently logged-in user. Let's check this functionality in the template that's being rendered for the new action—it's located in `app/views/story/new.rhtml`:

File: **03-new.rhtml** (excerpt)

```
<%= error_messages_for 'story' %>
<%= debug @story %>
<% form_for :story do |f| %>
  ...
<% end %>
```

The code I added between the `error_messages_for` and `form_for` statements is the `debug` helper provided by Rails:

```
<%= debug @story %>
```

The debug statement instructs Rails to output a YAML representation of the object that we pass as a parameter. In this case, because we're working from a view template, this output will be sent directly to the browser. Load the story submission form in your browser with this debugging code in place, and you should see something that resembles Figure 11.3.

The output should remind you of our test fixtures—it's formatted in YAML, after all. The debugging content that's shown in addition to our regular template output is a representation of `@story` that contains a new, unsaved `Story` object.

The debug helper automatically wraps its output in a `pre` element. By default, the contents of a `pre` element are displayed by the browser as pre-formatted text in a monospace font.

Figure 11.3. Looking at a YAML representation of `@story`

Within the YAML representation, you can spot that the `user_id` attribute lacks a value (in contrast to the `votes_count` attribute, for example, which has a value of 0). This means that the attribute isn't being set properly in the controller action, before the `new` template is rendered.

Time for me to come clean: here's the modified controller action that causes this problem:

File: **shovell-debug-01/app/controllers/story_controller.rb (excerpt)**

```
def new
  @story = Story.new(params[:story])
  #@story.user = @current_user

  if request.post? and @story.save
    ...
  end
end
```

As you can see, the line that sets the `user` attribute of the new `Story` object has been commented out. Asa result, no user will be assigned to the newly submitted story.

"But wait!" you might be thinking. "Wouldn't a test have caught this problem?"

Of course it would have.

Running the functional tests (using `rake test:functionals`) with the `@story.user = @current_user` line commented out, as it is above, would reveal a test failure, as Figure 11.4 shows.

The test that fails is the one that verifies that the submission of a new story stores the current user—obviously, it doesn't. The error message from the test even tells us that it expected a `User` object with a login of `patrick`; instead, it got a `nil` object.

Figure 11.4. Functional tests failing and revealing the broken code

```
○ ○ ○            Terminal — bash — 80x25 — ⌘3
nctional/story_controller_test.rb"
Loaded suite /opt/local/lib/ruby/gems/1.8/gems/rake-0.7.1/lib/rake/rake_test_loa
der
Started
..............................F..
Finished in 1.205805 seconds.

  1) Failure:
test_should_store_user_with_story(StoryControllerTest) [./test/functional/story_
controller_test.rb:100]:
<#<User:0x35366b4
 @attributes=
   {"name"=>"Patrick Lenz",
    "id"=>"1",
    "password"=>"sekrit",
    "login"=>"patrick",
    "email"=>"patrick@lenz.sh"}>> expected but was
<nil>.

35 tests, 88 assertions, 1 failures, 0 errors
rake aborted!
Command failed with status (1): [/opt/local/bin/ruby -Ilib:test "/opt/local...]

(See full trace by running task with --trace)
Core:~/shovell scoop$ ▌
```

What lesson can we take from this exercise? Well, if you equip your code with proper test coverage from the beginning, you'll have an easy and efficient way to spot an error in your code later.

If you've been following along (you have been following along, right?), you'll need to either remove the story with the broken user association, or fix the user association through the console by changing its user_id to 1.

Debugging Using Breakpoints

In the next example, we'll take a look at another problem that I've secretly introduced to our existing code. If you take a look at Figure 11.5, you'll notice that although we've provided a description for the new story we submitted, it doesn't show up on the final story page.

Figure 11.5. Story description missing from a newly submitted story

If you'd like to follow along with this example, copy the shovell-debug-2 folder from the code archive, and set it up using the same steps as we used for shovell-debug-1 (I'll even wait for you!).

"Ha!" I hear you laugh. "I learned in the last section that I just need to run the test suite and it'll tell me what's wrong!"

While that's a great idea, the reality is that when we run the full test suite with rake test from the application root, every single test passes, as if nothing were wrong; Figure 11.6 shows the results of running the test suite.

Figure 11.6. Running the test suite without errors

```
●○○          Terminal — bash — 80x25 — ⌘3
Started
................
Finished in 0.602583 seconds.

17 tests, 20 assertions, 0 failures, 0 errors
/opt/local/bin/ruby -Ilib:test "/opt/local/lib/ruby/gems/1.8/gems/rake-0.7.1/lib
/rake/rake_test_loader.rb" "test/functional/account_controller_test.rb" "test/fu
nctional/story_controller_test.rb"
Loaded suite /opt/local/lib/ruby/gems/1.8/gems/rake-0.7.1/lib/rake/rake_test_loa
der
Started
....................................
Finished in 1.249551 seconds.

35 tests, 88 assertions, 0 failures, 0 errors
/opt/local/bin/ruby -Ilib:test "/opt/local/lib/ruby/gems/1.8/gems/rake-0.7.1/lib
/rake/rake_test_loader.rb" "test/integration/stories_test.rb"
Loaded suite /opt/local/lib/ruby/gems/1.8/gems/rake-0.7.1/lib/rake/rake_test_loa
der
Started
.
Finished in 0.275391 seconds.

1 tests, 9 assertions, 0 failures, 0 errors
Core:~/shovell scoop$ []
```

What happened here? We'll need to find out. While we used statements to investigate specific objects and attributes in the previous example, in this case, we don't really know where to begin.

One tool that proves extremely useful as we explore the working environment of an application is the **breakpoint client**. You can use the breakpoint client, which operates a lot like the `console` script, to jump into your running application and inspect variables, run other code, step through your code line by line, and more. You can even use it to *change* objects and variables while the application is in the middle of executing.

To use the breakpoint client, we need to insert breakpoints in our application code. Execution of the application code stops as soon as one of these `breakpoint` statements is encountered. A `breakpoint` statement can be placed anywhere, including within any of our models, controllers, and views.

While you're in the breakpoint client, you can step through your code, one line at a time, and make whatever changes you need to figure out the cause of the problem. Once you're finished debugging, and exit the breakpoint client, execution of the application resumes as if nothing had interrupted it.

Be careful when changing code from the breakpoint client, though, since your changes will persist when your application resumes execution. It's like Marty McFly risking his birth by changing the past in *Back to the Future*...

Let's use the breakpoint client to find out a bit more about the misbehavior of our story submission form. To do so, add a `breakpoint` statement to the `new` action of `StoryController`, which is located at `app/controllers/story_controller.rb`, like so:

*File: **shovell-debug-02/app/controllers/story_controller.rb** (excerpt)*

```
def new
  @story = Story.new(params[:story])
  @story.user = @current_user
  if request.post? and @story.save
    breakpoint
    flash[:notice] = "Story submission succeeded"
    redirect_to :action => 'index'
  end
end
```

As soon as you submit the story submission form, you'll notice that your browser hangs. Your breakpoint is in action, and Rails is waiting for you to connect to it using the breakpoint client.

Use the following command from the application root to fire up the breakpoint client:

```
$ ruby script/breakpointer
```

You'll end up seeing a command prompt similar to that of the Rails console. But as the prompt prefix suggests, you're not looking at your application from the outside, as you do when using the Rails console—you're looking *out* from the *inside* of `StoryController`, as Figure 11.7 shows.

Figure 11.7. The breakpoint client

```
Terminal — ruby — 80x10 — ⌘3
Core:~/shovell scoop$ ruby script/breakpointer
Executing break point at /Users/scoop/shovell/config/../app/controllers/story_co
ntroller.rb:23 in `new'
irb(#<StoryController:0x35bb7e8>):001:0> @story.description
=> nil
irb(#<StoryController:0x35bb7e8>):002:0> █
```

At this point, you can examine parts of the working environment, such as the `@story` instance variable or the `params` hash. First up, we'll take a look at the new story object that's stored in the `@story` variable:

```
>> @story.description
=> nil
```

As you can see, even through we've entered a beautifully phrased story description into the form, the relevant `description` attribute of the new `story` object is `nil`, or empty.

Since each of the form fields ends up in the `params` hash, this will be the next stop on our debugging journey. As `params[:story]` contains all the submitted attributes for our new story object, we'll ask directly for the `description` attribute, like so:

```
>> params[:story][:description]
=> nil
```

Hmm, that attribute's empty as well. But the contents of that form field have to end up *somewhere*! Let's take a look at the `params` hash as a whole:

```
>> params
=> {"commit"=>"Save changes", "controller"=>"story",
        "action"=>"new",
    "story"=>{"name"=>"What is a Debugger?",
    "link"=>"http://en.wikipedia.org/wiki/Debugger"},
    "description"=>{"rows10"=>"A debugger is a computer program
                    that is used to test and debug other
                    programs."}, }
```

There it is—it's sitting at `params[:description]` for some reason. This indicates that the element names in our form must be incorrect.

Checking the form in `app/views/story/new.rhtml` reveals the cause of the problem:

File: **shovell-debug-02/app/views/new.rhtml** (excerpt)

```
<% form_for :story do |f| %>
  ...
  <p>
    description:<br />
    <%= text_area :description, :rows => 10 %>
  </p>
  ...
<% end %>
```

Instead of using the `FormBuilder` object provided by `form_for`, I altered the helper that generates the text area for the story's description, so that it uses the `text_area` helper directly. The change messed up the element name, and broke the application's ability to store the submitted story description.

Changing that line to the following fixes the error:

```
<%= f.text_area :description, :rows => 10 %>
```

To exit the breakpoint client for the current breakpoint, you can use the `exit` command or use the **Ctrl-D** keyboard shortcut. To exit the breakpoint client completely, press **Ctrl-C**. If you don't, Rails will keep on trying to connect to the next breakpoint in our application, even though we don't currently have one.

Now that that problem's solved, you can go ahead and remove the `breakpoint` statement from the `StoryController`.

Okay, so we've squashed the bug. Great. But why didn't our test suite report any errors? Well, first of all, `description` is not a required attribute according to the validations that we defined—we only specify that a `name` and a `link` are necessary for a story to be submitted successfully. Additionally, our test only checks for the presence of a specific number of form fields in the story submission form—it doesn't check individual attributes and element names. That's why our tests didn't reveal the error.

Armed with this knowledge, we can expand the test case for `StoryController` by adding one more test to `test/functional/story_controller_test.rb`:

File: **04-story_controller_test.rb** (excerpt)

```
class StoryControllerTest < Test::Unit::TestCase
  ...
```

```
  def test_should_include_description_field_on_new_form
    get_with_user :new
    assert_select 'form p textarea#story_description'
  end
end
```

This test confirms that a `textarea` element exists on the page, is properly nested, and has an element `id` of `story_description`.

Running our test suite with the error still in place now produces the expected test failure. And correcting the error allows the test to pass, as Figure 11.8 illustrates.

Figure 11.8. Expanding functional test coverage for the problem we found

Using the Rails Logging Tool

Rails comes with an internal logging tool for writing custom entries, triggered by specific events, to your application's log file.

While logging events can certainly be useful for debugging purposes (especially in a production environment, where you don't want to scare your users with the output of debugging code), event logging can also be of general interest. For instance, log entries can reveal usage patterns for your application, such as the times at which maintenance jobs start and end, or the frequency with which external services are accessed.

We'll use the Rails logging tool to implement an **access log** for our application—a log of the pages requested by users who are logged in. While web server logs allow for comprehensive analysis, they don't contain any details of the specific user that requested the page—this information can be particularly useful, either to the marketing department, or when you're trying to diagnose a problem that was reported by a particular user.

To implement the access log, we need to:

1. Create a call to the Rails internal logging system.

2. Place this call in an appropriate location in our application code so that it's executed for every page. This location must allow the code to determine whether or not a user is logged in.

We have a location that meets both of these requirements: the `fetch_logged_in_user` before filter, which lives in the `ApplicationController` class.

To document the page requests of our users, we use the `logger` object, which is available at any point in a Rails application. `logger` is used to write a new entry to the environment-specific log file. By default, we operate in the development environment, so the `logger` object will write new entries to the bottom of the log file `log/development.log`.

Like logging functionality in Java or other platforms, Rails logging can deal with a variety of severity levels. When you log an entry, it's up to you to decide how severe the event you're logging really is. The most common severity levels are `debug`, `info`, `warn`, and `error`.

Each of the Rails environments has different default settings for the severity levels that are written to the log file. In the production environment, which we'll cover in depth in Chapter 12, the default is the `info` level; in the development and testing environments, events of every level of severity are logged.

Here's the `fetch_logged_in_user` action in `app/controllers/application.rb` with an added `logger` statement:

File: **05-application.rb (excerpt)**

```
def fetch_logged_in_user
  return if session[:user_id].blank?
  @current_user = User.find_by_id(session[:user_id])
  logger.info "#{@current_user.login} requested
    #{request.request_uri} on #{Time.now}"
end
```

As you can see in the `logger` call above, we're using the `info` severity level to log these statements in all environments, including production. Specifying the severity level is simply a matter of calling the appropriately named instance method of the `logger` object.

The string that's written to the log file is actually a composite of three Ruby statements. First, we're logging the value of the `login` attribute for the current user:

```
logger.info "#{@current_user.login} requested
    #{request.request_uri} on #{Time.now}"
```

Then, we add the URL that the user requested (without the host and port; you'll see an example in a second), which is available from the `request` object that Rails provides:

```
logger.info "#{@current_user.login} requested
    #{request.request_uri} on #{Time.now}"
```

Lastly, the current date and time are added to the string:

```
logger.info "#{@current_user.login} requested
    #{request.request_uri} on #{Time.now}"
```

With these details in place, every page in our application will make an entry to the application log file. Here's a sample session:

```
patrick requested /story/new on Sun Oct 22 15:46:50 CEST 2006
patrick requested / on Sun Oct 22 15:47:24 CEST 2006
patrick requested /story/bin on Sun Oct 22 15:47:26 CEST 2006
patrick requested /story/show/my-shiny-weblog on Sun Oct 22
    15:47:29 CEST 2006
patrick requested /story/vote/5 on Sun Oct 22 15:47:38 CEST 2006
```

The `fetch_logged_in_user` method exits immediately if the current user hasn't logged in, so our log file displays only log entries from pages requested by users who were logged in when they used Shovell. Of course, you can customize log output to your heart's content, so if this format doesn't suit your needs, you could modify it to be more readable for humans, or more easily parsed by a Ruby script, for example.

Overcoming Problems in Debugging

While we've added a considerable number of tests to our application code so far, we certainly haven't covered *every* aspect of the application.

Whenever you fix a problem during the development of your application, take a moment to add a test to your test suite that verifies that the problem has been fixed—just like we did in the last section. Following this approach will ensure that you never receive another bug report for the same problem.

Another approach is to write a test to verify the problem *before* you attempt to fix it—this way, you can be sure that as long as your test fails, the problem still exists. It's entirely up to you to determine your own approach to the task of debugging, but try to not move on from any problem without having added a new test for it to your test suite.

Testing your Application

The test code that we've written so far has dealt mostly with the isolated testing of controller actions and model functionality. To test scenarios that involve multiple controllers and multiple models, Version 1.1 of Rails introduced a feature called integration testing.

Integration Tests

An **integration test** verifies the behavior of a number of controllers and models as a user interacts with the application. Integration tests tell a story about a fictitious user of our application—the user's login process, the links that person follows, and the actions that he or she takes.

When to Use an Integration Test

Some example scenarios that are ideally suited to testing via an integration test include:

❏ A visitor wants to submit a story, so he tries to access the story submission form. He is redirected to the login form because he hasn't logged in yet. After logging in using the login form, he's sent back to the submission form and submits a story.

❏ A given user is the fifth user to vote on a particular story. She knows that the threshold for stories to appear on the front page is five votes, so once she's voted, she visits the front page to check that the story she voted for appears there.

❏ A user submits a new story with a number of tags. After sending in her submission, she proceeds to the tag page for one of the tags she used on her submission, and checks that the story does indeed appear in the list.

As you can see, integration tests can be quite specific and detailed; writing Ruby test code to match the level of detail specified by the above scenarios is perfectly achievable.

Integration tests are highly dependent upon an application's business logic, so Rails doesn't offer a facility to automatically generate test templates like those we created for unit and functional tests. Let's begin writing our first integration test from scratch.

Creating our First Integration Test

First, we'll create a new file in which to store the test. Then, we'll set up a test case to implement the first of the scenarios that we just discussed—a user who is not logged in tries to submit a story. This scenario will be translated into Ruby code.

Every integration test class is stored in the `test/integration/` directory. Create a new file named `stories_test.rb` in this directory, and edit it to appear as follows:

File: **06-stories_test.rb**

```
require "#{File.dirname(__FILE__)}/../test_helper"
class StoriesTest < ActionController::IntegrationTest
  fixtures :stories, :votes, :users
  def test_story_submission_with_login
    get '/story/new'
    assert_response :redirect
    follow_redirect!
    assert_response :success
```

```
    assert_template 'account/login'
    post '/account/login', :login => 'patrick',
        :password => 'sekrit'
    assert_response :redirect
    follow_redirect!
    assert_response :success
    assert_template 'story/new'
    post 'story/new', :story => {
      :name => 'Submission from Integration Test',
      :link => 'http://test.com/'
    }
    assert_response :redirect
    follow_redirect!
    assert_response :success
    assert_template 'story/index'
  end
end
```

On the surface, this test resembles a regular functional test—the test performs an action, then asserts that the results of that action are as expected. In this case, the first action is to request a page; the test then verifies that the response code and the template used to render the page are as expected; it then continues with the rest of its actions.

However, instead of the `get` and `post` calls being based on specific controllers and their respective actions, page requests in an integration test take standard URLs (from which the domain is omitted, if appropriate). Why? Well, an integration test doesn't test a controller in complete isolation from its environment—it views the application as a whole, so other elements of the application, such as routing and the handover of control from one controller to another, are tested as well.

```
get '/story/new'
```

Another new tidbit in this test code is the `follow_redirect!` statement. At this point, the test assumes that a redirect was issued after the last `get` or `post` call (which we're asserting using `assert_response`, by the way). It also assumes that the URL to which a user is redirected—the story submission page—is followed in the test, hence the test's name.

```
follow_redirect!
```

Additionally, when we're verifying that an action renders the view template we expected, we must specify the path relative to the `app/views/` directory. Remember, we're not testing in isolation, so there's no "default" view directory:

```
    assert_template 'account/login'
```

Other than that, the test consists of plain old functional test code.

Running an Integration Test

Let's run this test to make sure it passes as we expect. Like unit and functional tests, integration tests are run with a `rake` command:

```
$ rake test:integration
```

Integration tests are executed along with your unit and functional tests when running the `rake test` command. Figure 11.9 shows the outcome of our test.

Figure 11.9. Running the integration tests

As you can see from this basic example, an integration test gives you the assurance that your application behaves independently of your functional and unit tests, and that all of your application's components are put through their paces in an automated manner.

Using Breakpoints in a Test

Just as we used breakpoints to jump into the running application at a pre-defined point, we can use breakpoints to jump into the application from within a test. This technique can be useful for determining why a test is failing, or for gaining insight into the resources available when we're writing tests.

Using breakpoints in tests is just as straightforward as using them in regular development mode: place the `breakpoint` statement at the point at which you want execution to halt. Contrary to the approach we used in development mode, however, you don't need to use the separate breakpoint client to "connect" to your application. When you're using breakpoints in tests, Rails presents you with the Rails console as soon as the `breakpoint` statement is encountered.

Here's an example of a breakpoint in action. I added a breakpoint to the integration test that we built in the previous section (as a reminder, this integration test is stored in `test/integration/stories_test.rb`):

File: **07-stories_test.rb (excerpt)**

```
class StoriesTest < ActionController::IntegrationTest
  ...
  def test_story_submission_with_login
    get '/story/new'
    breakpoint
    ...
  end
end
```

Let's run our suite of integration tests using the command `rake test:integration`. We're presented with the Rails console immediately after the new session has been created—just after the test requests the submission form for the first time. At this point, we're free to explore the environment—below are examples of the characteristics of our code that can be revealed using the console.

First, let's look at the cookies that have been set for the user that the test is impersonating:

```
>> cookies
=> {"_session_id"=>"19be51e81372877994bba056d20f671d"}
```

At the point at which the breakpoint appears, the user has not yet logged in, so no `user_id` value has been stored in the user's session:

```
>> session[:user_id]
=> nil
```

We can log in using the same statement that our test uses a few lines down—the return value shown here is the numeric HTTP response code for a redirect (which happens to be **302**). Enter this all on one line.

```
>> post '/account/login', :login => 'patrick',
   :password => 'sekrit'
=> 302
```

The user's session now contains a `user_id` value, as this code and Figure 11.10 show:

```
>> session[:user_id]
=> 1
```

Figure 11.10. A breakpoint used in a test

Breakpoints can be a great timesaver if you need to explore the environment surrounding an action in order to write better, more comprehensive tests. Without using breakpoints, exploring the environment would only be possible in a limited fashion—for example, by placing lots of `puts` statements in your tests and rerunning them countless times to get the information you need.

With breakpoints, however, you can interact with your models right there, without modifying huge chunks of code. This process is as easy as possible, which means the barriers to writing tests are reduced even further.

Revisiting the Rails Console

We've used the `console` script frequently in previous chapters, mainly to explore features as they were being introduced.

The console can also be used to play with your application in **headless mode**, in which you can interact with your application from the console just as a browser would interact with it. In conjunction with breakpoints in tests, which we talked about in the last section, this technique can be a good way to play around with your application in anticipation of creating a new integration test once you've worked out exactly what you want to do.

With integration tests in Rails 1.1 came a new object that's available by default in the `console` script: the `app` object. This object can be thought of as providing you access to an empty integration test. You're able to `get` and `post` to URLs, you have access to the session and cookies containers, and so on—just like a regular integration test.

Let's have a go at using the `app` object from the `console` script. You should recognize a lot of the methods that we're using here from the integration test that we built earlier in this chapter.

Initially, we're interested to know what kind of object `app` really is:

```
>> app.class
=> ActionController::Integration::Session
```

Next, let's fetch the front page of our application using the `get` action:

```
>> app.get '/'
=> 200
```

The return value is the HTTP response code that indicates a successful page request. We've been using the `:successful` symbol in its place in most of our tests until now.

Next, we'll use the `assigns` action to check the instance variable assignments that are made in the action we requested. In this case, we're looking at the number of elements in the `@stories` array:

```
>> app.assigns(:stories).size
=> 1
```

If we try to fetch the story submission form, we receive a redirect (HTTP code 302) as we're not yet logged in:

```
>> app.get '/story/new'
=> 302
```

When we receive the redirect, we can look at the URL to which the redirect is pointing using the following construct:

```
>> app.response.redirect_url
=> "http://www.example.com/account/login"
```

It's easy to follow the redirect that was just issued using the `follow_redirect!` method:

```
>> app.follow_redirect!
=> 200
```

We can also use the `post` method to log in with a username and password, and follow the resulting redirect:

```
>> app.post '/account/login', :login => 'patrick',
                              :password => 'sekrit'
=> 302
>> app.follow_redirect!
=> 200
```

Note that we didn't look at the `app.response.redirect_url` before we accepted the redirection. Here's how you can check the last URL you requested:

```
>> app.request.request_uri
=> "/story/new"
```

As it is, after all, an integration test, headless mode also provides you with access to the `session` and `cookies` variables:

```
>> app.cookies
=> {"_session_id"=>"c8302c71ec9329174a00a53273a53b8d"}
>> app.session[:user_id]
=> 1
```

Figure 11.11 shows a sample session in which the console is used in headless mode.

Figure 11.11. The console in headless mode

```
ruby — 80x25 — ⌘2
Core:~/shovell scoop$ ruby script/console
Loading development environment.
>> app.class
=> ActionController::Integration::Session
>> app.get '/'
=> 200
>> app.assigns(:stories).size
=> 1
>> app.get '/story/new'
=> 302
>> app.response.redirect_url
=> "http://www.example.com/account/login"
>> app.follow_redirect!
=> 200
>> app.post '/account/login', :login => 'patrick', :password => 'sekrit'
=> 302
>> app.follow_redirect!
=> 200
>> app.request.request_uri
=> "/story/new"
>> app.cookies
=> {"_session_id"=>"c8302c71ec9329174a00a53273a53b8d"}
>> app.session[:user_id]
=> 1
>>
```

As you can see, headless mode is a great tool for checking out the possible ways in which you might develop an integration test. Once you're satisfied with your findings, you can open up your text editor and transform your console results into an automated test. Easy!

Benchmarking your Application

As software developers, it's our job to know which part of our application is doing what—if an error arises, we can jump right in and fix it. However, knowing *how long* each part of our application is taking to perform its job is a completely different story.

Benchmarking, in software terms, is the process of measuring an application's performance, and taking steps to improve it based on that initial measurement. The benchmarking process usually involves **profiling** the application—monitoring it to determine where bottlenecks are occurring—before any changes are made to improve the application's performance.

While I won't cover the profiling and benchmarking of a Rails application in every gory detail (it's a topic to which an entire book could easily be devoted), I'll give you an introduction to the tools that are available for the job. Keep in mind that your first Rails application is unlikely to have performance problems in its early stages—the objective with your first application (or at least the first *version* of your application) should be to get the functionality right the first time; *then* you can worry about making it fast.

Taking Benchmarks from Log Files

When it's running in development and testing modes, Rails provides a variety of benchmarking information in its log files, as we saw briefly in Chapter 5. For each request that's served by the application, Rails notes all of the templates rendered, database queries performed, and the total time that it took to serve the request.

Let's examine a sample request to understand what each of the log entries means. This example deals with a request for the Shovell homepage:

```
Processing StoryController#index (for 127.0.0.1 at 2006-09-13
    12:03:52) [GET]
```

This line represents the start of the block of logging for a single page request. It includes:

❑ the names of the controller and action

❑ the IP address of the client requesting the page (127.0.0.1 being the equivalent of localhost)

❑ the time the request came in

❑ the request method that was used (GET in this case)

Rails also logs the session ID of the request, as well as the parameters that the user's browser provided with the request:

```
Session ID: c8302c71ec9329174a00a53273a53b8d
Parameters: {"action"=>"index", "controller"=>"story"}
```

Each of the next three entries in our sample log file corresponds to a database query issued by the application. Each entry lists the time (in seconds) that the application took to execute the query:

```
Story Columns (0.001504)   SHOW FIELDS FROM stories
SQL (0.000659)   SELECT count(*) AS count_all FROM stories
              WHERE (votes_count >= 5)
Story Load (0.000224)   SELECT * FROM stories
              WHERE (votes_count >= 5) ORDER BY id DESC
              LIMIT 0, 10
```

In the first of these log entries, Rails has asked the database for the column information of the stories table. The second query represents a request made by the Rails pagination helper, which simplifies the handling of large result sets. The final line is a simple query to display Story data.

Each of the following lines corresponds to a rendered template; when Rails renders a layout template, it explicitly says so by logging Rendering within:

```
Rendering within layouts/application
Rendering story/index
```

A summary entry appears at the end of each page request:

```
Completed in 0.05800 (17 reqs/sec) | Rendering: 0.00893 (15%) |
    DB: 0.00468 (8%) | 200 OK [http://www.example.com/]
```

This summary contains totals for the time spent by each of the areas of the application that were responsible for serving the request. The total time that was taken to serve the request is mentioned along with the *potential* number of requests to this particular action that your application might be able to handle per second:

```
Completed in 0.05800 (17 reqs/sec) | Rendering: 0.00893 (15%) |
    DB: 0.00468 (8%) | 200 OK [http://www.example.com/]
```

This value should be taken with a grain of salt, however—in reality, calculating an accurate estimate of the number of requests that an application can handle in parallel involves more than simply dividing 60 seconds by the time it takes to serve a single request.

Additionally, Rails tells us the amount of time that was spent rendering templates and talking to the database—these figures are listed both in seconds, and as percentages of the total time that was spent completing the task:

```
Completed in 0.05800 (17 reqs/sec) | Rendering: 0.00893 (15%) |
    DB: 0.00468 (8%) | 200 OK [http://www.example.com/]
```

You don't need to be a mathematician to figure out that a whopping 77% is missing from these numbers! One of the reasons for this difference is that serving the request took only a couple of milliseconds. These numbers come from my version of Shovell, which is quite a small application, and the benchmark calculation gets a little wacky when it calculates time information using such small numbers. In the meantime, Figure 11.12 shows the log file from a complete page request:

Figure 11.12. Benchmarking information in the log file

```
●●●          Terminal — bash — 80x25 — ⌘3
Vote Load (0.000631)   SELECT * FROM votes WHERE (votes.story_id = 6)
SQL (0.000179)   BEGIN
Story Update (0.000806)    UPDATE stories SET `permalink` = 'the-ruby-language'
, `user_id` = 1, `link` = 'http://www.ruby-lang.org/', `votes_count` = 0, `name`
= 'The Ruby Language' WHERE id = 6
SQL (0.000301)   COMMIT
Vote Load (0.000635)   SELECT * FROM votes WHERE (votes.story_id = 7)
SQL (0.000203)   BEGIN
Story Update (0.000436)    UPDATE stories SET `permalink` = 'rails-manuals', `u
ser_id` = 1, `link` = 'http://manuals.rubyonrails.org/', `votes_count` = 0, `nam
e` = 'Rails Manuals' WHERE id = 7
SQL (0.000181)   COMMIT
Vote Load (0.000593)   SELECT * FROM votes WHERE (votes.story_id = 8)
SQL (0.000172)   BEGIN
Story Update (0.000355)    UPDATE stories SET `permalink` = 'welcome--debugger-
', `user_id` = NULL, `link` = 'http://en.wikipedia.org/wiki/Debugger', `votes_co
unt` = 0, `name` = 'Welcome, Debugger!' WHERE id = 8
SQL (0.000174)   COMMIT
SQL (0.000360)   UPDATE schema_info SET version = 5
SQL (0.000465)   SELECT version FROM schema_info
Migrating to AddStoryCreationDateAndDescription (6)
SQL (0.008726)   ALTER TABLE stories ADD `created_at` datetime
SQL (0.008619)   ALTER TABLE stories ADD `description` text
SQL (0.000423)   UPDATE schema_info SET version = 6
SQL (0.000354)   SELECT version FROM schema_info
```

For all the comfort and speed that Rails provides developers, it does have its drawbacks. The framework certainly requires a large amount of CPU time in order to do its job of making your life easy, which is another explanation for the missing milliseconds in the timing calculation above. However, the overhead used by the framework won't necessarily increase greatly as your code becomes more complicated, so with a larger application, these numbers become more accurate.

In any case, it's important to take a look at your log files every now and then to get an idea of your application's performance. As I mentioned, take these numbers with a grain of salt—learn to interpret them by changing your code and comparing the new numbers with previous incarnations of the code. This will help you gain a feel for how your changes affect the speed of your application. You should not, however, use them as absolute measures.

Manual Benchmarking

While the default information presented by the Rails log files is great for providing an overview of how long a certain action takes, the log files can't provide timing information for a specific group of code statements. For this purpose, Rails provides the benchmark class method, which you can wrap around any block of code that you'd like to benchmark.

As an example, let's add benchmarking information for the story fetcher implemented in the fetch_stories method of our StoryController, which is located in app/controllers/story_controller.rb:

File: **08-story_controller.rb (excerpt)**

```ruby
class StoryController < ApplicationController
  ...
  def fetch_stories(conditions)
    self.class.benchmark('Fetching stories') do
      @stories = Story.find :all,
        :order => 'id DESC',
        :conditions => conditions
    end
  end
end
```

As you can see, the benchmark class method simply wraps around the Story.find statement. As benchmark is a class method, rather than an instance method, we have to call it with a prefix of self.class:

```ruby
self.class.benchmark('Fetching stories') do
  ...
end
```

The textual argument provided to benchmark is the text that Rails writes to the log file, along with the timing information:

```ruby
self.class.benchmark('Fetching stories') do
  ...
end
```

When you request Shovell's front page or upcoming stories queue now (both pages make use of the fetch_stories method we just modified), you should see that the corresponding benchmark entries are added to the log file at `log/development.log`. The sample log file in Figure 11.13 shows how this looks.

Figure 11.13. The output from manual benchmarking

```
000                 Terminal — bash — 80x10 — %1
Fetching stories (0.02599)
Fetching stories (0.02602)
Fetching stories (0.02529)
Fetching stories (0.29043)
Fetching stories (0.01435)
Fetching stories (0.00765)
Fetching stories (0.00756)
Fetching stories (0.00921)
Fetching stories (0.00787)
Core:~/shovell scoop$
```

Using manual benchmarks in this way can give you a feel for the amount of time required to execute certain parts of your code. Additionally, `benchmark` logs events with a severity of `debug` by default—as production mode does not log statements that have a severity of `debug`, `benchmark` statements in your code will not be calculated and won't slow your production application down.

Summary

In this chapter, we've dealt with some of the less-glamorous—but very helpful—aspects of software development. We used `debug` statements to inspect certain objects in our views, we used the log files written by Rails to document certain occurrences in Shovell, and we used breakpoints to explore our application at run-time.

We also covered the topic of integration tests—broad, scenario-based tests that have the ability to go beyond the isolated testing of models and controllers.

Finally, we talked briefly about the benchmarks that Rails provides by default, and explored a manual approach to benchmarking a specific group of statements.

In the next (and final!) chapter, we'll take Shovell into production mode and discuss the options available for deploying a Rails application for the whole world to use!

Deployment and Production Use

When Rails applications start to fledge, you, as their guardian, have to take extra care to make sure they can fly ... although, admittedly, the term "roll" would be a little more correct in the Rails context!

In this final chapter, we'll review the variety of components involved in the process of deploying a Rails application to a production system. Following that, we'll look at what's required to fine-tune an application's deployment so that it's able to cope with a moderate amount of traffic.

The Implications of "Production"

Back in Chapter 4, when we discussed the different environments Rails provides for each stage of an application's lifecycle, we barely scratched the surface of what it means to flip the switch between the development and production environments.

In a nutshell, moving to the production environment results in four major changes to the way in which our application is run:

The Ruby classes that make up your application are no longer reloaded *on each request*.

Ruby's reloading of each class on each request is a nice feature of the development environment, because it allows you to make rapid changes to your application code and see the effects immediately. However, when your application's in production mode, the primary requirement is that it's *fast*, which isn't a goal that can be accomplished by reloading Ruby classes over and over again. To gain the effects of any changes you make to code while the application's in production mode, you'll need to restart the application. The only exceptions to this rule are view templates, which are just that—templates for outputting your application's data. You don't need to restart your application in order to gain the effects of the changes you make to templates.

The production environment doesn't log every single database communication that's executed by your application.

This restriction was put in place for performance reasons, and to save you from buying new hard drives just to store your log files. In the production environment, Rails logs items with a severity level of `info` or higher by default (skipping those with a severity of `debug`). While it might make sense to skip items with a severity of `info` later on, when our application first enters production we're still at a point at which the inner workings of our application are of interest, so we'll leave the default level of reporting unchanged for now.

Your application's users receive short, helpful error messages; they're not presented with the stack trace.

Obviously, the beautifully detailed stack trace that you investigate when you find an error in your code is not something you want users of your application to see. Fear not! Rails never throws stack traces at users while it's in production mode. Instead, you can use the Exception Notification plugin to dispatch an email to the administrators of the system to notify them of a potential problem in the code.[1] The email includes the same detailed stack trace you'd see in your browser if you were still in development, as Figure 12.1 illustrates. With the error notification taken care of, you can simply use a generic error page within your application to let users know that an error has occurred and the administrators have been notified.

---

[1] http://dev.rubyonrails.org/browser/plugins/exception_notification

Figure 12.1. An example email resulting from the Exception Notification plugin

```
Subject:  [ERROR] messaging#read (NoMethodError) "undefined method `update_attribute' for
          nil:NilClass"
   Date:  October 20, 2006 12:16:01 PM GMT+02:00
     To:  Lenz Patrick

A NoMethodError occurred in messaging#read:

  undefined method `update_attribute' for nil:NilClass
  [RAILS_ROOT]/app/models/message_observer.rb:28:in `after_create'
```

Caching is available for pages, actions, and page fragments.

To improve the performance of your application, you can cache its pages, actions, and even fragments of pages. This means that the fully rendered page (or fragment) is written to the file system as well as being displayed in the user's browser. The next request that's responded to by this page, action, or fragment is served without the data that it contains needing to be recalculated. Rails's caching features are especially useful in situations in which your pages don't contain user-specific content, and everyone sees the same pages.

In the following sections, we'll talk about the server software components that are well suited for production use and take a look at what we can do to make Shovell happy and healthy in a production environment.

Choosing a Production Environment

Until now, we've trusted WEBrick to serve up our application. So why wouldn't we just stick with it as we move Shovell to our production system?

There are a couple of reasons: first of all, WEBrick is only capable of serving a single request at a time. If multiple users simultaneously access a Rails application served by WEBrick, their requests will be queued and dealt with one at a time, in turn. Sooner or later, this queue will become a huge performance problem.

Additionally, WEBrick isn't the best option for serving static content such as CSS, JavaScript, or images. Each of these static elements would have to go through the same processing chain (and suffer the same single-request-at-a-time limitation) as would a request to your Rails application for a dynamically generated page. These limitations render WEBrick unsuitable for production use.

Common production setups comprise two parts: a "front-end" web server that's best suited to serving static content (such as CSS files, JavaScript, and images), and a separate "back-end" component that handles the dynamic pages generated by the Rails application. This process is depicted in Figure 12.2.

Figure 12.2. Architecture of a Rails application

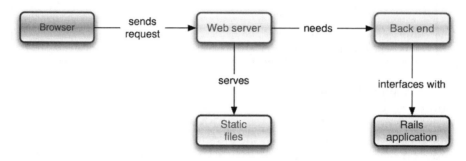

I used quotes when mentioning the terms front-end and back-end because on the Web these terms usually refer to the client and server respectively. However, in this case we're talking about two members of a web server team: the front-end server performs load balancing as well as serving static files, and the back-end component serves dynamic pages. Note that the back-end component is a persistent Ruby interpreter process—it never quits. As soon as the interpreter finishes servicing one request, it waits for the next.

The differences in the available back-end components can be described in terms of the protocol (or dialect) that the front-end web server has to speak in order to communicate with the Ruby process. We'll explore the back-end options in a moment, after we consider the available web servers.

Web Server Options

Back in the days when the World Wide Web wasn't dynamic at all—everyone edited their web pages with a text editor and uploaded HTML files to a server connected to the Internet—web server software didn't have much else to do than serve static content. For this reason, web servers are still very good at that today.

Some things have changed, though. For instance, it's now much easier to make web servers communicate with the components that deliver dynamically generated pages—such as those created by web applications written in Perl, PHP, Python, and Ruby.

Let's take a look at three web server software packages that are available to use with Rails applications under the terms of various free software licenses.[2] Several commercial web servers that support Rails applications are also available, but for the sake of simplicity and relevance, we'll only be looking at open source options.

Apache

With 62.5% market share, the free Apache web server written and maintained by the Apache Software Foundation is certainly the de-facto standard on the web server software market.[3] Apache is a good all-purpose, cross-platform web server. It's used by most web hosting providers, and therefore will be the focus of the hands-on part of this chapter.

Apache has many strengths, one of which is the huge number of extensions that are available to expand its feature set. It also has a robust interface for back-end services, a useful URL rewriter, and extensive logging capabilities. It's available as free software under the Apache license[4].

lightTPD

Often abbreviated to "lighty" to keep tongues intact, lightTPD is one of the more recent arrivals in the ever-expanding web server software market.[5] It was first created in 2003 by Jan Kneschke as a proof-of-concept that web servers could be secure and fast while treating kindly the resources of the hosting server. Since then, lightTPD has become a very popular choice among Rails developers who run it on their own servers; hosting companies, on the other hand, haven't yet embraced it for use in shared hosting environments.

lightTPD is free software under the BSD (Berkeley Software Distribution) license.[6] Apart from needing very little memory and CPU to do its job, lightTPD has excellent support for SSL, a flexible configuration file, and virtual-hosting capabilities.

---

[2] When we say "free software," we're referring to free software as defined by the Free Software Foundation [http://www.fsf.org/licensing/essays/free-sw.html].

[3] http://httpd.apache.org/

[4] http://www.apache.org/licenses/

[5] http://www.lighttpd.net/

[6] http://www.opensource.org/licenses/bsd-license.php

nginx

Another relatively new player in this market is nginx (pronounced "engine x"), a high-performance HTTP and proxy server that was originally developed by Igor Sysoev to power several high-traffic sites in Russia.[7] Due to the fact that it only recently appeared on the radar outside of Russia, English documentation is sparse at the time of writing. However, many translation efforts have commenced.

Recent performance evaluations have revealed that nginx is indeed the leader of the pack in terms of raw speed, with Apache and lightTPD scoring second and third place, respectively. However, due to the lack of English documentation, many developers and hosting companies may not consider a switch to nginx for some time to come.

Apart from outstanding performance, nginx also offers excellent proxy and caching capabilities, SSL support, and flexible configuration options. nginx is also available under the BSD license.

Back-end Options

As we've already discussed, regular web servers excel at serving static files. However, in order to interface with our Rails application and handle dynamically generated pages, they need a server software component that's specifically designed for the task. This may be a software module that's shipped with the web server, or it may be one that's available as a third-party extension. Here's a list of the back-end component options that are currently available for Rails applications.

The mod_ruby Extension

Exclusively available for use on the Apache web server, the mod_ruby extension provides an embedded Ruby interpreter that executes Ruby (and Rails) scripts, which, in turn, serve dynamically generated content to the outside world.[8]

mod_ruby has never really been used as a production-quality back end for Rails applications because its architecture entails some major drawbacks that prevent multiple Rails applications from being run on the same server. This makes it an especially poor choice for shared hosting environments.

---

[7] http://nginx.net/
[8] http://www.modruby.net/

The SCGI Protocol

An abbreviation for Simple Common Gateway Interface, the SCGI protocol is commonly used to serve dynamic content provided by Python web applications.[9] It can also be used to serve content provided by Rails applications, but hasn't been widely adopted for this purpose.

Implementations of SCGI are available as a third-party extension for the Apache web server and support for the protocol is built into the lightTPD web server.

The FastCGI Protocol

Until recently, FastCGI was the de-facto standard for deploying Rails applications.[10] FastCGI, a variation of the Common Gateway Interface (CGI), operates by starting one or more persistent processes of the language interpreter (in our case, Ruby) when the application in question is started up. The web server then communicates with these processes through the FastCGI protocol to serve dynamic pages.

FastCGI is often used when the machine the web server is running on is separate from the machines running the application. The FastCGI processes are started on the application servers, and the web server is instructed to connect to those processes using TCP/IP.

Support for FastCGI is provided by third-party extensions for the Apache web server and is built into the lightTPD web server, among others. Due to limitations that are present in the Apache extensions, FastCGI and Apache don't get along very well at times. Despite its excellent performance, FastCGI has been the victim of a number of stability problems, and is definitely a configuration headache.

Mongrel

The new kid on the block is Mongrel, created by Zed A. Shaw.[11] Mongrel uses a different approach to interface with the web server. Unlike options such as SCGI and FastCGI, both of which use a rather complex communication protocol, Mongrel uses plain HTTP.

---

[9] http://python.ca/nas/scgi/
[10] http://www.fastcgi.com/
[11] http://mongrel.rubyforge.org/

Due to Mongrel's pure-HTTP nature, many have used it to replace WEBrick in their development setups. While its performance isn't quite on par with that of FastCGI, it definitely outperforms WEBrick, boasts production-level robustness, and is *really* easy to use for Rails deployment.

Mongrel is compatible with every web server that's equipped with a proxy module to pass incoming HTTP requests on to other services. Apache, lightTPD, and nginx all have this capability.

Because Mongrel's so easy to install and use, and doesn't require complex protocols to interface with your preferred web server, it's an ideal choice for the hands-on part of this chapter. So, let's learn how to deploy Shovell using Apache and Mongrel!

Deploying Shovell

As you've seen, Rails applications can be deployed using various combinations of web servers and back-end services. Since most hosting providers use the Apache web server, and Mongrel is the simplest solution with decent performance (it definitely has the best speed to complexity ratio, bar none), we'll use this combination to deploy the Shovell application.

The hands-on part of this chapter will consist of a process that contains many steps. Initially, we'll install Mongrel using RubyGems, and use Mongrel instead of WEBrick in development mode. This will give us an initial impression of what using Mongrel is all about.

Our next task will be to configure Apache as a proxy to Mongrel to serve our application in production mode. This setup will be sufficient to handle a moderate amount of traffic to our application.

Step 1: Installing Mongrel

The simplest of all the steps in the deployment process is the installation of Mongrel using the RubyGems system. As I mentioned above, we'll begin by switching over to Mongrel on our local machine, replacing WEBrick as the development application server.[12]

---

[12] You might be wondering why we haven't been using Mongrel instead of WEBrick from the very beginning of this book. The reason is that, at the time of writing, Mongrel is a separate install and I didn't want to make matters more complicated than they needed to be when you were just finding your feet with Ruby.

Execute the following command to install the Mongrel gem. It downloads the gem from the RubyForge servers, then installs it on your system along with its dependencies:

```
$ gem install mongrel --include-dependencies
```

Mac OS X users: You might need to use the `sudo` command to gain administrative privileges when running the command above (`sudo gem install mongrel`).

Windows users: Make sure you start the Ruby console from the Instant Rails application—otherwise, the `gem` executable will not be within your search path.

Unfortunately, the gem installation will throw a *huge* list at you. The list contains two entries for every version of Mongrel that was ever released: one for Windows (labeled "win32") and one for all other operating systems (labeled "ruby"). I encourage you to choose the most recent release that's appropriate for your platform. If you use a Mac, your screen will appear similar to the display in Figure 12.3.

Figure 12.3. Installing Mongrel

After you enter the number that's appropriate to the release you want, and hit the **Enter** key, the RubyGems system will download the requested packages from the RubyForge site. If yours is a Windows system, the download will comprise a single package that contains a ready-to-use version of Mongrel. For all other operating systems, Mongrel will be freshly compiled for your computer; two additional packages on which Mongrel depends will also be installed. The completed installation will appear as shown in Figure 12.4.

Figure 12.4. Completing the Mongrel installation

```
● ● ○              bash — 80x25 — ⌘2
. -I/opt/local/lib/ruby/1.8/i686-darwin8.7.2 -I/opt/local/lib/ruby/1.8/i686-darw
in8.7.2 -I.  -O -pipe -I/opt/local/include -c tst_insert.c
gcc -fno-common -O -pipe -I/opt/local/include  -fno-common -pipe -fno-common  -I
. -I/opt/local/lib/ruby/1.8/i686-darwin8.7.2 -I/opt/local/lib/ruby/1.8/i686-darw
in8.7.2 -I.  -O -pipe -I/opt/local/include -c tst_search.c
cc -dynamic -bundle -undefined suppress -flat_namespace -L/opt/local/lib   -L"/o
pt/local/lib" -o http11.bundle http11.o http11_parser.o tst_cleanup.o tst_delete
.o tst_grow_node_free_list.o tst_init.o tst_insert.o tst_search.o  -lruby -lc  -
lpthread -ldl -lobjc

make install
/usr/bin/install -c -m 0755 http11.bundle /opt/local/lib/ruby/gems/1.8/gems/mong
rel-0.3.13.4/lib

make clean
Successfully installed mongrel-0.3.13.4
Successfully installed daemons-1.0.1
Successfully installed gem_plugin-0.2.1
Installing ri documentation for mongrel-0.3.13.4...
Installing ri documentation for daemons-1.0.1...
Installing ri documentation for gem_plugin-0.2.1...
Installing RDoc documentation for mongrel-0.3.13.4...
Installing RDoc documentation for daemons-1.0.1...
Installing RDoc documentation for gem_plugin-0.2.1...
Core:~ scoop$
```

At this point, a new command is available on your system: `mongrel_rails`. We'll use this command to start and stop the Mongrel server. It can be viewed as a replacement for `ruby script/server`, which we've been using to start the WEBrick server.

Make sure that no WEBrick processes continue to lurk on your system, then navigate to the application root in your console window. Execute the following command to start Mongrel for Shovell in development mode:

```
$ mongrel_rails start -B
```

Like WEBrick, Mongrel will start up and listen for connections on port 3000. The -B argument instructs Mongrel to launch in debug mode and to log all the requests it receives in the terminal window, as can be seen in Figure 12.5. To verify that Shovell is indeed working properly under Mongrel, use your web browser to connect to the usual URL: http://localhost:3000/.

Figure 12.5. Running Shovell under Mongrel

```
●○○              ruby — 80x20 — ⌘2
Core:~/shovell scoop$ mongrel_rails start -B
** Starting Mongrel listening at 0.0.0.0:3000
** Installing debugging prefixed filters.  Look in log/mongrel_debug for the fil
es.
** Starting Rails with development environment...
** Rails loaded.
** Loading any Rails specific GemPlugins
** Signals ready.  TERM => stop.  USR2 => restart.  INT => stop (no restart).
** Rails signals registered.  HUP => reload (without restart).  It might not wor
k well.
** Mongrel available at 0.0.0.0:3000
** Use CTRL-C to stop.
127.0.0.1 - [Sat, 23 Sep 2006 20:05:10 GMT] "GET / HTTP/1.1"
127.0.0.1 - [Sat, 23 Sep 2006 20:05:11 GMT] "GET /favicon.ico HTTP/1.1"
```

You may or may not notice that our application is a little snappier than it was under WEBrick,[13] although our development of Shovell certainly hasn't reached a high level of complexity yet, nor does it use any images at this point. Still, many Rails developers have permanently replaced the installation of WEBrick on their development machines with Mongrel, and if you like what you've seen so far, so should you!

Step 2: Moving to the Production System

The time has come to leave our development machine and switch to the machine that will provide a home to Shovell in production mode. Don't worry if you

---

[13] At this point we are running Mongrel in debug mode, which is *much* slower than production mode. If Mongrel doesn't appear to be running noticeably faster than WEBrick at this point, don't fret.

haven't found a hosting provider to host your Rails applications yet—you can just keep this section in mind for later reference.

Due to the fact that there are countless variations of server setups, we'll have to assume a few things for the sake of this walk-through introduction, including the following:

❑ The operating system of the server is Linux.

❑ You either have superuser privileges (root) on the system, or know someone who does (even if that's the tech support guy from your hosting provider).

❑ Ruby and Rails have been installed on the server using a similar process to that outlined in the Linux section of Chapter 3.

❑ Mongrel has been installed using the `gem install mongrel` command described earlier in this chapter.

❑ MySQL has been installed and your databases (at least, the one configured for the production environment in `config/database.yml`) have been created.

❑ Apache Version 2.2 is installed and running.[14]

❑ The Apache configuration is stored in the directory `/etc/httpd/` (if it's located elsewhere, you'll need to adapt the pathnames I mention).

❑ The Apache installation has the following extension modules available and enabled: `mod_proxy`, `mod_proxy_balancer`, `mod_deflate`, and `mod_rewrite`.

❑ You have access to the production system through a remote shell, preferably Secure Shell (SSH).

❑ You have the ability to upload files to the production system through either FTP or SSH.

❑ You have an available Internet domain name or a subdomain[15] on which to host your application.

---

[14] Versions 1.3 and 2.0 should work to a certain extent. However, the proxy_balance extension is only available in Version 2.2. Even the Apache Foundation recommends Version 2.2 as the *best you can get*, so why bother with anything else?

[15] Assuming `domain.com` is your domain name, `shovell.domain.com` would be a subdomain of it.

Okay, now that we have our assumptions clear, we can begin.

As we're starting out with a totally empty database on the production system, we need to recreate the database structure we've established on our development machine; you'll find it in the file db/schema.rb. Just to be sure that this file is up to date, run the following rake task on your development machine before you start to copy the files:

```
$ rake db:schema:dump
```

Assuming you see no errors when executing this command, your schema.rb file should now be up to date.

At this point, we need to transfer our application code to the production system. As I mentioned, we can achieve this task in a variety of ways. I'll use the file transfer capabilities provided by the SSH protocol to transfer the files; another common option would involve the use of FTP.

In any case, you need to copy the full directory structure that houses Shovell to the production system (minus the files from the log and tmp subdirectories, which contain output from the application in development mode; that output isn't required to run the application in production mode). Where you place the application's directory structure doesn't really matter, either. I've put mine into the subdirectory rails in my user account's home directory, as depicted in Figure 12.6, so the full path to my application is /home/scoop/rails/shovell.

Once we've finished transferring the application code, we need to set up the database structure on the production system. Again, this can be accomplished with a rake task. However, this time, we need to prepare the production part of the environment, instead of the development and test parts.

Figure 12.6. Transferring Shovell to the production system

All Rails scripts (in the `script` subdirectory) and all available `rake` tasks in your application will check whether an environment has been specified; if it hasn't, these scripts and tasks will assume you're using the `development` environment. To identify explicitly the environment in which you'd like to work, you must declare the `RAILS_ENV` environment variable, as illustrated in Figure 12.7.

Let's set up the database structure in the production database (which is `shovell_production`, as configured in `config/database.yml`). Log into the production system through a remote shell like SSH, and execute the following command:[16]

```
$ rake db:schema:load RAILS_ENV=production
```

---

[16] If you're wondering why we're not using the `rake db:migrate` command that we used during development to bring our database up to date, the reason is that once the total number of migrations becomes sizeable, iterating over every one to deploy an application can take quite a long time!

Figure 12.7. Creating the database structure

```
scoop@flubber:~/rails/shovell$ rake db:schema:load RAILS_ENV=production
(in /home/scoop/rails/shovell)
-- create_table("stories", {:force=>true})
   -> 0.4514s
-- create_table("taggings", {:force=>true})
   -> 0.0052s
-- create_table("tags", {:force=>true})
   -> 0.0418s
-- create_table("users", {:force=>true})
   -> 0.0222s
-- create_table("votes", {:force=>true})
   -> 0.0322s
-- initialize_schema_information()
   -> 0.0034s
-- columns("schema_info")
   -> 0.0023s
scoop@flubber:~/rails/shovell$
```

By specifying RAILS_ENV=production on the rake command line, we're instructing rake to operate on the production database (and environment) instead of the development equivalents.

This environment variable is an application-wide, but slightly tedious, method of specifying the desired environment. A few of the common Rails commands—for example, ruby script/console—also take the environment name as a direct argument. Let's use the Rails console now to create an initial user for the production version of Shovell:

```
$ ruby script/console production
```

The message Loading production environment, which displays when we execute this command, indicates that the console session is connecting to the production database. Next, let's create a new User object; the results of this command are shown in Figure 12.8:

```
>> User.create :login => 'patrick', :password => 'sekrit'
=> #<User:...>
```

Figure 12.8. Creating a first production user

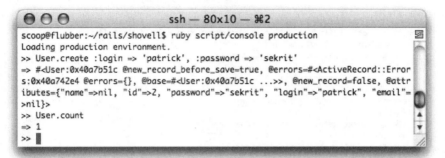

```
scoop@flubber:~/rails/shovell$ ruby script/console production
Loading production environment.
>> User.create :login => 'patrick', :password => 'sekrit'
=> #<User:0x40a7b51c @new_record_before_save=true, @errors=#<ActiveRecord::Error
s:0x40a742e4 @errors={}, @base=#<User:0x40a7b51c ...>>, @new_record=false, @attr
ibutes={"name"=>nil, "id"=>2, "password"=>"sekrit", "login"=>"patrick", "email"=
>nil}>
>> User.count
=> 1
>>
```

Armed with a ready-made production database, we can now launch Mongrel similarly to the way we launched it on our development machine in the section called "Step 1: Installing Mongrel". This will ensure that both Mongrel and the application behind it are working on the production system.

Move to the application root (/home/scoop/rails/shovell, in my case) and execute the following command:

```
$ mongrel_rails start -e production
```

Yes, that's yet another syntax for specifying the environment we want to be in!

Mongrel will fire up and wait for requests on port 3000, just as it did on the development machine. However, now our application is running in the production environment, and will be quite a bit faster than it was in the development environment.

Depending on the firewall configurations employed by your hosting provider, you may or may not be able to connect to this port from the Internet. On a shared host, you might not even be able to *start* Mongrel on port 3000—it might be reserved for another user. In this case, you'll need to ask your web host's tech support team for a port number on which you can run your Rails application, then pass this port number to Mongrel using the -p argument:

```
$ mongrel_rails start -e production -p 3333
```

Let's see how your application looks in production mode. Fire up a web browser and open http://<*hostname*>:3000/, where *hostname* is the fully qualified domain name of the production system. In my case, for example, I'll connect to http://poocs.net:3000/.

You should see the Shovell front page pictured in Figure 12.9. No stories are listed as yet, because we left them in the development database on the development machine. However, you should be able to log in with the credentials of the user that you just created using the console. Excellent!

Figure 12.9. Shovell served by Mongrel

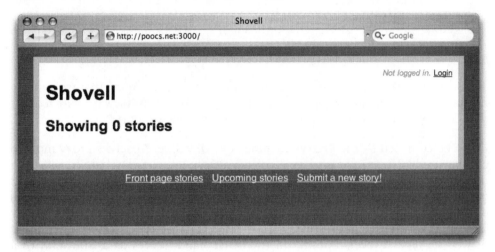

Step 3: Setting Up Apache

Although Shovell is now being served successfully by a single Mongrel process in production mode, a scenario in which our users have to type in an explicit port number in order to access the Shovell application is far from ideal.

Our next goal is therefore to set up Apache as a web server for Mongrel, so that Apache can pass incoming requests to the Mongrel process—technically referred to as a **proxy through**. This setup makes it possible to run multiple Rails applications (be they our own, or the applications of other users on the same system) on a single IP address: Apache decides (based on the configuration we give it) which requests to forward to each application.

To do this, we'll add the following configuration directives to the end of our Apache configuration file, /etc/httpd/httpd.conf:[17]

---

[17] Typically, the Apache configuration is split into many smaller files. However, in shared hosting setups, each user usually has his or her own configuration file, which is used for specific configuration directives concerning that user's own web sites and applications. In such cases, you should obviously

File: **httpd.conf (excerpt)**

```
<VirtualHost *:80>
    ServerName shovell.poocs.net
    ProxyRequests Off
    <Proxy *>
        Order deny,allow
        Allow from all
    </Proxy>
    ProxyPass / http://localhost:3000/
    ProxyPassReverse / http://localhost:3000/
</VirtualHost>
```

This is the simplest of all possible proxy configurations. Assuming that we're using the shovell subdomain of poocs.net, we instruct Apache to forward *every* request that comes in directly to the Mongrel process running on port 3000.

Don't be confused by the ProxyRequests Off directive. Apache's proxy module can be used as a *forward* and as a *reverse* proxy. A forwarding proxy acts as a middleman for your web browser when it connects to sites on the Internet (something you might have used in a corporate environment). The proxy answers only those requests that originate from a known group of browsers (usually identified by their IP addresses) and forwards them on to an arbitrary number of web servers. A reverse proxy, on the other hand, serves as a front-end to a known service, such as our Mongrel process. It handles incoming requests from an arbitrary number of browsers that might be scattered all over the planet.

The ProxyRequests Off directive turns off the forwarding proxy capabilities, while the ProxyPass and ProxyPassReverse directives turn the reverse proxy capabilities on.

To activate these configuration changes, we need to instruct Apache to reload its configuration file, which we usually achieve using the command apachectl reload.

For this setup to work flawlessly, we need to make sure the Mongrel process continues to run at all times, without us having to keep the terminal window open. Before the Linux and Unix folks scream "Use screen!," let me tell you that we can run Mongrel as a background process by invoking the mongrel_rails command with the -d argument, like so:

```
$ mongrel_rails start -d -e production
```

---

put the directives mentioned in this section into the appropriate configuration file, rather than using the global one.

Now that this has been executed, Mongrel is happily sitting in the background, waiting for requests to reach it. If you need to stop or restart your Mongrel process (restarting is especially useful if you made changes to the application code, which a Rails application in production mode can't reload on the fly), use the appropriate variant of the `mongrel_rails` command:

```
$ mongrel_rails stop
$ mongrel_rails restart
```

Sure enough, connecting to http://shovell.poocs.net/ with a browser displays the Shovell front page shown in Figure 12.10. Well done: you've successfully deployed your application!

Figure 12.10. Shovell proxied through Apache

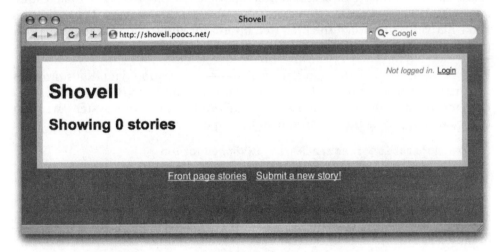

Alternatives for Session Storage

When you start thinking about performance and load distribution, the next logical step is to consider the performance of the session container.

As we discussed in Chapter 9, Rails creates a new session for every visitor, logged in or not, by default. Each session is stored in a single file (one file is created per session) in the application's `tmp` subdirectory.

However, the situation becomes awkward when multiple processes write to the same file at the same time—a problem that's encountered when requests that use the same session are processed simultaneously by separate Mongrel processes.

For this reason, Rails supports alternative session storage containers, two of which we'll look at in this section.

The `ActiveRecord` `Store` Session Container

The most popular option after the file-based default, the `ActiveRecord Store` session container stores all session data safely within a table in your database. While this is not as fast as other options, using `ActiveRecord Store` takes care of the problems that arise when multiple processes attempt to access a single file. It also allows sessions to be accessed from multiple machines—an essential feature for applications that are large enough to require multiple servers. These abilities make ActiveRecord `Store` the preferred option for applications that attract low-to-medium levels of traffic, so let's configure Shovell to use it now.

First, we need to make room in our database for the session data. Rails provides a shortcut for this job in the form of a `rake` task, and in so doing removes any need for manual table creation. As we're still on the production system, we need to include the production environment option explicitly:

```
$ rake db:sessions:create RAILS_ENV=production
```

This command will create a new migration file that contains the Ruby code necessary to create an appropriate `sessions` table that will hold our session data. The migration can then be applied using the regular `rake` task `db:migrate`:

```
$ rake db:migrate RAILS_ENV=production
```

Figure 12.11 shows the output of these migrations being applied.

Next, we need to let Rails know that we want to use the `ActiveRecord Store` instead of the default file-based session container. We can tell it the good news via the `config/environment.rb` file; simply remove the comment mark in front of the following line:

```
config.action_controller.session_store = :active_record_store
```

Figure 12.11. Creating the sessions table

```
ssh — 80x16 — ⌘2
scoop@flubber:~/rails/shovell$ rake db:sessions:create RAILS_ENV=production
(in /home/scoop/rails/shovell)
      exists  db/migrate
      create  db/migrate/008_add_sessions.rb
scoop@flubber:~/rails/shovell$ rake db:migrate RAILS_ENV=production
(in /home/scoop/rails/shovell)
== AddSessions: migrating ====================================================
-- create_table(:sessions)
   -> 0.0737s
-- add_index(:sessions, :session_id)
   -> 0.2228s
-- add_index(:sessions, :updated_at)
   -> 0.0270s
== AddSessions: migrated (0.3249s) ===========================================

scoop@flubber:~/rails/shovell$ 
```

As soon as you restart the application (using `mongrel_rails restart`), sessions will be stored in the SQL database.

Be aware that the changes you make to `config/environment.rb` will have global effects. If you want to limit this configuration change to a specific environment (for example, you want it to affect the production environment only), add the line above to the environment-specific configuration file located at `config/environments/production.rb`. If you make the change on your development machine (or copy the application code back and forth between it and your production server), be sure to run the migration in order to add the sessions table to your development database.

The MemCached Store Session Container

Another popular option for session storage is the `MemCached Store` session storage container.[18] With `MemCached`, a piece of software originally developed by Danga Interactive for the LiveJournal blog-hosting service, sessions are stored in the available memory on your server—nothing is ever written to disk.

This approach is obviously a lot faster than writing each session to the hard disk or to a database (which will eventually be written to a hard disk as well). However, the setup instructions for `MemCached` are slightly more complicated than the

---

[18] http://www.danga.com/memcached/

`ActiveRecord Store` option we saw above, and the software provides little extra value for an application the size of Shovell. I'll leave you to review the setup instructions on the Ruby on Rails Wiki.[19]

Further Reading

We've done it! Our application is ready for initial public consumption, and the hands-on parts of this book have come to an end. However, I'd like to alert you to a few additional Rails features and extensions that may come in handy in your future encounters with Rails applications.

Caching

Depending on the project budget and the availability of hardware, every Rails application can only serve so many dynamic pages at any given time. If your app happens to receive traffic numbers that exceed these limits, you'll have to consider your options for tackling this problem.

Rails' built-in caching options vary in their levels of granularity. The simplest of all possibilities is to cache whole pages in the form of HTML files. What Rails does in such cases is to take the output that's sent to the browser, and store it in a file on the server's hard disk. This file can then be served directly by Apache without even bothering Mongrel (provided that your setup is configured appropriately). This saves Rails from re-generating page content over and over again even though the content may not have changed between successive requests for the same page. Another option allows you to cache the outputs of single actions and even fragments of views (a sidebar, for example).

Caching can do wonders to improve your application's performance. However, take care to ensure that the relevant sections of the cache are flushed when pages change, otherwise your users will receive outdated content. Additionally, using cached pages may not be feasible if your application depends on a lot of user-specific content—for instance, in an application whose page content changes depending on who's using it.

The Rails documentation for the caching feature is available online.[20]

---

[19] http://wiki.rubyonrails.com/rails/pages/HowtoChangeSessionStore
[20] http://ap.rubyonrails.com/classes/ActionController/Caching.html

Version Control and Deployment Management

Software development projects usually progress at a rapid pace—a truth that's even more relevant in the case of web applications. There are no strict version numbers; new features are continuously being implemented while, at the same time, bugs are fixed. Updated source code must be deployed easily and quickly. Developer resources typically need to be distributed across projects in a flexible manner.

And developers make mistakes. Not on purpose, of course—but we're all human.

Version control and deployment systems have been developed to address these issues; popular options include Subversion[21] and Capistrano.[22]

Subversion

Subversion is a general-purpose version control (or source control) system that's available for free under an open source license. This package is highly recommended for use in any software development project.

Using Subversion, you can access the project code at any point in time and you can view any code revision that was made to your project. All changes are tracked, and no modification is irreversible or destructive. Subversion also allows for the easy updating of a given copy of the project's code (for example, the copy that resides on the production system) with changes that were made elsewhere (on your development machine, perhaps).

Capistrano

Capistrano is a deployment and management system that was written in Ruby by Jamis Buck, one of the Rails core members. Capistrano can be used only with projects that are version controlled through a system such as Subversion.

Capistrano is designed to assist you in a number of ways:

❏ It facilitates the deployment of application code to your production server, along with the necessary maintenance tasks (such as restarting the Mongrel processes after the code has been updated).

---

[21] http://subversion.tigris.org/
[22] http://manuals.rubyonrails.com/read/book/17

❑ It provides a means by which you can revert to the last "known good" code base if errors appear, or put up a maintenance banner when you need to perform database repairs.

❑ It supports the deployment of application code to *multiple* servers simultaneously.

Errors by Email

We've talked briefly about the fact that Rails will never annoy your users with extensive stack traces if an error occurs in your application. Instead, it will display a polite message to inform the user that the request couldn't be processed successfully.[23]

But what if you want to *fix* such errors instead of silently ignoring them? You could certainly comb through your log files every day, checking for unusual activity. Better yet, you could install the `exception_notification` plugin, which hooks into your application and sends you an email whenever something unusual happens.

The plugin can be installed using the `script/plugin` utility. Documentation that explains how to customize its behaviour is available online.[24]

Summary

In this final chapter, we've plowed through the variety of options available for deploying Rails applications to production systems.

We opted to use the combination of Apache and Mongrel to deploy Shovell. In three simple steps, we took the Shovell application code to the production system, initialized the production database, and started serving requests with a single Mongrel process. It doesn't get much easier than that!

Once Shovell was running happily in its new environment, we looked at some alternative session storage containers and found that the `ActiveRecord Store` suited our needs by storing session data in our SQL database.

---

[23] The default templates for these messages can be found in `public/404.html` and `public/500.html`.

[24] http://dev.rubyonrails.org/svn/rails/plugins/exception_notification/README

Finally, I provided a few pointers to more advanced information on some particularly relevant aspects of Rails application development and deployment.

I hope you've found value in the time you've spent with this book, and that you're now able to go forth and build upon what you've learned. Now's the time to get out there and use your knowledge to build an application that changes the Internet!

Index

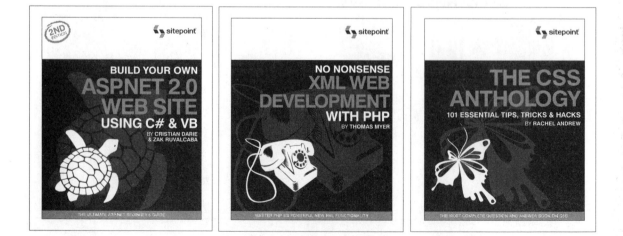